The Source® for

by Nancy B. Swigert

Disorder	Age
■ dysarthria	■ adults

Evidence-Based Practice

- Effective speech treatment for individuals with dysarthria has been documented through group treatment studies, single-subject studies, and case reports. Study outcomes measure improvements in:

  - increased muscle strength and control
  - improved respiration and phonation for adequate voice
  - improved consonant precision and intelligibility (ASHA, 2008; Yorkston et al., 2001)

- Speech production adequacy can improve, often with a focus on the physiological systems of speech (Hanson, Yorkston, & Beukelman, 2004).

- Speech supplementation strategies (e.g., letter cues, topic cues, gestures) may be useful for speakers with severe or profound dysarthria (Hanson, Yorkston, & Beukelman, 2004).

- Listener skills, attitudes, and experiences affect the range of intelligibility for speakers with severe dysarthria. Listeners must be trained as active participants in the communication process (Hanson, Yorkston, & Beukelman, 2004).

- ASHA's National Outcomes Measurement System (NOMS) shows that outpatient speech therapy services [for dysarthria] are associated with improved intelligibility and communication functioning (ASHA, 2008).

The Source for Dysarthria incorporates these principles and is also based on expert professional practice.

References

American Speech-Language-Hearing Association (ASHA). (2008). Treatment efficacy summaries: Dysarthria. Retrieved April 15, 2009, from http://www.asha.org/public/EfficacySummaries.htm

Hanson, E.K., Yorkston, K.M., & Beukelman, D.R. (2004). Speech supplementation techniques for dysarthria: A systematic review. *Journal of Medical Speech-Language Pathology, 12*(2), ix-xxix.

Yorkston, K.M., Spencer, K.A., Duffy, J.R., Beukelman, D.R., Golper, L.A., Miller, R.M., et al. (2001). Evidence-based medicine and practice guidelines: Application to the field of speech-language pathology. *Journal of Medical Speech-Language Pathology, 9*(4), 243-256.

LinguiSystems

LinguiSystems, Inc.
3100 4th Avenue
East Moline, IL 61244
800-776-4332

FAX: 800-577-4555
Email: service@linguisystems.com
Web: linguisystems.com

Printed in the U.S.A.

ISBN 10: 0-7606-0162-3
ISBN 13: 978-0-7606-0162-4

About the Author

Nancy B. Swigert, M.A., CCC-SLP, received her master's degree from the University of Tennessee, Knoxville. She is the Director of Swigert & Associates, Inc., a private practice which has been providing services in the Lexington, Kentucky area for over 17 years. The practice is contracted by Central Baptist Hospital in Lexington to run their in-patient and out-patient Speech-Language Pathology Department. That is where Nancy spends the majority of her time.

In addition to administering the private practice and the department, Nancy spends much of her time providing patient care. She evaluates and treats adults with motor speech disorders in acute care, skilled nursing facilities, and home health settings. Nancy has also authored *The Source for Dysphagia* for LinguiSystems and she lectures extensively at the state, regional, and national level on dysphagia and on functional outcomes.

Nancy is the Past President of the Kentucky Speech-Language-Hearing Association and the Council of State Association Presidents. She is very active in the American Speech-Language-Hearing Association, serving as the project officer for the Treatment Outcomes Project since 1994 and as ASHA President in 1998.

Dedication

To Keith, who for 22 years has been my source of support and encouragement.

To the scholars in the area of motor-speech disorders, whose work (cited frequently in this book) provides the foundation for clinical intervention.

Acknowledgment

I am indebted to Timothy Coleman, M.D., neurologist and friend, for reviewing this manuscript for accuracy. I am also grateful to him for referring patients with dysarthria to me for evaluation and treatment.

A special thanks to Lonnie Wright and Jeff Kurz, librarians extraordinaire, who were able to find each and every reference I needed as I reviewed the literature in preparation to write this book.

Illustrations by Leslie Dunlap

Table of Contents

Introduction

There are many challenges faced when working with patients who present with a dysarthria.

- There is no such thing as *a* dysarthria. There are many different types of dysarthria.

- Some dysarthrias are caused by an acute event and respond fairly well to treatment whereas other dysarthrias are related to degenerative diseases and require an entirely different type of intervention.

- We lack a significant number of efficacy studies to prove that how we treat patients with dysarthria really works.

- There are techniques which may help the patient with dysarthria compensate for decreased intelligibility, but it's very difficult to get the patient to use the techniques on a consistent basis.

I'm sure many of you had the same reaction in graduate school that I did when using the Darley, Aronson, and Brown text (*Motor Speech Disorders*, 1975) with the descriptions of the characteristics of the dysarthrias. When studying those lists, my head began to swim and I began to think that all patients with dysarthria presented with imprecise consonants, hypernasality, decreased rate, etc. It's a challenge to develop skill in differentiating between the types of dysarthria. However, this is an important skill as the treatment varies related to the type of dysarthria and its etiology.

The Source for Dysarthria is written to help you improve the services you provide to patients with dysarthria. It provides a refresher on the neurology of dysarthria as well as tips and techniques for assessing dysarthria and planning treatment. This book is based on a perceptual framework. That is, it is based not on the results of an instrumental assessment (as most of us have no access to instrumentation when working with patients), but instead is based on refining our listening skills and helping us make decisions about diagnosis and treatment based on what we hear. *The Source for Dysarthria* is also designed to help you relate perceptual symptoms to specific physiologic causes.

I hope you find this book useful in two ways. When you encounter an interesting and challenging patient, please take *The Source for Dysarthria* from your shelf and look through the chapters on neurology, evaluation, and treatment planning to help you make decisions about the patient's care. Second, since there are many activities in the book designed to be used with patients, I hope you will take the book into your therapy sessions and use the goals and treatment objectives, descriptions of activities to achieve those treatment objectives, and patient handouts (marked with a shaded box at the top of the page) on a regular basis.

It takes great skill on the part of a speech-language pathologist to accurately evaluate a patient with dysarthria and make an appropriate diagnosis, to plan the kind of intervention needed, and to choose treatment objectives and activities that will help the patient achieve the goals you have set. I hope *The Source for Dysarthria* will help you refine your skills in each of those areas.

Nancy

Chapter 1
Introduction and Neurology

What is dysarthria?

There have been many approaches to describing and defining dysarthria. When we explain dysarthria to patients or their families, we may say that dysarthria is speech that is slurred or hard to understand and is caused by damage to the control center in the brain. However, we know that this is a simplistic explanation which focuses too much on the articulation aspects and not on the other components.

Rosenbek and LaPointe (1985) describe the dysarthrias as "a group of related motor speech disorders resulting from disturbed muscular control over the speech mechanism."

We must keep in mind that the dysarthrias affect more than the ability to produce consonants and vowels (i.e. articulation). The disturbed muscular control can result in difficulties in respiration, phonation, resonance, articulation, and prosody.

Which systems are affected by dysarthria?
- Respiration
- Phonation
- Resonance
- Articulation
- Prosody

There are also different problems with the muscular control that result in these difficulties. The muscles can be paralyzed or weak, they can have too much or too little tone (spastic or flaccid), or they can be uncoordinated.

What can be wrong with the muscles?
- paralyzed (can't move at all)
- weak (can't move well)
- spastic (too much tone; tight)
- flaccid (not enough tone; flabby)
- uncoordinated

The movements can also be impaired in different ways: the muscles can move too far or not far enough, they can move in the wrong direction, they can move with too much or too little strength, they can move at the wrong time in the sequence, or they can stop moving.

What can be wrong with the muscle movements?

- overshoot (move too far)
- undershoot (can't move all the way to the target)
- move in wrong direction
- move with too much strength
- move with too little strength
- move with poor timing
- involuntary movements

Darley (1983) provides a good summary definition of dysarthria, "Dysarthria refers to a group of speech disorders involving any or all of the basic motor speech processes — respiration, phonation, resonance, articulation, and prosody — resulting from disturbances in muscular control due to damage to the central or peripheral nervous system always evidenced by some degree of weakness, slowness, incoordination or alteration of muscle tone of the speech apparatus."

The Veteran's Association Task Force indicates that dysarthria is a disorder of speech resulting from neurological damage. They specify that the general signs are impaired speech intelligibility and naturalness. This definition points out that although a patient may present with a disease such as multiple sclerosis or Parkinson's disease that typically results in dysarthria, the patient does not have a dysarthria unless you hear it. This definition elaborates that you must hear:

- impaired intelligibility
- impaired naturalness
- perceived imprecision

Etiology and Course of Disease

Yorkston (1996) indicates that dysarthrias are also defined by their etiology and their course. Dysarthrias may be acquired or congenital. They may follow several different courses. It is important to be aware of the courses of dysarthria because the treatment plan is largely dictated by the course the disorder is following. Dysarthrias may be:

- developmental (e.g., cerebral palsy)
- recovering (e.g., post stroke)
- stable (e.g., long term post stroke)
- degenerative (e.g., Amyotrophic Lateral Sclerosis)
- exacerbating-remitting (e.g., multiple sclerosis)

Yorkston's breakdown can be compared to another more common schema which divides the dysarthrias by their course into:

- non-progressive (would include developmental and recovering; may include some exacerbating-remitting)
- degenerative (degenerative and may include some exacerbating-remitting)
- chronic (stable)

In Chapter 3 we discuss the differences in approaches to treatment for dysarthrias based on their etiology and their course.

Causes of Dysarthria

Different types of lesions or damage in the central and peripheral neurons system cause different types of dysarthria. The following is a brief description of selected disorders which often cause dysarthria.

Non-Progressive Dysarthrias

1. *Cerebrovascular Accident (CVA)*

   Strokes can either be *ischemic* or *hemorrhagic*. An ischemic stroke can be caused by blockage of a major blood vessel in the brain from a clot.

- If the clot is in the brain itself, it is called a *thrombus*.
- If the clot is formed in the heart and travels to the brain, it is called an *embolus*.
- Strokes may also be described as *lacunar*. Lacunar strokes usually result from chronic hypertension and involve smaller infarcts.

Hemorrhagic strokes are usually caused by:

- hypertension (subarachnoid hemorrhage)
- a fall or injury (intracerebral hemorrhage)
- ruptured vessel (intracerebral hemorrhage)
- an arteriovenous malformation

After a stroke, a patient can have a very mild transient dysarthria if the stroke is on one side. If the lesion is bilateral, the patient can have a severe permanent spastic dysarthria. If the stroke affects the brain stem, the patient may have a resulting flaccid dysarthria. If the stroke is in the cerebellum, the patient may have an ataxic-like dysarthria.

CVA: *Unilateral cortical lesion*

If the lesion to the corticobulbar fibers is unilateral, there will be weakness of the articulators on the opposite side. This usually results in a mild dysarthria that often resolves spontaneously. If the lesion affects the pyramidal and extrapyramidal tracts unilaterally, the result may be unilateral upper motor neuron dysarthria.

CVA: *Bilateral cortical lesions*

Bilateral lesions to the corticobulbar fibers can produce a permanent dysarthria after a stroke. This results in a spastic dysarthria called pseudo-bulbar palsy.

2. *Traumatic Brain Injury (TBI)*

It is not surprising that the type of dysarthria that results from a TBI depends largely on the location and severity of the brain injury. Therefore, you may observe any type of dysarthria including ataxic dysarthria, spastic dysarthria, or flaccid dysarthria.

TBIs are classified either as a closed head injury or an open head injury (in which there is a penetration into the brain such as from a bullet or knife).

3. *Brain Tumor*

A brain tumor can cause dysarthria, as can the result of intervention for brain tumor whether the intervention be excavation of the tumor, radiation therapy, or chemotherapy. If the tumor is removed and not expected to return or grow, the dysarthria would then be expected to be non-progressive. The type of dysarthria you will observe is largely dependent on the location and extent of the tumor.

4. *Cerebral Palsy*

Cerebral Palsy is caused by an insult in the central nervous system during the prenatal or perinatal period. Although the injury occurs around the time of birth, complications can arise throughout the patient's life.

Chronic Dysarthrias

Any of the dysarthrias described above as non-progressive can be considered chronic when the onset is not recent, and there is no chance for more improvement in function. For instance, a spastic dysarthria caused by a stroke two years prior would be considered chronic. Developmental or congenital disorders would also be considered chronic. The dysarthria associated with cerebral palsy is chronic when there is no further improvement of function and treatment, if any, is compensatory in nature.

Degenerative Dysarthrias

1. *Parkinson's disease*

   Patients with Parkinson's disease have a very high prevalence of dysarthria. Parkinson's can affect laryngeal and velopharyngeal function, oral articulation, and overall intelligibility.

   Parkinsonism is due to a loss of neurons in the basal ganglia which produce dopamine, the substantia nigra which is related to the basal ganglia, and the brain stem. It is sometimes divided into three subgroups:

   1) idiopathic Parkinson's disease
   2) secondary Parkinson's disease caused by toxins, infections, drugs, or sometimes multiple strokes
   3) system degeneration such as Progressive Supranuclear Palsy or Shy-Drager Syndrome

   It is important to be aware of the effects of the medications prescribed for Parkinson's. Do your best to time intervention after the medication has been administered in order to achieve the best results.

2. *Progressive Supranuclear Palsy*

   This is an extrapyramidal syndrome and the symptoms include ophthalmoplegia (paralysis of the eye muscles), rigidity of the neck, pseudobulbar palsy, and a severe spastic dysarthria.

3. *Dystonia*

   This is a group of motor disorders characterized by abnormal involuntary movements and postures. The spasms are usually associated with voluntary motor activity.

   Not all individuals with dystonia have a dysarthria, but if the dystonia involves the face, larynx, or mouth, some dysarthria may be observed. As would be expected, if the dystonia involves the larynx, there may be problems with pitch being too low, pitch variability, and decreased phonation time. Some patients may show a vocal harshness or strained quality and others may show a slow speaking rate. If the muscles of the face and mouth are involved, there might be imprecise consonant production and breakdowns in articulation.

4. *Huntington's disease*

   This is a degenerative disorder of the nervous system and includes features of chorea, dementia, and a history of familial occurrence. The disease appears between 35 and 40 years of age.

   Individuals with Huntington's disease may have little to no dysarthria when their choreic movements (i.e., involuntary and irregular) are occurring in the limbs and body. However, if the choreic movements involve the respiratory muscles, oral muscles, and facial muscles, speech may be severely unintelligible. Patients may have a highly variable pattern of articulation or they may have periods of hypernasality, harshness, breathiness, and variations in loudness. Rate of speech is altered. Stress seems equalized and inappropriate silences appear.

5. *Wilson's disease*

This is a rare hereditary disease caused by the body's inability to process the dietary intake of copper. Neurologic abnormalities include tremor, drooling, dysphagia, a mask-like face, incoordination, and tremor. Patients usually have a mixed dysarthria with some ataxic, some spastic, and some hypokenetic features.

6. *Amyotrophic Lateral Sclerosis (ALS)*

This is a progressive degenerative disease of both the upper motor neurons (UMNs) and lower motor neurons (LMNs). UMN symptoms include muscle weakness, increased tone, and pseudobulbar palsy. LMN symptoms include muscle weakness, muscle atrophy, and diminished reflexes.

Individuals with ALS also present with a mixed dysarthria (spastic and flaccid). When the patient becomes weaker, the flaccid symptoms usually become more apparent because the excessively weak muscles can no longer show these spastic symptoms.

Patients with ALS show reduced respiratory support for speech, oftentimes presenting a low pitch. If the symptoms are more spastic, patients will show a harsh, strangled voice. If the symptoms are more flaccid, patients will show a breathy, monotone voice. Other symptoms of patients with ALS include hypernasality, nasal emission, and decreased articulation.

7. *Friedreich's Ataxia*

This is one of a heterogenous group of degenerative spinocerebellar disorders. Friedreich's Ataxia usually predominantly affects the spinal cord. There are some that predominantly affect the cerebellum, and others that predominantly affect the brain stem.

Generally these patients have a reduced intelligibility with monoloudness, inappropriate silences, imprecise consonants, and vocal harshness with pitch breaks.

8. *Multiple Sclerosis*

This is a disease of the white matter of the central nervous system characterized by progressive neurological deficits and a remitting and relapsing course. Not all patients with multiple sclerosis exhibit a dysarthria. Those that do may have hypernasality, impaired articulation, harsh vocal quality with pitch and loudness variations, and inappropriate phrasing with exaggerated stress.

9. *Myasthenia Gravis*

This is an auto-immune disorder that is characterized by abnormal fatiguability and by weakness in the skeletal muscles. This is due to electrical impulses not being transmitted from nerve to muscle. How significant a dysarthria really is depends on how severe the disorder is and also how well it is controlled with medication.

Because the symptoms are caused by weakness in muscles of the palate, tongue, and larynx, these patients' speech usually includes hypernasality, deteriorating articulation, and reduced level of loudness. If the patient is not receiving pharmacological treatment, then the deciding characteristic is that the patient's speech deteriorates with fatigue.

It is particularly important that treatment for patients with this disorder be timed after the patient is given medications. They should be able to perform much more appropriately in therapy at that time.

Neurology of Dysarthria

It is beyond the scope of this book to provide extensive information about the neurological basis of dysarthria. However, it is important to understand the major systems and pathways in the brain and nervous system that control the speech processes. With a better understanding of this information, you can:

- plan better treatment
- give more accurate information about prognosis
- understand references in medical records
- knowledgeably discuss patient care with other health care providers

There are two major systems in the central nervous system: *pyramidal* (sometimes called direct pathway) and *extrapyramidal* (sometimes called indirect pathway). The pyramidal system controls voluntary movements and is made of three tracts: *corticospinal, corticobulbar*, and *corticopontine*. Damage to any of these tracts can result in a dysarthria. (See Table 2, page 16.)

Pyramidal

Corticospinal: This tract is comprised only of upper motor neurons. This means that they never leave the neuraxis (i.e., contained solely within the brain, brain stem, and spinal cord). The corticospinal tract controls the distal muscles like the limbs and digits. Innervation is mostly contralateral. It travels through the internal capsule and decussates or crosses over in the medulla. Unilateral upper motor neuron damage to this tract usually results in transient or mild effects on speech.

Corticobulbar: This tract has upper motor neurons and lower motor neurons (those that send axons into the peripheral nerves — cranial and spinal). This tract also travels through the internal capsule and decussates at various levels. The upper motor neurons have ipsilateral and contralateral fibers. Therefore, the lower motor neurons have mostly bilateral innervations (Table 1) and are called the final common pathway. Damage to the upper motor neurons (corticospinal or corticobulbar tract) results in spastic or hypertonic movements.

Damage to the lower motor neurons in the corticobulbar tract keeps the neural impulses from being transmitted to the muscles, so the result is a flaccid, hypotonic muscle. Fasciculations are a sign of lower motor neuron damage.

Understanding the corticobulbar tract, with its upper and lower motor neurons, is challenging. Pages 14 and 15 contain some examples and graphic representations to help clarify how the corticobulbar tract functions and what the relationship is between the upper and lower neurons.

Corticopontine: This tract travels to the pontine nuclei and then interacts with the cerebellum.

Cerebellum

The cerebellum maintains proper posture and balance in walking, sequential movements of eating, and rapid, alternating movement like those in speech. Our voluntary movements

Table 1

Cranial Nerve	Upper Motor Neuron (UMN) Innervation
Trigeminal (V)	bilateral

Facial (VII)
    upper face
    lower face
	bilateral
	mostly contralateral

Glossopharyngeal (IX)	bilateral
Vagus (X)	bilateral
Accessory (XI)	bilateral
Hypoglossal (XII)	mostly contralateral

would be clumsy and uncoordinated without assistance from the cerebellum. Damage to the cerebellum results in ataxia.

Extrapyramidal

The extrapyramidal system is a set of pathways that connect subcortical motor nuclei. These indirect pathways include the basal ganglia. The extrapyramidal system is concerned with coarse, stereotyped movements and has more influence over proximal (midline) than distal (peripheral) muscles. This system maintains tone and posture. Damage in the extrapyramidal system yields involuntary movement disorders or dyskinesias (tremor, chorea, athetosis, dystonia, myoclonus, or tardive dyskinesia).

Summary

Now that we have reviewed some of the basics and terminology of the neurology of dysarthria, we'll discuss descriptions of the dysarthrias related to the site of lesion. This information is most clearly presented in a table format. The tables on pages 17-23 are organized by site of lesion (e.g. pyramidal — upper motor neuron) and then describe the possible effects you will hear and see in the five processes of speech (respiration, phonation, resonance, articulation, and prosody).

These tables should serve as a reference document to you. *The Source for Dysarthria* is organized by the five processes of speech: respiration, phonation, resonance, articulation, and prosody. You will be guided to treat based on your perceptual judgments of what you hear and observe. However, it's not enough to simply treat what you hear. You must also understand the site of lesion and course of the disorder, or you may treat a patient with poor prognosis for improvement the same as you would treat a patient with a good prognosis, just because they happen to sound the same at a certain point in time.

The charts may also help you make a differential diagnosis so that you can plan appropriately.

The Corticobulbar "Highway" System

Try to picture the relationship between the upper motor neurons and the lower motor neurons like a highway system (Diagram 1). Picture two major expressways (I-75 from Cincinnati and I-64 from Louisville). Instead of passing by Lexington, imagine they dead end in Lexington. There are two exits to Lexington, one to the East side of the city and one to the West. I-75 and I-64 have to share the ramps to exit into Lexington. That ramp is the final common pathway to that side of town. Understanding this relationship helps to make clear why lesions in a certain location cause the kind of damage we see.

UMN Damage with Bilateral Innervation to LMN

For example, a wreck on I-75 (Diagram 1, Wreck A, the expressway from Cincinnati) would cause a decrease in the number of cars exiting on either ramp to Lexington, but cars from the other major highway I-64 (Louisville) would be unaffected. There would be some impact on both ramps, but continuing input to both ramps.

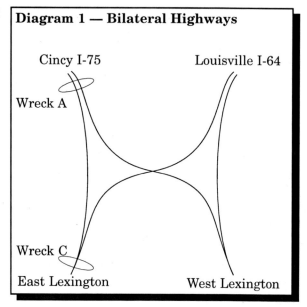

Diagram 1 — Bilateral Highways

Cincy I-75   Louisville I-64

Wreck A

Wreck C

East Lexington   West Lexington

A lesion to the upper motor neuron controlling one of the cranial nerves which has bilateral control such as the glossopharyngeus, would cause some weakness in the tongue, but some function would be maintained because of control from the opposite side where there is no lesion. (Diagram 2 - Lesion A).

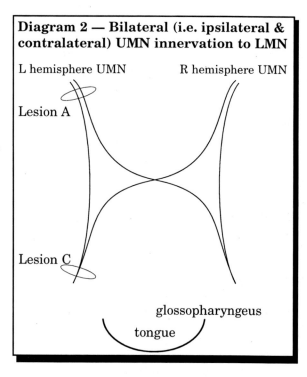

Diagram 2 — Bilateral (i.e. ipsilateral & contralateral) UMN innervation to LMN

L hemisphere UMN   R hemisphere UMN

Lesion A

Lesion C

glossopharyngeus
tongue

UMN Damage with Contralateral Innervation to LMN

Diagram 3 illustrates contralateral control. In our traffic example, I-75 and I-64 would each have separate exit ramps leading to different sides of Lexington. That is, I-75 would exit only to West Lexington and I-64 to East Lexington. So a wreck (Wreck B) on I-75 would lead to loss of traffic flow into one side of Lexington.

Damage to the UMN control of the hypoglossal, as in a CVA, results in the tongue being weak and deviating to the weak side opposite the lesion because of this contralateral control. (Diagram 4, Lesion B)

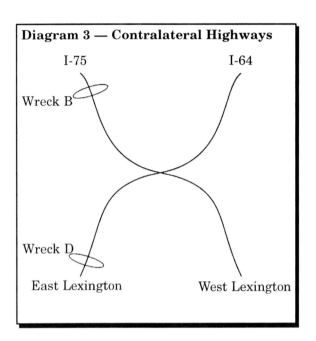

Diagram 3 — Contralateral Highways

LMN Damage with Bilateral or Contralateral UMN Input

Using either Diagram 1 or 3, damage to the exit ramp will essentially stop traffic flow to one side of the city. In Diagram 1, if there were a wreck (C), traffic from bilateral highways (I-75 and I-64) would be stopped at the ramp to East Lexington — the final common pathway. In Diagram 3, a wreck at D would cause traffic from the highway opposite the side of the ramp (the only highway that feeds that ramp), to stop to that side of the city. Whether you have one or two highways feeding the East Lexington exit ramp, a wreck on that ramp stops all traffic to that side of the city.

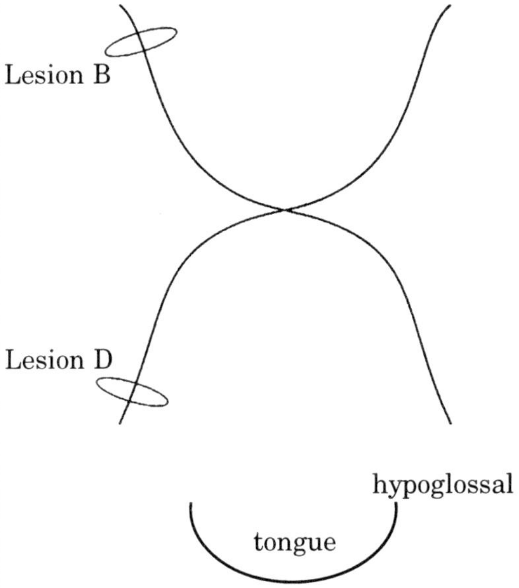

Diagrams 2 and 4 illustrate that damage to the LMN (whether there is bilateral control as in Diagram 2, Lesion C, or contralateral control only as in Diagram 4, Lesion D) stops innervation on that side. Lesions to the lower motor neurons, the final common pathways, result in atrophy and fasciculations on the same side as the lesion because this is the only pathway to that side of the structure. (Lesions C and D)

Diagram 4 — Contralateral UMN innervation of LMN

Pyramidal and Extrapyramidal Systems

Table 2

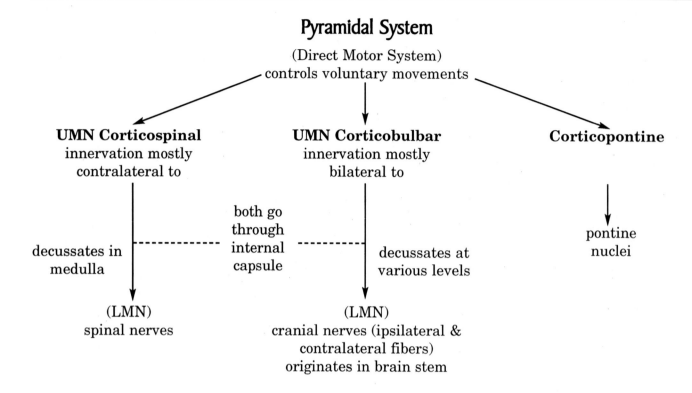

Pyramidal System

(Direct Motor System)
controls voluntary movements

UMN Corticospinal
innervation mostly
contralateral to

decussates in
medulla

(LMN)
spinal nerves

both go
through
internal
capsule

UMN Corticobulbar
innervation mostly
bilateral to

decussates at
various levels

(LMN)
cranial nerves (ipsilateral &
contralateral fibers)
originates in brain stem

Corticopontine

pontine
nuclei

Extrapyramidal System (Indirect Motor System) UMN*

Set of pathways that connect subcortical motor nuclei, includes basal ganglia

- concerned with coarse stereotyped movements
- maintains tone and posture
- more influence over proximal (midline) than distal (peripheral) muscles

Points to Remember:
- UMN never leave neuraxis — contained within brain, brain stem, and spinal cord
- LMN sends motor axons into peripheral nerves, the final common pathway

*Extrapyramidal system has UMN, but most authors mean the UMN in the corticobulbar and corticospinal tracts in the pyramidal system when they use the term UMN.

Site of Lesion: Pyramidal

Type of Dysarthria	Respiration	Phonation	Resonance	Articulation	Prosody
Spastic: Pseudobulbar (UMN)	may have reduced volumes, difficult to separate from what is caused by poor laryngeal valving	strained, strangled low pitch; some pitch breaks; little loudness variation	hypernasality, but usually not nasal emission	imprecise consonants	reduced stress; maybe excess and equal stress; slow rate
Flaccid: Bulbar (LMN)	decreased respiratory support secondary to muscle weakness	if unilateral damage in brain stem, voice will depend on where cord is (e.g., paramedian) bilateral cord involvement: breathy, audible inspiration, monoloudness	hypernasal and nasal emission	imprecise articulation, especially tongue tip plosives and fricatives	prosodic insufficiency, monotone
Flaccid: LMN Myasthenia Gravis	respiratory weakness	progressively more breathy, decreased intensity	hypernasal and nasal emission	imprecise articulation	monopitch
Flaccid: LMN (Vth)	none	none	none	unilateral: none bilateral: imprecise bilabials, labiodentals, linguadentals, lingual-alveolars, distorted vowels	unilateral: none bilateral: slow rate

Site of Lesion: Pyramidal

Types of Dysarthria	Respiration	Phonation	Resonance	Articulation	Prosody
Flaccid: LMN (VIIth)	none	none	none	unilateral: mild distortion bilabials, labiodentals, fricatives and affricates bilateral: distortion or inability to produce bilabials and labiodentals; possible vowel, lingual fricatives and affricates distorted	unilateral: none bilateral: slow rate
Flaccid: LMN (Xth) pharyngeal		unilateral: breathiness, hoarseness, diplophonia, reduced pitch and loudness bilateral: breathiness, aphonia, inhalatory stridor	unilateral: no affect to mild-moderate hypernasality and nasal emission bilateral: severe hypernasality, nasal emission, imprecise pressure consonants, short phrases secondary to nasal air wastage	bilateral: weak pressure consonants	
Flaccid: LMN (Xth) superior & recurrent		unilateral: breathiness or aphonia, reduced loudness, low pitch, diplophonia, rapid vocal flutter on vowel prolongation bilateral: all characteristics worse, monopitch			

Site of Lesion: Pyramidal

Types of Dysarthria	Respiration	Phonation	Resonance	Articulation	Prosody
Flaccid: LMN (Xth) Superior		unilateral: breathiness or hoarseness, mild inability to change pitch, loudness mildly reduced bilateral: mild to moderate breathiness and hoarseness, decreased loudness, inability to change pitch, low pitch, short phrases secondary to poor laryngeal valving			
Flaccid: LMN (Xth) Recurrent		unilateral: breathiness, hoarse voice quality, decreased loudness, diplophonia, pitch breaks bilateral: inhalatory stridor with airway compromise, voice fairly good, short phrases secondary to poor laryngeal valving			
Flaccid: LMN (XIIth) Nerve Lesions			bilateral: may be perceived as abnormal secondary to tongue falling back in oral cavity	unilateral/bilateral: imprecise articulation of lingual phonemes	slow rate

Site of Lesion: Pyramidal

Type of Dysarthria	Respiration	Phonation	Resonance	Articulation	Prosody
right hemisphere CVA					flattened intonation and monotone, reduced pitch and loudness variation, reduced or abnormal intonation, poor expression of irony and sarcasm, lack of emphasis, reduced affect and emotion

Site of Lesion: Extrapyramidal

Type of Dysarthria	Respiration	Phonation	Resonance	Articulation	Prosody
hypokinetic (not enough movement), Parkinson's disease	decreased support	hoarseness, breathiness, tremors, decreased loudness	some have hypernasality	changes in manner, "artic undershoot"	increased rate, palilalia (compulsive repetition of syllables), monopitch, monoloudness, short rushes of speech
hyperkinetic (too much movement), essential organic voice tremor		regular tremor of alternating pitch and loudness, low pitch, pitch breaks			monotone, rate may be slowed
hyperkinetic (too much movement), Chorea: Sydenham's, Huntington's	sudden forced inspiration and expiration	strained, strangled; excess loudness variation; voice stoppages and errors	hypernasality	imprecise consonants, distorted vowels, irregular articulatory breakdowns	decreased variable stress, prolonged intervals, variable rate, inappropriate silences
hyperkinetic (too much movement), dystonia and athetosis	poor respiratory support in athetosis	harsh, strained, strangled; possible intermittent breathiness; voice stoppages secondary to involuntary movements; excess loudness variations; audible inspiration; monoloudness	hypernasality	variable articulation, imprecise consonants, vowel distortions	short phrases with prolonged intervals, variable rate, monotone

Site of Lesion: Mixed — Pyramidal (UMN) and Cerebellar

Type of Dysarthria	Respiration	Phonation	Resonance	Articulation	Prosody
Spastic - Ataxia Multiple Sclerosis	decreased breath support	impaired loudness control; harsh, breathy quality	may have hypernasality	impaired articulation	inappropriate phrasing, impaired emphasis, increased stress, impaired pitch control
Progressive Supranuclear Palsy		hoarseness	nasal emission	imprecise articulation	excess and equal stress, slow rate, monopitch

Site of Lesion: Mixed - Pyramidal UMN/LMN

Type of Dysarthria	Respiration	Phonation	Resonance	Articulation	Prosody
Spastic/Flaccid ALS	decreased respiratory support	UMN damage: low pitch; harsh, strained, strangled voice with wet vocal quality LMN damage: breathy, monoloudness	hypernasality (not nasal emission)	imprecise consonants	decreased stress, decreased rate, prosodic insufficiency, prolonged phonemes breathy, monotone

Site of Lesion: Mixed – Pyramidal/Extrapyramidal

Type of Dysarthria	Respiration	Phonation	Resonance	Articulation	Prosody
unilateral upper motor neuron		harshness		imprecise consonants, irregular articulatory breakdowns	slow rate

Site of Lesion: Cerebellum

Type of Dysarthria	Respiration	Phonation	Resonance	Articulation	Prosody
Ataxia	speaks on low air	may be normal; may have excessive loudness variations; harshness; monoloudness		imprecise consonants; vowel distortion; irregular articulatory breakdowns	some patients have slow rate; excess and equal stress; bursts of increased intensity after pauses; phoneme and pause prolongation; monotone

Chapter 2
Evaluation of Dysarthria

The basis of any treatment plan is formed by a thorough diagnostic evaluation. Orlikoff (1992) indicates that an evaluation is indicated when:

- a patient has been given a certain medical diagnosis or decision about a medical condition
- the patient's speech is unintelligible
- the patient's speech is unnatural

Framework for Assessment of Dysarthria

When considering evaluation and management of dysarthria, it may be useful to use the framework suggested by the World Health Organization (WHO). This definition is undergoing revision, but provides us with a useful way to consider managing the care of patients with dysarthria. WHO describes three levels:

- impairment: the abnormality of structure or function at the organ level, in this case the stroke or other neurological disorder with resulting brain damage that has caused the dysarthria
- disability: the effect that impairment has had on function; in dysarthria, this would be the reduced ability to speak on the phone, give verbal directions, etc.
- handicap: the effect the disability can have on the individual's ability to participate in social situations

Too often our assessments focus only at the impairment level. That is, we look carefully at what is wrong with the muscles and not enough at the level of disability and handicap. We should be looking more at how the impaired musculature has affected speech and the ability to communicate (level of disability) and the patient's quality of life as a result of the impairment (level of handicap).

A different conceptual framework proposed by Coster and Haley (1992) can be used. They propose a four-level framework for functional assessment. The chart on the following page illustrates the framework.

Level of Function/Disablement	Assessment Questions	Assessment Questions Specific to Management of Dysarthria
social participation/societal performance (societal disadvantage)	To what extent is the individual included in or restricted from participating in the activities and opportunities typically expected of or available to an individual of this age and culture?	To what extent is the individual able to participate in activities in the home or community using verbal communication or another method of adapted or alternative communication?
complex task performance (disability)	To what extent is the individual currently meeting expectations for the performance of important (complex) tasks expected of peers in this culture and context?	To what extent is the individual able to meet the expectations to engage in conversation, talk on the phone, and perform other speech tasks (whether adapted or not)?
activity performance (functional limitations)	What are the individual's current strengths and limitations in performance of specific activities required to accomplish the major tasks expected of him?	What are the individual's current strengths and limitations in performing specific communication tasks such as saying short phrases and sentences intelligibly?
basic structures and processes (impairment)	What is the status (intactness) of the basic processes or components necessary for the performance of daily tasks and activities?	What is the status of the patient's lingual strength, lip strength and movement, phonation time, etc.?

As can be seen, activity performance and complex task performance in this framework are an elaboration of the WHO classification of disability. Impairment remains impairment in both of the schema and societal disadvantage equates to handicap from the WHO schema.

It's important to keep in mind that in the management of dysarthria, we shouldn't stay at the impairment level alone, although many of the activities in this book are designed to help facilitate improvement of those basic structures and processes. In addition, we shouldn't focus just on the disability (or disability and functional limitations) level which would be helping the patient compensate for lost function in real world situations. Instead, we must include in our management of individuals with dysarthria a consideration of the handicap (societal disadvantage) of having unintelligible or impaired intelligibility of speech and decreased ability to communicate.

Purposes of Evaluation

Is there a problem?

The first goal of an evaluation is to determine if the patient has a dysarthria.

What type of problem?

The second goal is to determine the specific disorder the patient has. This includes distinguishing a dysarthria from another motor speech disorder such as apraxia or, more specifically, determining which type of dysarthria the patient has. Once the determination has been made that the patient has a dysarthria, it's important to determine the type. This information will help you provide an appropriate prognosis and develop appropriate techniques for intervention.

Wertz and Rosenbek (1992) state that knowing the type of dysarthria is important to help confirm or rule out specific neurological diagnoses and may even aid in the localization of the lesion. It is also important to be able to determine dysarthric speech from apraxic speech as the two disorders share some features. For example, patients with dysarthria and apraxia may both produce imprecise consonants. The prosody of a patient with apraxia may sound similar to the disturbed prosody of ataxia.

Is the problem amenable to treatment?

Although it may not necessarily occur during the first evaluation session, stimulability testing is very important. This will help you determine which characteristics are amenable to treatment. Tasks of stimulability should focus on areas of deficit of function (that is, disability) rather than at the impairment level. For instance, if the patient is perceived as hypernasal, it's not important to know if he can move his palate better, but it is important to know if he can compensate for the hypernasality, perhaps by opening his mouth wider to reduce the perception of hypernasality. Some stimulability tasks are listed

under each physiologic component on pages 49-58.

What is the impact on function?

How does the dysarthria affect the patient's ability to perform functional tasks such as talking on phone, answering questions, or requesting information from strangers?

What is the impact on the patient's particpation in activities?

Is the patient able to take part in activities at her residence or in the community?

Is it possible to determine the type of dysarthria if you know the cause/etiology?

Not necessarily. As is apparent from studying the charts provided in the next chapter, many times one etiology can be the cause of a variety of different types of dysarthria. The following etiologies can cause any type of dysarthria: vascular disease, degenerative disease, traumatic brain injury, and surgical trauma.

Duffy (1995) provides some clues from the etiology concerning the type of dysarthria. For instance:

- tumors rarely cause hyperkinetic dysarthria
- toxic and metabolic disturbances rarely cause flaccid and unilateral upper motor neuron dysarthria
- infectious and inflammatory conditions do not often cause dysarthria of any type
- demyelinating diseases may cause any type of dysarthria, but rarely cause hypokinetic dysarthria
- anatomic malformations are usually associated with flaccid dysarthria
- neuromuscular junction disorders, muscle disease, and neuropathy cause flaccid dysarthria

Instrumentation or Perceptual Evaluation

There appears to be a wide range of opinions concerning the need for the use of instrumentation in the assessment of dysarthria. Orlikoff (1992) states that speech assessments tend to be based on what is heard (i.e., the perceptual features), but cautions that this has led to subjective categorizations of speech disorders. He and other authors point out the importance of using instrumentation.

Yorkston, Beukelman, and Bell (1988) state that a problem with using only perceptual assessment not backed up by any instrumental assessment is that it can fool you into forgetting to look at the nature of the problem. They provide an example that a speaker may use short phrases with only a few syllables or words per breath group for any number of reasons. It could be an underlying respiratory problem with poor respiratory support. It could be observed in a patient who has spastic dysarthria who is trying to compensate to push past the spasticity and, therefore, can only get out a few syllables at a time. It could also be related to velopharyngeal incompetency with air wastage through the nasopharynx.

Therefore, it can be dangerous to simply listen to what you hear and make a judgment since there can be many causes for the same perceptually-based problem. Instrumental assessments can help you better identify the reason for or nature of the impairment.

Orlikoff points out that physical measures help to describe the dysarthria at the level of impairment, but a perceptual evaluation can help document the disability. There is fairly extensive instrumentation which can be used to assess:

- respiratory structure and function
- laryngeal structure and function
- vocal tract structure and function

Even Orlikoff, however, admits that there is not a direct relationship between the physiology and the perceptual characteristic.

On the other hand, Duffy (1995) and others point out that all that is needed for an assessment of dysarthria is:

- light
- tongue blade
- small mirror
- stopwatch
- audio/video recorder

Wertz and Rosenbek (1985) defend a perceptual evaluation of motor speech disorders stating that "dysarthrias do not exist unless you can hear . . . them." They discuss the rationale, validity, and reliability of specific perceptual measures. Their position is not meant to demean acoustical or physiological methods of evaluation of dysarthrias. They agree that it is important to determine the type of dysarthria rather than simply stating that the patient presents with a dysarthria, but they encourage SLPs not to be distracted from listening to the patient's overall speech.

McNeil (1986) also argues that listening to a patient's speech is a more valid tool to assess dysarthria than instrumental measures. And, of course, the grandaddy of all dysarthria studies by Darley and his colleagues (1975) was based on perceptual judgments.

Perceptual Assessment Framework

It is beyond the scope of this book to describe the instrumentation which can be used to help in the assessment of a dysarthria. These are described nicely in other sources such as *Clinical Management of Dysarthric Speakers* by Yorkston, Beukelman, and Bell (1988). In addition, most clinicians in most clinical settings do not have easy access to such instrumentation. Typically the only instrumentation used when completing evaluations at bedside, in the clinic, or in the patient's home is a tape recorder.

The framework for this book is that of a perceptual analysis. This perceptual analysis must be paired with a careful study of the case history and presenting symptoms to help you recognize the presence of a dysarthria and then to determine which type of dysarthria exists. Remember that different treatment techniques may be recommended for the same perceptual symptom based on the physiology that is causing the symptom.

Testing Components vs. Listening to Speech

Components

Testing speech motor functions with vowel prolongation, nonsense syllables, and diadochokinetic rates may yield results that are different from those gained with linguistically meaningful stimuli.

The value of testing individual components of the speech mechanism is well known. For example, holding the jaw in a fixed position with a bite block between the teeth is used to test independent function of the lips and tongue. Better speech performance with the jaw stabilized suggests that jaw abnormalities are contributing to the poor speech. Poorer speech with the jaw stabilized suggests the jaw is assisting or compensating for the tongue and/or lips or biting on the block results in a spread of hyperactivity to the tongue and/or lips and affects their movement. Poorer performance with the jaw fixed may also indicate that the client has lost adaptive control.

An additional caution in interpreting component functions of the speech mechanism is that they may appear reasonably good on a component-by-component basis but look and sound quite poor collectively. Netsell (1983) points out the reasons for this:

- Component analysis does not test the overall coordination of the speech mechanism. You can lessen this concern by using meaningful speech stimuli that place primary demands on one component and minimal requirements on the other. For example, in testing lip function, use of the words *mom* and *momma* places emphasis on lip movement and lesser demands on the velopharynx, tongue, larynx, and respiratory system.

- When you add up small deficiencies, they can equal poor overall function.

- Some components may appear severely involved in the presence of fairly adequate speech. The individual may be compensating for these more severe malfunctions and, therefore, treatment of the individual problems may not be advised.

Speech Samples

When listening to samples of a patient's speech, be aware of several pitfalls.

1. You may hear certain perceptual characteristics from patients only during certain speech samples.

2. Some aspects of speech influence how you hear other aspects of speech. For instance, if a patient has a severe disorder in the production of individual phonemes, it may be difficult to perceptually determine that you are also hearing hypernasality.

3. Be careful when assessing a dysarthria by perceptual symptoms so as not to ignore the fact that many different medical problems can result in hearing the same type of speech disorders perceptually.

Commercial Tests of Dysarthria

There are several assessments of dysarthric speech available commercially. *The Assessment of Intelligibility of Dysarthric Speech* (Yorkston and Beukelman, 1981) and the *Computerized Assessment of Intelligibility of Dysarthric Speech* (Yorkston, et al., 1984) were designed to measure intelligibility in a clinical setting. They allow you to calculate a patient's "communication efficiency" by dividing the number of intelligible words produced in a minute by what the authors state is the number of normal intelligible words per minute (190).

Since these tests measure intelligibility (functional speech), they assess the disability more than the impairment. These assessments provide an objective measure of sentence and single-word intelligibility during a reading or imitative task (speaking rate combined with intelligibility). The authors contend that this is a useful means of distinguishing mildly dysarthric from normal speakers.

The Frenchay Dysarthria Test was developed in the United Kingdom by Pamela Enderby (1983). This test uses a form similar to a bar graph to rate the following areas:

- reflex
- respiration
- lips
- jaw
- palate
- laryngeal
- tongue
- intelligibility

The patient is asked to complete specific motor tasks which are then scored on a scale that ranges from normal function to no function. When the bar graph is filled in, it can be compared to typical patterns for patients with:

- upper motor neuron lesions
- lower motor neuron lesions
- extrapyramidal disorders
- cerebellar dysfunctions
- mixed upper and lower motor neuron lesions

The *Perceptual Dysarthria Evaluation* (Forms A, B, C-1, and C-2) on pages 32-35 will provide you with a starting point in evaluating a patient. Instructions for completing the forms can be found on pages 36-41.

Informal Assessments

Beginning on page 49, there are descriptions of informal methods of assessment of dysarthria which may be utilized:

- to supplement the *Perceptual Dysarthria Evaluation* (PDE)
- to supplement information obtained through a commercial test
- in combination with instrumental measures

For each physiologic component (e.g., respiration, phonation, resonance, articulation, and prosody), you are provided with:

- a chart summarizing what you may hear and what might be causing it. Note that the same perceptual symptom (e.g., decreased loudness) may have several physiologic causes (e.g., weak respiratory muscles or abnormal tone). Use the information you obtain about each component during the evaluation to plan treatment by using the disorder-based charts in Chapter 3 or the *Symptoms by Dysarthria Types* charts at the end of Chapters 4-8.
- informal tasks for assessment — some of these are also found on the PDE
- questions to keep in mind as you make judgments about each physiologic component
- stimulability tasks to help determine if the functional problem can be changed

Using the framework of impairment, disability, and handicap, remember that many of the tasks described assess the impairment (i.e., which muscles aren't working well). We must also assess the disability (i.e., the impact that the impairment has on the patient's ability to perform specific speech tasks). This is particularly related to assessing intelligibility such as in the word and sentence repetition tasks and in conversational speech tasks used to assess prosody.

We should also make some attempt, particularly if it is a chronic or progressive disorder, to assess the resultant handicap. That is, to what extent has the patient withdrawn from participating in activities of daily living because of the dysarthria? Appendix A (page 59) may be helpful in obtaining this information.

Perceptual Dysarthria Evaluation

Patient _____   Patient # _____
Date of birth _____ Age _____   Date of evaluation _____
Physician _____   Date of onset _____
Medical diagnosis related to speech disorder _____
_____

Associated neurological symptoms reported _____
_____

Patient complaint/impact on function _____
Previous treatment _____

Observation by (physiologic) Component	Goals/Treatment Objectives
RESPIRATION	_____ Patient will improve respiratory support and the use of respiration for speech. Stimulable _____ *Treatment Objectives*
PHONATION	_____ Patient will maximize use of phonation to improve communication skills. Stimulable _____ *Treatment Objectives*
RESONANCE	_____ Patient will reduce the amount of perceived hypernasality/nasal emission to increase intelligibility. Stimulable _____ *Treatment Objectives*
ARTICULATION	_____ Patient will improve articulation to increase intelligibility. Stimulable _____ *Treatment Objectives*
PROSODY	_____ Patient will improve use of prosody to increase intelligibility and produce speech. Stimulable _____ *Treatment Objectives*
ENVIRONMENT	Environmental Modification _____ Speaker and listener will improve environment in which communication takes place. *Treatment Objectives*

Diagnosis _____
Recommendations   ____ S/L Therapy   ____ Cognitive/Language Eval   ____ Dysphagia Eval
                  ____ no therapy indicated   Frequency _____
Long-term goals   ____ achieve intelligible verbal speech   ____ achieve natural-sounding speech
                  ____ verbal communication via augmentation
                  ____ alternative form of communication: _____
Patient/Family Goals _____

_____   _____
Speech-Language Pathologist   Date

Patient _____ Patient # _____

ASHA Functional Communication Measure/Speech Production

Level 0   unable to test

Level 1   Production of speech is unintelligible.

Level 2   Spontaneous production of speech is limited in intelligibility; some automatic speech and imitative words or consonant/vowel (CV) combinations may be intelligible.

Level 3   Spontaneous production of speech consists primarily of automatic words or phrases with inconsistent intelligibility.

Level 4   Spontaneous production of speech is intelligible at the phrase level in familiar contexts; out of context speech is generally unintelligible unless self-cueing and self-monitoring strategies are applied.

Level 5   Spontaneous production of speech is intelligible for meeting daily living needs; out of context speech requires periodic repetition, rephrasing, or provision of a cue.

Level 6   Spontaneous production of speech is intelligible in and out of context, but the production is sometimes distorted.

Level 7   Production of speech is normal in all situations.

Positive expectation to begin service _____

_____

_____

_____

Need for skilled service _____

_____

_____

_____

Frequency of service _____

Duration of service _____

Discharge Plan _____

_____

I certify that the above patient requires therapy services, is under a plan of care established or reviewed every 30 days by me, and requires the above treatment specified on a continuing basis with the following changes:

Physician Notice: (circle one)   I do / do not find it necessary to see this patient within the next 30 days.

_____   _____
              Physician   Date

Perceptual Dysarthria Evaluation

Patient _____   Date_____

Oral-Motor Evaluation

1. **Structure**
   Note any abnormalities _____

edentulous	yes	no	dentures	yes	no
			dentures in during eval	yes	no

2. **Assessing Jaw, Lips, and Tongue**
   Jaw Control ____ CNA   + / -

Labial Function	____ CNA			
lip spread /i/	+/-	lip round /u/	+ / -
lip closure at rest		lip smacking	+ / -
symmetry	+/-		
droop	R L		

Lingual Function	____ CNA		
protrusion	+ / -	retraction	+ / -
lick lips	+ / -	lateralization to corners	R + / - L + / -
lateralization to buccal cavity	R + / - L + / -	elevation of tip	+ / -
elevation of back	+ / -		

3. **Velar Function** _____ CNA
   prolonged /a/: symmetry during evaluation   + / -

4. **Reflex** _____ CNA
   swallow reflex   + / -

Cognition/Communication   ___ CNA

Orientation	day _____	date _____	year _____	place _____
follows one-step directions	+/-	with cues	without cues	
follows two-step directions	+/-	with cues	without cues	
Expressive language	gestures/points	uses single words	uses phrases	confused speech
Short-term memory				
Can patient retell techniques?	yes	no		
Hearing acuity	right _____	left_____		
wears hearing aid(s)	yes	no		
hearing aid(s) in for eval	yes	no		

AMRs	**Rhythm**	**Rate**	**Accuracy**
/pʌ pʌ pʌ/	regular / irregular	slow / normal / fast	precise / imprecise
/tʌ tʌ tʌ/	regular / irregular	slow / normal / fast	precise / imprecise
/kʌ kʌ kʌ/	regular / irregular	slow / normal / fast	precise / imprecise

SMRs			
/pʌ tʌ kʌ/	regular / irregular	slow / normal / fast	precise / imprecise

Perceptual Dysarthria Evaluation

Form C-2

Patient _____ Date_____

Prolong /a/
Characteristics
observed:
_____ time in seconds
_____ breathy   _____ harsh   _____ hoarse
_____ tremor   _____ inhalatory stridor _____ diplophonia
_____ voice arrest   _____ decreased loudness _____ strained/strangled

Reading and/or Conversation	Characteristics Observed
Respiration	_____ reduced loudness _____ monoloudness _____ short phrases _____ impaired loudness control _____ sudden inspiration/expiration
Phonation	_____ breathy _____ harsh _____ hoarse _____ monopitch _____ low pitch _____ monoloudness _____ reduced loudness _____ short phrases _____ audible inspiration _____ strained/strangled _____ pitch breaks _____ voicing errors _____ excessive loudness variations
Resonance	_____ hypernasal _____ nasal emission
Articulation	_____ imprecise consonants _____ irregular breakdowns _____ distorted vowels specific errors: _____
Prosody	_____ reduced stress _____ monotone _____ excess & equal stress _____ bursts of loudness _____ slow rate _____ fast rate _____ variable rate _____ prolonged intervals _____ prolonged phonemes _____ short rushes _____ poor intonation

Contrastive Stress

"Todd likes apples."   To indicate stress, patient uses:
_____ increased pitch   _____ patient does not indicate stress
_____ increased loudness
_____ pauses

Stress testing (1-100) _____

Patient-initiated compensatory strategies _____

_____

Perceptual Dysarthria Evaluation Instructions

Completing Form A   (Use this form in all settings.)

Identifying Information

Complete this part of the form before beginning the evaluation.

- Physician: Who ordered the evaluation?

- Date of onset: It's important to note the date of onset of the event which caused or exacerbated the dysarthria. Knowing the length of time since the onset may help you determine whether the patient is a candidate for treatment.

- Medical diagnosis related to speech disorder: Although the patient may carry many diagnoses, be sure to list the medical diagnosis which is the probable cause of the dysarthria.

- Associated neurological symptoms reported: Look through the neurological evaluation or other physicians' notes to find any other related neurological symptoms. The associated symptoms related to a specific diagnosis are listed on the disorder-based charts in Chapter 3. The symptoms might include things like:

excessive muscle tone	loss of skilled movement
hypotonia	decreased range of motion
rigidity	drooling
unpredictable movements	cognitive deficits
falling	weakness
atrophy and fasciculations	dysphagia
resting tremor	bradykinesia
mask-like face	gait problems
sensory deficits	pseudobulbar affect

- Patient complaint/impact on function: Find out from the patient what it is about the speech disorder that bothers the patient the most, and how it impacts on the patient's ability to function on a daily basis. The questions in Appendix 1 can help the patient focus on this issue.

- Previous treatment: It's important to note if the patient has had previous treatment, when it was, how long the patient was treated, what the response to treatment was, and why the patient was discharged.

Complete the rest of Form A after you have evaluated the patient.

Observations by Component

Write down a phrase or two to describe your impression of each of the components.

Goals/Treatment Objectives

Check any goals you plan to address with the patient. Also check Stimulable if you think the patient is stimulable for achieving that goal.

Using the information in Chapters 4-8, select appropriate treatment objectives that will help the patient achieve the goals you have chosen. You can either write them in by number and letter code (e.g., AR 1, 4; RSN 7, 9) or actually write out the objectives. If you write in the codes, but need to have the treatment objectives written out, you can save time by copying appropriate pages from Chapters 4 - 8, circling the treatment objectives, and attaching them to the report.

Note that most patients will need the environmental goal "Speaker and listener will improve environment in which communication takes place" with certain treatment objectives selected. This goal is repeated in Chapters 4 - 8 with the only change being on the last treatment objective (EM 8) as you may want to write in the specific external aid(s) needed by the patient.

Diagnosis

With the information in Chapter 2 and the disorder-based charts in Chapter 3, try to make a differential diagnosis about the type of dysarthria presented.

Recommendations

Indicate any and all therapy or evaluations that are needed or whether no treatment is necessary.

Long-Term Goals

Long-term goals indicate where you think the patient will be at the conclusion of treatment. Patients now receive therapy in many settings across the continuum of care (e.g., starting in acute care settings, then perhaps in sub-acute or skilled nursing, later in home health, etc.) You may not work with the patient long enough to achieve the long-term goal(s). You may make predictions about where you think the patient will be at the end of treatment/end of the continuum as it is entirely possible that other SLPs will be helping the patient reach the long-term goals.

Patient/Family Goals

Encourage the patient and his family to discuss what their goals are for the patient. Provide counseling if their goals seem unrealistic based on your prognosis. Remember, however, that if a patient doesn't agree with the goals you set, he probably won't work to achieve them.

Completing Form B

This form is to be used in addition to Form A in a skilled nursing facility or outpatient setting when an M.D. signature is needed.

ASHA Functional Communication Measure/Speech Production

The Functional Communication Measures (FCMs) are seven-point scales designed to allow a quick rating of the patient's functional skills. This FCM is one of many for the adult population which is part of the ASHA National Outcomes Measurement System (NOMS). Circle the level you think best describes the patient's speech at this time.

Positive Expectation

Medicare in particular wants you to document why you have enrolled the patient in treatment. What gave you an expectation that the patient would change? Statements like the following may be used to describe the patient:

- Patient alert and cooperative.
- Patient motivated to improve intelligibility.
- Patient stimulable to improve articulation and resonance.
- Patient frustrated by decreased intelligibility and willing to learn compensatory strategies.
- Patient received only brief period of previous treatment and responded well.

Need for Skilled Service

Describe why the patient needs the services of a certified/licensed SLP and not just anyone (e.g., family member) to practice with them or remind them to slow down. Statements like the following can be used:

- Without intervention, the patient won't be able to achieve adequate respiratory support for connected speech.
- Without intervention, the patient won't be able to speak loudly enough to be heard.
- Without intervention, the patient's speech will remain unintelligible.
- Without intervention, the patient's speech won't sound natural.

Frequency of service

How often do you plan to see the patient? In the acute phase of a disease, it may be appropriate to see the patient twice a day. Once the patient is through the acute phase, it may be more appropriate to adjust the schedule to once a day or several times a week.

Duration of service

How long do you predict the patient will need your services? You can list this in weeks or months.

Discharge Plan

You should be thinking about when you will be able to discharge the patient from the time of the initial evaluation. Statements like the following are helpful:

- Patient will be discharged when all short term goals are met.
- Patient will be discharged when speech is intelligible to strangers 85% of the time.
- Patient will be discharged when able to independently communicate with an alternative form of communication.
- Patient will be discharged when speech sounds natural and no longer calls attention to itself.

| Completing Forms C-1 and C-2 | (Use both of these forms regardless of setting.) |

Oral-Motor Evaluation

Examining a patient's ability to use oral-motor skills in isolation yields information about strength, speed, and accuracy of movements, but it many not necessarily tell how the patient will be able to use these same structures for speech. Be sure to wear gloves when peforming any oral-motor evaluation.

1. **Structure**
    Carefully examine for any structural abnormalities of the lips, tongue, gums, and hard and soft palates.

    Find out if the patient has no teeth (edentulous). If this is the case, note whether the patient has dentures and whether the dentures were worn during your evaluation.

    You may have to help the patient clean his dentures and put them in if he wants to wear them during the evaluation. If the patient has had a stroke with hemiparesis, he'll probably try to put the dentures in the side of his mouth in which he still has feeling, catching them on the side of the mouth with no feeling. If you help the patient put his dentures in, start on the weaker side.

    Sometimes a patient doesn't want to wear his dentures for an evaluation. If he hasn't worn them for a while, they may not fit or they may even cause some gagging.

2. **Assessing Jaw, Lips, and Tongue**
    Circle + if the movements appear to be within normal limits. A decrease in strength, speed, amplitude, or accuracy indicates you should circle -. CNA means that you could not assess.

    Jaw Control
    Assess the patient's ability to open his jaw adequately and to maintain good jaw closure.

    Labial Function
    Assess the patient's range of motion when asked to repeat /i/ and /u/. Note lip closure at rest, indicating if there is symmetry or droop on either side. Have the patient smack his lips. Observe for strength and symmetry.

    Lingual Function
    Demonstrate any of the following tasks if the patient doesn't understand your instructions:
    - protrusion/retraction: Ask the patient to stick her tongue out as far as she can and then retract it entirely within her mouth.
    - lick lips: Ask the patient to lick her lips all the way around in a circular motion.
    - lateralization to corners: Ask the patient to put her tongue to the corners of her lips.
    - lateralization to buccal cavity: Ask the patient to put her tongue in the buccal cavity on each side.
    - elevation of tip: Ask the patient to place her tongue tip on her alveolar ridge with her mouth open and jaw steady.
    - elevation of back: Ask the patient to produce /k/ with as much force as possible.

3. **Velar Function**

Using a tongue depressor to stabilize the patient's tongue and a penlight to light the oral cavity, ask the patient to produce a prolonged /a/. Watch for symmetry on elevation of the velum.

4. **Reflex**

Ask the patient to swallow. If the oral cavity is very dry, you may need to stop and clean the patient's mouth (oral care) before the patient will be able to swallow.

Cognition/Communication

- Orientation: Ask the patient to identify the day, date, year, and place.

- One-step directions: Ask the patient to follow some basic one-step commands such as "Close your eyes," "Point to the door," and "Pick up the spoon." Note whether the comments are followed accurately and whether cues are needed.

- Two-step directions: Ask the patient to follow several two-step commands such as "Open your mouth and touch your head," or "Point to the door and pick up the pencil." Again note whether the patient needed cues to accurately follow the directions.

- Expressive language: Provide a judgment about the patient's basic expressive language skills.

- Short-term memory: If the patient is going to use any compensatory techniques to improve intelligibility, indicate whether the patient is able to restate them.

- Hearing acuity: Note whether the patient's hearing has been informally or formally assessed. Add any observations about hearing acuity that may interfere with dysarthria treatment. For example, does the patient fail to follow a direction because he can't hear it accurately? Note whether the patient wears hearing aids and whether he is wearing them for your evaluation.

AMRs (Alternate Motion Rates)

How a patient produces alternate motion rates can tell you a great deal about his dysarthria. Ask the patient to repeat each sound as quickly and as evenly as possible. Model each of the AMR series for the patient. Note if the rhythm is regular or irregular; if the rate is slow, normal, or fast; and if the accuracy is precise or imprecise.

SMRs (Sequential Motion Rates)

Provide the same instructions as for the AMRs. Make the same observations about rhythm, rate, and accuracy.

Prolong /a/

Ask the patient to say /a/ and hold the sound for as long as possible. Note the time in seconds. An average adult should be able to hold the sound for approximately 20 seconds. If the patient can only sustain production of a vowel for a few seconds, it may mean that respiratory support for speech is reduced. It may also mean that the patient has poor laryngeal valving, wasting a lot of air because the vocal folds aren't closing tightly or may indicate poor velopharyngeal valving. Check any characteristic observed about the patient's phonation.

Reading and/or Conversation

Each of the five (physiologic) components should be observed in either reading or conversation. This can be done at the beginning of the evaluation when you're asking the patient questions to obtain background information or can be done more formally later in the evaluation. You can also use the Grandfather Passage (Appendix D, page 62) for reading, or use questions to elicit conversation (Appendix E, page 63).

- Respiration: Check any of the characteristics listed which may indicate reduced control for respiration or incoordination of respiration.

- Phonation: You have already made some assessments of phonation when listening to the patient prolong /a/. Now listen to conversational speech or reading to determine how phonation is perceived in connected speech. Check any characteristics you observe.

- Resonance: You have probably also made an initial impression of resonance when the patient produced /a/. However, listen for assimilation nasality, hypernasal resonance, and nasal emission in connected speech. Check any characteristics you observe.

- Articulation: Have the patient read a list of words or sentences (Appendices B and C, pages 60 and 61) or just listen to conversational speech. Check any characteristics you observe. If there seems to be a pattern of errors on specific sounds or classes of phonemes, list them.

- Prosody: Listen for the appropriate use of rate, stress, and intonation. Stress will be tested more completely on the contrastive stress activity which follows.

Contrastive Stress

Have the patient repeat the sentence "Todd likes apples." Then use the following questions to assess the patient's use of contrastive stress.

| Clinician: | Does Sue like apples? | Clinician: | Does Todd like grapes? |
| Patient: | <u>Todd</u> likes apples. | Patient: | Todd likes <u>apples</u>. |

| Clinician: | Does Todd hate apples? |
| Patient: | Todd <u>likes</u> apples. |

If you hear any change in stress at all, check whether the patient seems to be using increased pitch, increased loudness, a pause, or any combination of these to indicate a change in stress. If the patient is not indicating stress, note that.

Stress Testing/Effects of Fatigue

Some types of dysarthria result in an exacerbation of symptoms as an effect of fatigue. Asking the patient to count from 1 - 100 may reveal better articulation, phonation, resonance, etc. at the beginning and worse skills by the time the patient reaches 100. Describe any effects of fatigue.

Patient-initiated Compensatory Strategies

The patient may have found some ways to improve intelligibility and compensate for decreased function. List any strategies the patient is using.

Sample: Perceptual Dysarthria Evaluation

Form A

Patient __D.A.__ Patient # _____

Date of birth __3-1-20__ Age __77__ Date of evaluation __10-9-97__

Physician __Brooks__ Date of onset __8-26-97__

Medical diagnosis related to speech disorder __Cerebellar hemorrhage__

Associated neurological symptoms reported __hypotonia, ataxic gait__

Patient complaint/impact on function __biting tongue; sounds drunk__

Previous treatment __acute and sub-acute care__

Observation by (physiologic) Component | Goals/Treatment Objectives

RESPIRATION

_____ Patient will improve respiratory support and the use of respiration for speech. Stimulable _____

Treatment Objectives

PHONATION

voice sounds harsh with loudness bursts

__✔__ Patient will maximize use of phonation to improve communication skills. Stimulable __✔__

Treatment Objectives

PH 21, 24

RESONANCE

_____ Patient will reduce the amount of perceived hypernasality/nasal emission to increase intelligibility. Stimulable _____

Treatment Objectives

ARTICULATION

distorted vowels, irregular articulatory breakdowns

__✔__ Patient will improve articulation to increase intelligibility. Stimulable __✔__

Treatment Objectives

AR 29, 30, 38, 39, 41, 46 (s blends, l blends, s, z, ʃ ,tʃ)

PROSODY

excess and equal stress; slow rate — bursts of increased loudness

__✔__ Patient will improve use of prosody to increase intelligibility and produce speech. Stimulable _____

Treatment Objectives

PR 17, 18, 19, 20, 34

ENVIRONMENT

Pt doesn't wait to gain listener's attention

Environmental Modification

__✔__ Speaker and listener will improve environment in which communication takes place.

Treatment Objectives

Diagnosis __Ataxic dysarthria__

Recommendations __✔__ S/L Therapy _____ Cognitive/Language Eval _____ Dysphagia Eval

_____ no therapy indicated Frequency __5x week; B.I.D.__

Long-term goals _____ achieve intelligible verbal speech __✔__ achieve natural-sounding speech

_____ verbal communication via augmentation

_____ alternative form of communication: _____

Patient/Family Goals __To improve naturalness of speech__

_____ _____
Speech-Language Pathologist Date

Sample: Perceptual Dysarthria Evaluation

Patient D.A.   Patient #_____

ASHA Functional Communication Measure/Speech Production

Level 0   unable to test

Level 1   Production of speech is unintelligible.

Level 2   Spontaneous production of speech is limited in intelligibility; some automatic speech and imitative words or consonant/vowel (CV) combinations may be intelligible.

Level 3   Spontaneous production of speech consists primarily of automatic words or phrases with inconsistent intelligibility.

Level 4   Spontaneous production of speech is intelligible at the phrase level in familiar contexts; out of context speech is generally unintelligible unless self-cueing and self-monitoring strategies are applied.

(Level 5) Spontaneous production of speech is intelligible for meeting daily living needs; out of context speech requires periodic repetition, rephrasing, or provision of a cue.

Level 6   Spontaneous production of speech is intelligible in and out of context, but the production is sometimes distorted.

Level 7   Production of speech is normal in all situations.

Positive expectation to begin service   Pt very cooperative and motivated to improve.

_____

_____

_____

Need for skilled service   Without intervention, pt's speech will remain distorted and difficult to understand.

_____

_____

_____

Frequency of service   5x wk B.I.D.

Duration of service   4-6 wks, then probably decrease to QD

Discharge Plan   when pt's speech sounds natural

I certify that the above patient requires therapy services, is under a plan of care established or reviewed every 30 days by me, and requires the above treatment specified on a continuing basis with the following changes:

Physician Notice: (circle one)   I do / do not find it necessary to see this patient within the next 30 days.

_____   _____
            Physician   Date

Sample: Perceptual Dysarthria Evaluation

Patient _D.A._   Date _10/9/97_

Oral-Motor Evaluation

1. **Structure**
   Note any abnormalities _____
   edentulous (yes)   no   dentures (yes)   no
                                                  dentures in during eval (yes)   no

2. **Assessing Jaw, Lips, and Tongue**
   Jaw Control   ___ CNA   ⊕/ -

   Labial Function   ___ CNA
   lip spread /i/   ⊕ /-   lip round /u/   ⊕/ -
   lip closure at rest   lip smacking   ⊕/ -
      symmetry   ⊕/ -
      droop   R L

   Lingual Function   ___ CNA
   protrusion   ⊕/ -   retraction   ⊕/ -
   lick lips   ⊕/ -   lateralization to corners   R ⊕ -   L ⊕/ -
   lateralization to buccal cavity   R⊕/ -   L⊕/ -   elevation of tip   ⊕/ -
   elevation of back   ⊕/ -

3. **Velar Function**   ___ CNA
   prolonged /a/: symmetry during evaluation   ⊕/ -

4. **Reflex**   ___ CNA
   swallow reflex   ⊕/ -

Cognition/Communication   ___ CNA

Orientation   day ✔   date ✔   year ✔   place ✔
follows one-step directions   ⊕/ -   with cues   without cues
follows two-step directions   ⊕/ -   with cues   without cues
Expressive language   gestures/points   uses single words   (uses phrases)   confused speech
Short-term memory
Can patient retell techniques? (yes)   no
Hearing acuity   right _____   left_____
wears hearing aid(s) ⓇR (yes)   no
hearing aid(s) in for eval (yes)   no

AMRs	Rhythm	Rate	Accuracy
/pʌ pʌ pʌ/	regular / (irregular)	(slow) / normal / fast	precise / (imprecise)
/tʌ tʌ tʌ/	regular / (irregular)	(slow) / normal / fast	precise / (imprecise)
/kʌ kʌ kʌ/	regular / (irregular)	(slow) / normal / fast	precise / (imprecise)

SMRs			
/pʌ tʌ kʌ/	regular / (irregular)	(slow) / normal / fast	precise / (imprecise)

Sample: Perceptual Dysarthria Evaluation

Patient ___D.A._____ Date_____

Prolong /a/
Characteristics
observed:

___15___ time in seconds
_____ breathy   ✔ harsh   _____ hoarse
_____ tremor   _____ inhalatory stridor   _____ diplophonia
_____ voice arrest   _____ decreased loudness   _____ strained/strangled

Reading and/or Conversation	Characteristics Observed		
Respiration	_____ reduced loudness _____ monoloudness _____ short phrases _____ impaired loudness control _____ sudden inspiration/expiration		
Phonation	_____ breathy ✔ harsh _____ hoarse _____ monopitch _____ low pitch _____ monoloudness _____ reduced loudness _____ short phrases _____ audible inspiration _____ strained/strangled _____ pitch breaks _____ voicing errors ✔ excessive loudness variations		
Resonance	_____ hypernasal _____ nasal emission		
Articulation	✔ imprecise consonants ✔ irregular breakdowns ✔ distorted vowels specific errors: _s blends, l blends, s, z, ∫ , t∫)_		
Prosody	_____ reduced stress _____ monotone ✔ excess & equal stress ✔ bursts of loudness ✔ slow rate _____ fast rate _____ variable rate _____ prolonged intervals _____ prolonged phonemes _____ short rushes _____ poor intonation		

Contrastive Stress

"Todd likes apples."   To indicate stress, patient uses:
_____ increased pitch   _____ patient does not indicate stress
_____ increased loudness
_____ pauses

Stress testing (1-100) ___WFL_____

Patient-initiated compensatory strategies ___none_____

Sample: Perceptual Dysarthria Evaluation

Form A

Patient __R.J.__

Patient # _____

Date of birth __9-25-30__   Age __67__

Date of evaluation __9-30-97__

Physician __Coleman__

Date of onset __9-28-97__

Medical diagnosis related to speech disorder __Bilateral brain stem stroke__

Associated neurological symptoms reported __Bilateral UE and LE weakness__

Patient complaint/impact on function __Difficulty making himself understood__

Previous treatment _____

Observation by (physiologic) Component	Goals/Treatment Objectives
RESPIRATION Pt. uses short phrases.	✔ Patient will improve respiratory support and the use of respiration for speech. Stimulable ✔ *Treatment Objectives* RSP 2, 4, 13, 14, 15, 16
PHONATION Pt's voice is breathy and is difficult to hear.	✔ Patient will maximize use of phonation to improve communication skills. Stimulable _____ *Treatment Objectives* PH 1, 5, 7, 8
RESONANCE mild hypernasality	_____ Patient will reduce the amount of perceived hypernasality/nasal emission to increase intelligibility. Stimulable _____ *Treatment Objectives*
ARTICULATION imprecise articulation and reduced intelligibility	✔ Patient will improve articulation to increase intelligibility. Stimulable ✔ *Treatment Objectives* AR 17, 20, 21, 39, 45, 46 (p, b, t, d, s, ʃ), 49
PROSODY Pt is monotone.	✔ Patient will improve use of prosody to increase intelligibility and produce speech. Stimulable _____ *Treatment Objectives*
ENVIRONMENT Wife has decreased hearing which complicates communication.	Environmental Modification ✔ Speaker and listener will improve environment in which communication takes place. *Treatment Objectives* EM 3, 6

Diagnosis __moderate flaccid dysarthria__

Recommendations   ✔ S/L Therapy   _____ Cognitive/Language Eval   _____ Dysphagia Eval
_____ no therapy indicated   Frequency __Daily B.I.D.__

Long-term goals   ✔ achieve intelligible verbal speech   ✔ achieve natural-sounding speech
_____ verbal communication via augmentation
_____ alternative form of communication: _____

Patient/Family Goals __To be able to converse with family and staff__

_____   _____
Speech-Language Pathologist   Date

Sample: Perceptual Dysarthria Evaluation

Patient _R.J._____   Date _9/30/97_____

Oral-Motor Evaluation

1. **Structure**
   Note any abnormalities _____
   edentulous   (yes)   no   dentures   (yes)   no
                                               dentures in during eval   yes   (no)

2. **Assessing Jaw, Lips, and Tongue**
   Jaw Control   ____ CNA   (+)/ -

   Labial Function   ____ CNA
   lip spread /i/   + /(-)   lip round /u/   + /(-)
   lip closure at rest   lip smacking   + /(-)
     symmetry   (+)/ -
     droop   R L

   Lingual Function   ____ CNA
   protrusion   (+)/ -   retraction   (+)/ -
   lick lips   + /(-)   lateralization to corners   R (+)/ -   L (+)/ -
   lateralization to buccal cavity   R(+)/ -   L + / -   elevation of tip   + /(-)
   elevation of back   + /(-)

3. **Velar Function**   _____ CNA
   prolonged /a/: symmetry during evaluation   (+)/ -

4. **Reflex**   _____ CNA
   swallow reflex   (+)/ -

Cognition/Communication   ____ CNA

Orientation	day ✔	date ✔	year ✔	place ✔

Orientation   day ✔   date ✔   year ✔   place ✔
follows one-step directions   (+)/ -   with cues   without cues
follows two-step directions   (+)/ -   with cues   without cues
Expressive language   gestures/points   uses single words   (uses phrases)   confused speech
Short-term memory
Can patient retell techniques?   (yes)   no
Hearing acuity   right _____   left_____   _appears adequate_
wears hearing aid(s)   yes   (no)
hearing aid(s) in for eval   yes   no

AMRs	**Rhythm**	**Rate**	**Accuracy**
/pʌ pʌ pʌ/	(regular)/ irregular	(slow)/ normal / fast	precise /(imprecise)
/tʌ tʌ tʌ/	(regular)/ irregular	(slow)/ normal / fast	precise /(imprecise)
/kʌ kʌ kʌ/	(regular)/ irregular	(slow)/ normal / fast	precise /(imprecise)

SMRs			
/pʌ tʌ kʌ/	(regular)/ irregular	(slow)/ normal / fast	precise /(imprecise)

Patient __R.J._____   Date _____

Prolong /a/   __6__ time in seconds
Characteristics   _✔_ breathy   ____ harsh   ____ hoarse
observed: ____ tremor   ____ inhalatory stridor ____ diplophonia
                         ____ voice arrest   ____ decreased loudness ____ strained/strangled

Reading and/or Conversation	Characteristics Observed		
Respiration	_✔_ reduced loudness ____ monoloudness _✔_ short phrases ____ impaired loudness control ____ sudden inspiration/expiration		
Phonation	_✔_ breathy ____ harsh ____ hoarse _✔_ monopitch ____ low pitch ____ monoloudness _✔_ reduced loudness ____ short phrases ____ audible inspiration ____ strained/strangled ____ pitch breaks ____ voicing errors ____ excessive loudness variations		
Resonance	_✔_ hypernasal ____ nasal emission		
Articulation	_✔_ imprecise consonants ____ irregular breakdowns ____ distorted vowels specific errors: _p, b, t, d, s, ʃ_____		
Prosody	____ reduced stress _✔_ monotone ____ excess & equal stress ____ bursts of loudness ____ slow rate ____ fast rate ____ variable rate ____ prolonged intervals ____ prolonged phonemes ____ short rushes ____ poor intonation		

Contrastive Stress

"Todd likes apples."   To indicate stress, patient uses:
____ increased pitch   ____ patient does not indicate stress
_✔_ increased loudness
____ pauses

Stress testing (1-100)   loudness continues to decrease _____

Patient-initiated compensatory strategies   Pt spells some words when he isn't understood. _____

_____

Evaluating Respiration

What can be wrong?	What will you hear?
weakness of respiratory muscles	reduced overall loudness, monoloudness short phrases
abnormal tone	reduced overall loudness, monoloudness impaired loudness control
incoordination of respiratory muscles	sudden forced inspiration/expiration speaking on low air

Assessing Respiration

1. Listen to how loud the patient's speech is. If the patient has very soft speech, it's likely that respiratory support is compromised.
2. Ask the patient to count from 1-20 on one breath. A patient with adequate respiratory support (and adequate laryngeal valving) should be able to do this without difficulty.
3. Ask the patient to produce /a/ starting very softly and becoming very loud.
4. Listen to the patient's conversational speech to determine how many syllables the patient is producing on a breath group. The normal number of syllables produced is between 12 and 20. Keep in mind, however, that decreased number of syllables per breath group can also mean the patient has poor laryngeal valving and is losing air because of a laryngeal disorder, or has poor velopharyngeal closure which allows air to escape out the nose.

Questions to Ask Yourself as You Make Judgments About Respiration

1. Does the patient exhibit a normal respiratory pattern (inhaling for between 1 and 2 seconds and exhaling between 6 and 12 seconds)?
2. Does the patient initiate speech at the beginning of the exhalation?
3. Is the patient able to use pauses to make a point or does the patient breathe in every time he pauses?
4. Are there any observed exaggerated maneuvers such as lifting the shoulders during inhalation?
5. Does the speaker seem to run out of air before inhaling?
6. How many words or syllables does the patient produce in one breath?
7. How long is each breath group?
8. Does the patient pause at appropriate places in the utterance to take a new breath?

Stimulability

- Ask the patient to take a bigger breath and start talking at the beginning of the exhalation.

Evaluating Phonation

What can be wrong?	What will you hear?
weakness in laryngeal musculature	breathiness, hoarseness, monopitch decreased loudness, short phrases, audible inspiration
reduced tone in laryngeal muscles	breathiness, hoarseness, monotone, decreased loudness, low pitch
increased tone in laryngeal muscles	strained, strangled dysphonia; harshness; low/high pitch; monoloudness; pitch breaks
incoordination of laryngeal movements	inappropriate pitch changes, inconsistent hoarseness, voicing errors, tremors, excessive loudness variations, audible inspiration

Assessing Phonation

1. Listen to the patient's spontaneous cough or ask the patient to cough. A weak cough may indicate decreased tone or strength in the larynx.

2. Ask the patient to produce /a/ and hold it as long as he can.
   - a strained, strangled vocal quality may indicate that the patient has a spastic disorder, but may also indicate that the patient is pushing very hard to try to make up for weakness
   - tremors may indicate essential voice tremor
   - a breathy vocal quality may indicate reduced vocal fold closure

3. Ask the patient to sing a few notes up or down the musical scale. Listen for smooth changes between the notes.

4. Reading or conversation allows you to listen for any of the characteristics.

Questions to Ask Yourself as You Make Judgments About Volume, Pitch, and Quality

1. Is the patient too loud or too soft?

2. Can the patient maintain a consistent and appropriate level of loudness throughout the utterance?

3. Does the patient's loudness decrease towards the end of the utterance?

4. Can the patient shout?

5. Can the patient speak quietly?

6. Does the patient complain of becoming fatigued when talking for long periods of time and trying to maintain loudness?

7. Is the patient using too low a pitch?
8. Does the patient sound monotone?
9. Does the patient's voice break?
10. Does the patient's voice tremor?
11. Does the patient's voice sound harsh and rough?
12. Does the patient's voice sound weak and breathy?

Stimulability

- Ask the patient to speak louder or softer.
- Ask the patient to match your pitch.

Evaluating Resonance

What can be wrong?	What will you hear?
weakness of velopharyngeal mechanism	hypernasality or nasal emission
increased tone	hypernasality

Assessing Resonation

1. Have the patient prolong /i/ or /i-u/ and alternately occlude the patient's nose by squeezing on his nostrils. If resonance is normal, it should sound the same whether the nostrils are being squeezed or not.

2. Have the patient repeat a sentence with many nasal sounds (e.g., "Many men may mourn him.") and one with no nasal sounds (e.g., "Bob's puppy was cute."). There should be a distinctly different sound between these two sentences. If the sentence with non-nasal sounds is perceived as nasal, then there is a problem.

3. If nasal emission is suspected, place a mirror under the patient's nose and ask the patient to produce a consonant-vowel sequence with a pressure consonant such as "see see see see see."

4. Observe the movement of the soft palate by holding the patient's tongue down with a tongue depressor and asking him to produce a series of /a/ sounds. If the palate does not appear to be moving well, but you don't hear hypernasality, then this is probably not an area you will need to treat.

    (Note: Assessing velopharyngeal closure in non-speech tasks such as whistling or blowing has no documented relationship to the use of the velopharyngeal port for speech.)

Questions to Ask Yourself as You Make Judgments About Resonance

1. Does the patient sound hypernasal?
2. Does air escape audibly through the nose?
3. Does the patient's speech sound less hypernasal on sentences with no nasal sounds?

Stimulability

*   Ask the patient to open her mouth very wide during speech to try to reduce the perception of hypernasality.
*   Ask the patient to repeat word pairs with nasal and non-nasal sounds to make them sound as different as possible (e.g., "my pie," "nice dice").

Evaluating Articulation

What can be wrong?	What will you hear?
decreased strength, (i.e. weakness)	imprecise consonant production
decreased coordination	irregular articulation breakdowns, distorted vowels
decreased range of motion	imprecise consonant production, distorted vowels
increased tone	imprecise consonants
unpredictable movements	irregular articulation breakdowns, distorted vowels

Assessing Articulation

Assess oral movements unrelated to speech. (Note: The use of oral structures for non-speech tasks has not been documented to have a correlation with how the same structures will be used during speech).

1. Ask the patient to pucker and then smile. Look for any asymmetry. One easy way to watch for asymmetry is to see if the fold between the end of the nose and the corner of the lips appears flatter on one side.

   Resistance: Ask patient to maintain the pucker while you try to pull his into a smile. Ask patient to maintain a smile while you try to pull his lips forward into a pucker.

2. Ask the patient to smack his lips together. Listen for sharp clarity to the sound.

3. Ask the patient to puff up his cheeks and keep air in the mouth without it leaking out through his lips.

   Resistance: Squeeze the patient's cheeks to try and force air out.

4. Ask the patient to stick his tongue straight out of his mouth. Observe to see if it is at midline. Remember that if there is a unilateral weakness in the tongue, the tongue will deviate toward the weaker side. This is because the stronger side of the tongue is pushing and the weaker side can't push.

   Resistance: Ask the patient to protrude his tongue and push against a tongue blade.

5. Ask the patient to open his mouth and maintain the opening while elevating the tip of his tongue to his top teeth and then to his bottom teeth. If the patient is using jaw assist for this, it usually means there is some weakness of the tongue. Try to stabilize the jaw by holding it with your hand or using a bite block.

6. Ask the patient to lateralize the tip of his tongue to each corner of his lips. If there is unilateral weakness, the patient may not be able to lateralize the tip of his tongue all the way into the corner on the weaker side.

    Place your finger on the patient's cheek. Ask the patient to lateralize his tongue inside his cheek to touch where your finger is. Look to see if the patient can move his tongue that far back on either side.

    Resistance: Ask the patient to push the tip of his tongue out against the tongue blade on either side. Ask the patient to push against your finger with his tongue in his cheek. Feel for the strength with which the patient can push against your finger.

7. Ask the patient to imitate tongue clicking (the sound you make when shaking your finger at a misbehaving child) and tongue popping (the sound you make if you are trying to imitate the sound of a horse galloping). The patient's inability to make these sounds may indicate weakness, especially at the tongue tip and blade.

8. Ask the patient to say /k/ with as much force as possible. Weakness on this task can indicate weakness at the back of the tongue.

    Resistance: Put a tongue blade at the dorsum of the tongue and ask the patient to try to produce /k/ while you push down on his tongue with the tongue blade.

As stated above, movement of the lips and tongue in non-speech activities may have no direct correlation to how well the lips and tongue will move for speech. Therefore, the best assessment of the lips and tongue for speech will be through evaluation of the patient's articulation skills.

9. Ask the patient to repeat /pʌ -pʌ -pʌ / as fast and as evenly as possible to assess speech alternate motion rates. Observe the oral mechanism on this rapid, coordinated task. Repeat with /tʌ -tʌ -tʌ / and /kʌ -kʌ -kʌ /.

10. Ask the patient to repeat /pʌ -tʌ -kʌ / as fast and as evenly as possible to assess sequential motion rate.

11. Have the patient read or repeat words, phrases, sentences, or paragraphs. The list of words and sentences in Appendices 2 and 3 can be used, as can word lists or sentences from more formal articulation tests. Appendix 4 is the familiar Grandfather Passage which can be used to assess reading in a paragraph.

12. Engage the patient in conversation. This is one of the best ways to assess the patient's functional use of articulation. You can ask the patient specific questions (although then the context is known and it may be a little easier to understand the patient) or simply engage in conversation. Appendix 5 provides some questions to stimulate conversation.

    Be sure to note related information about the situation in which the conversation took place. You may want to tape record the conversational sample for a more complete analysis at a later time.

    - Was the patient sitting up or lying down?
    - Was there background noise which could have interfered with intelligibility?
    - Was the patient wearing dentures?

Questions to Ask Yourself as You Make Judgments About Articulatory Skills

1. Are there certain sounds that the patient consistently misarticulates?
2. Are the patient's alternate motion rates (AMRs) and sequential motion rates (SMRs) slow?
3. Are patient's AMRs and SMRs irregular in rhythm?
4. To what extent is impaired articulation compromising intelligibility?

Stimulability

*   Ask the patient to imitate production of specific consonants.
*   Ask the patient to over-articulate a phrase.

Evaluating Prosody

What can be wrong?	What will you hear?
increased or decreased tone in laryngeal muscles; decreased range of motion; unpredictable movement	reduced stress, excess and equal stress
decreased strength, coordination and range of motion of lips and tongue	slow rate
weakness of respiratory muscles, abnormal tone of respiratory muscles, reduced tone in larynx	monotone/prosodic insufficiency
decreased respiratory support; unpredictable movements	prolonged intervals
decreased coordination of articulators, incoordination of laryngeal movements, decreased tone	prolonged phonemes
decreased respiratory support	increased rate
nasal air wastage, decreased respiratory support	short rushes of speech
increased tone	poor intonation
decreased coordination	poor pitch control
poor laryngeal valving, decreased respiratory strength	short phrases

Unlike the previously described perceptual symptoms which had a one-to-one relationship with a physiologic component (e.g., respiration, phonation, resonance, articulation), prosody is produced through a coordination of the respiratory, phonatory, and articulatory components. Therefore, the column "What can be wrong?" is less easy to distinguish.

Perhaps the best way to assess prosody (includes stress, intonation, rate, and rhythm) is by listening to a sample of conversational speech. It is very helpful to tape record a sample. If the patient has problems with articulation, it's difficult to separate the misarticulations you hear from problems with one of the parameters of prosody. When assessing rate and rhythm, listen to see if the articulation time, pause time, or both are appropriate.

Assessing Prosody

1. Stress

    a. Pretend to misunderstand something a patient has said and ask for clarification. Use an instance where it would be logical for a patient to use stress to correct your misperception. For example, you might ask the patient what her children's names are. She might tell you "My daughter is Mary and my son is John." You could repeat, "So your daughter is John and your son is Mary." You would expect her to correct this using stress by saying "My <u>son</u> is John." Look for opportunities to use this technique in conversational speech.

    b. Contrastive stress drills can be used as a perceptual assessment of stress and rhythm. (See Appendix A-1, pages 211-216.) An advantage of using contrastive stress drills over observations of spontaneous speech is your ability to control length and phonetic context which minimizes the effect of inadequate articulation on the prosodic features of stress. A disadvantage may be the limited generalization of the patient's speaking behavior in contrastive stress drills to conversational speech. Just because a patient can add stress to clarify a short response does not mean that he will do so spontaneously.

    Ask the patient to repeat a specific sentence and change the meaning, such as "Sue likes to cook breakfast." Ask the patient to make it sound like it's breakfast that she likes to cook and nothing else. Listen to see if stress is being achieved on the right syllables and how the patient is achieving stress. That is, is she able to increase the volume and change pitch slightly to achieve this stress? Is the patient using stress at both the word and sentence level?

2. Intonation

    Ask the patient to say a sentence with different meanings. For example, ask the patient to repeat the sentence "You remembered my birthday" and to make it sound like a question. Then have the patient say the sentence as if surprised.

    Observe whether pitch changes are appropriate and whether the patient sounds monotone or is able to actually vary the intonation.

3. Rate and Rhythm

    These are best assessed through listening to conversational speech.

Questions to Ask Yourself as You Make Judgments About Rate, Rhythm, Stress, and Intonation

1. Rate and Rhythm

    a. Is the rate appropriate?

    b. If not, is the articulation time, pause time, or both inappropriate?

    c. Is the rhythm smooth and natural sounding, or choppy?

2. Stress
   a. Is stress being achieved on the right syllables?

   b. Is stress observable at both the word and sentence level?

   c. How is stress being achieved?

3. Intonation
   a. Are pitch changes appropriate?

   b. Can the patient achieve a variety of intonation contours?

Stimulability

- Ask the patient to slow his speaking rate, perhaps using a pacing technique.
- Ask the patient to repeat contrastive stress drills after you. (e.g., Fred baked a pie. <u>Fred</u> baked a pie. Fred <u>baked</u> a pie. Fred baked a <u>pie</u>.)
- Ask the patient to repeat basic intonation patterns (e.g., "Is it time to go?" (rising inflection) or "I didn't see him." (falling inflection)).

Assessing Disability and Handicap

Ask the patient the following questions to assess dysarthria at the disability and handicap level.

1. What bothers you about your speech? _____

   _____

2. When do you have the most trouble making yourself understood?

   _____ on the phone

   _____ talking to strangers

   _____ in noisy situations

   _____ other: _____

3. Do you avoid situations because of your speech? If so, describe._____

   _____

   _____

4. How has your speech problem affected interactions:

   with family _____

   with friends _____

   at work _____

Based on Lubinski, R. "Dysarthria: A Breakdown in Interpersonal Communication" in Vogel, D. and Cannito, M. (eds.). *Treating Disordered Speech Motor Control*, Austin, TX: PRO-ED, 1991.

The Source for Dysarthria   59

Words for Reading or Imitation to Assess Articulation

	Initial Position	Medial Position	Final Position
Bilabials	pie boy	happy cabin	up tub
Alveolars	to door	eating under	out bed
Velars	car go	walking hugging	wake big
Sibilants	sit zoo shoe —	icy buzzer washer measure	bus was push garage
Affricates	chair jump	watching edgy	much fudge
Glides	wall you like	away onion pillow	— — ball
/s/ Blends	stop smile skin slow	rusty dismiss biscuit bracelet	lost — ask pencil
/l/ Blends	clean floor plane	o'clock cornflakes apply	buckle careful apple

Sentences for Imitation to Assess Articulation

Bilabials

1. She was happy he picked it up.
2. The boy was scrubbing the tub.

Alveolar

3. Tom was eating out on the patio.
4. Did you put the box under the bed?

Velars

5. Carl was walking around the lake.
6. Gary was hugging the big dog.

Sibilants

7. Sally wore a lacy dress.
8. The zoo has two buzzards.
9. Are you sure he crashed into the bush?
10. Measure the back wall of the garage.

Affricates

11. He is watching the children eat lunch.
12. The major jumped onto the bridge.

Glides

13. Move away from the wall.
14. Do you like onions?
15. I'd like a gallon of lemonade.

/s/ Blends

16. Steve was lost on the dusty road.
17. The basement smelled smoky.
18. There is a basket on his desk at school.
19. When he fell asleep, his pencil slid to the floor.

/l/ Blends

20. At one o'clock, give a nickel to the clerk.
21. Be careful! Don't get cornflakes on the floor.
22. He planted poplar and apple trees.

You wish to know all about my grandfather. Well, he is nearly 93 years old, yet he still thinks as swiftly as ever. He dresses himself in an old black frock coat, usually several buttons missing. A long beard clings to his chin, giving those who observe him a pronounced feeling of the utmost respect. When he speaks, his voice is just a bit cracked and quivers a bit. Twice each day he plays skillfully and with zest upon a small organ. Except in the winter when the snow or ice prevents, he slowly takes a short walk in the open air each day. We have often urged him to walk more and smoke less, but he always answers, "Banana oil!" Grandfather likes to be modern in his language.

- What happened that caused your speech problem?
- Have you had therapy for this problem before?
- Are you working/retired?
- What do you/did you do for a living?
- Where do you live?
- Have you lived there all your life?
- What do you like to do in your spare time?
- Do you have any children? Tell me about them.
- Where did you go to school?
- What do you like to watch on TV?

Questions for Patients Living in the Community

- When you get out of the house, where do you like to go?
- What are your favorite restaurants in town?

Questions for Patients in Long-Term Care

- What activities do you participate in here?
- Tell me about friends/family who come to visit.

Chapter 3
Planning Treatment

Having completed the diagnostic evaluation of your patient, you must now make some important decisions about the management of the patient's dysarthria:

- Should you treat?
- When should you treat?
- What should you treat?
- What should you treat first?

You must also select goals and appropriate treatment objectives for the patient. It is very important to involve the patient and significant others in the patient's life when setting goals. You can develop the most elaborate treatment plan, select appropriate treatment objectives, and work hard toward achieving the objectives, but if the patient doesn't understand the goal or agree with the goal, then you may see little or no progress. It's important to be realistic about expected results so as not to mislead the patient.

How Do You Know When to Treat?

The questions of when, and even if, to treat are not easy to answer. Some factors to consider are:

1. *What is the patient's medical status?* In acute care settings, you may be consulted to see an individual with a new onset dysarthria while their medical condition is still unstable. If the patient is less than optimally alert and is only able to work inconsistently, it may be better to wait until the patient's condition stabilizes before initiating treatment.

2. *Is the patient's condition progressive or non-progressive?* If the patient's condition is progressive, you must know the rate at which deterioration might be expected and the predicted course of the disease. It may be appropriate to evaluate the patient and initiate short-term treatment to show the patient how to maintain skills or to slow deterioration of skills.

   You may also be providing augmentative or alternative forms of communication. It may also be entirely appropriate to re-assess the patient and provide intervention at other intervals during the course of the disease. This is called appropriate staging of intervention. Goals and techniques for treating individuals with degenerative dysarthria may be very different from goals and techniques for non-progressive disorders either in the acute or chronic stages.

It is crucial to be prepared to provide emotional support to the patient and family. Environmental modification goals may be particularly appropriate for these patients. It is also very important to keep in mind the overall goal of maintaining some form of communication for the patient as the disease progresses. More detailed information about treatment for progressive disorders like ALS, Parkinson's disease, Huntington's disease, and multiple sclerosis can be found in *Management of Speech and Swallowing in Degenerative Disorders* by Yorkston, Miller, and Strand (1995).

3. *If the disorder is non-progressive, is the dysarthria acute or chronic?* If the dysarthria is acute and the patient is alert, stable, and ready to participate in therapy, then the goals of therapy may be to improve physiologic function as much as possible and at the same time introduce compensatory strategies.

The term *chronic* applies when the neurological event which caused the dysarthria happened long ago and the patient is referred to you past the point of any reasonable expectation to improve physiologic support. For instance, a patient in a long-term care facility who has been unintelligible for years may be referred to you for intervention. At this point, the most appropriate goals and treatment objectives would probably be to help the patient compensate for the loss of function and to make modifications in the environment to increase the patient's ability to participate in activities of daily living.

4. *Does the patient have other diagnoses?* For instance, if the patient has global aphasia and severe dysarthria, he has a poorer prognosis for learning how to compensate for decreased intelligibility. Other diseases such as Huntington's Chorea have common mental and behavioral problems. Because of this, patients are unable to fully participate in therapy and, therefore, are often not good candidates for treatment.

McHenry, Wilson, and Minton (1994) nicely summarize the challenges faced when planning intervention of patients with dysarthria when the dysarthria is caused by traumatic brain injury. These same challenges often apply to individuals who had a stroke or other neurological event causing their dysarthria. They point out that the patient's premorbid characteristics may be exacerbated by their injury.

The patient's physiological status should also be considered. The patient may now be dealing with impairments in a variety of physiologic systems. Cognitive deficits such as memory deficits and decreased ability to attend to tasks can interfere with progress in therapy. The patient's psychosocial status may also have a great impact on his progress in therapy. The patient may or may not be willing to implement strategies that would help him improve intelligibility if he thinks the strategies will make him more noticeable in a group.

You might consider conducting a short trial therapy period to determine if the patient is going to respond to treatment. This can be of value to help determine the patient's potential. Many patients can show short-term gains on very specific treatment objectives but, because of other confounding factors such as decreased cognitive skills, do not carry over these gains into daily activities.

5. *What about patients with mild dysarthria?* The general rule to use to decide whether to initiate treatment is to determine if the dysarthria is impairing intelligibility. However, there are many patients who have intact cognitive skills and present with a mild dysarthria that they find unacceptable. These individuals often use their speech extensively and are bothered by the mild distortions which they perceive more than any of their listeners. Remember Van Riper's definition:

> "Speech is defective when it deviates so far from the speech of other people that it calls attention to itself, interferes with communication, or causes its possessor to be maladjusted. We can condense this definition into three adjectives: speech is defective when it is conspicuous, unintelligible or unpleasant."

With that definition in mind, treating patients with mild dysarthria, at least to the point of instructing them in activities and exercises that they can complete independently to help improve their speech, is appropriate.

Note: As with any speech or language disorder, the ASHA Code of Ethics should guide you to fully inform the patient of the possible effects of services and provide these services only when benefit can reasonably be expected. You must not guarantee the results of any treatment, but may make a reasonable statement of prognosis.

Efficacy of Treatment

One of the impacts managed care has had on the practice of speech-language pathology is the increasing demand that we prove that the treatment we are providing works. We are encouraged to stay abreast of the latest research in the area of motor speech disorders so we are prepared to answer questions from payors and consumers.

A good place to familiarize yourself with efficacy research in motor speech disorders is the Supplement on "Treatment Efficacy: Part I" that appeared in the October 1996 issue of the *Journal of Speech and Hearing Research*. Yorkston provides a good review of the literature on treatment of dysarthria related to Parkinson's disease, ALS, stroke, traumatic brain injury, and cerebral palsy.

In the chapters which follow, efficacy studies will be referenced which document the effectiveness of treatment for specific physiologic components.

Framework for Management

Keeping in mind the framework described in Chapter 1 (i.e., impairment, disability, handicap) for assessment and management, management activities and specific goals can be divided into the following categories:

1. Facilitation Techniques

    These are activities designed to reduce the level of impairment or improve basic physiologic function. Some of the goals in each of the following chapters may be designed to do this. Examples of facilitation techniques include:

    Respiration: pushing and pulling exercises

    Phonation (laryngeal function): hard glottal attack

    Resonance: blowing exercises

Articulation: lingual and labial strengthening exercises

Prosody: goals for reducing impairment are typically not indicated for prosody since disorders of stress, intonation, rate, and rhythm are usually problems caused by the individual's inability to use physiologic function that has not been disrupted. In addition, there is no one-to-one correspondence between a prosodic disturbance (like rate) and a single physiologic function.

Rosenbek and LaPointe (1985) talk about physiologic support for speech. They describe it as the cumulative effect of the potential to produce speech that resides within the speech structures and their neurological supply. Dysarthric speakers have a reduced range of physiologic support. Rosenbek and LaPointe agree with Canter (1965) that physiologic support should be increased whenever possible. Canter states that before we teach a patient to make the best use of what he has (compensations), we should first try to improve the physiological support (facilitation techniques).

2. Compensatory Techniques

   Compensations are designed to help an individual use his residual function. These techniques reduce the disability or improve function on specific activities. Examples of compensation activities to help improve overall function might include:

   Respiration: using shorter breath groups

   Phonation (laryngeal function): intense high level phonatory effort

   Resonance: exaggerated mouth opening

   Articulation: exaggerated consonant production

   Prosody: reducing rate

3. Environmental Management

   The third level of dysarthria management, helping to reduce societal disadvantage or handicap, is not broken down by physiological components.

   Remember that you aren't just treating impaired muscles or decreased intelligibility, but you are helping to manage an individual's ability to participate in activities of daily living.

   It is very important to involve the patient's family and significant others in treatment, especially if it appears that the dysarthria will be long-standing in nature. Working with the patient and significant others provides an excellent opportunity for counseling and teaching strategies to enhance communication. Focus on what the speaker can do and what listeners can do. Broader goals and activities addressing these strategies are described later in the chapter.

   Duffy (1995) points out the importance of thinking in the larger context of communication rather than strictly thinking about the individual components of speech. Remember that when individuals without dysarthria talk, they are communicating through their speech as well as a variety of nonverbal cues and gestures. Thinking about communication rather than speech will help you broaden your goals. It will also help you to consider bringing in the patient's communication partners and working with them to help them learn to understand the patient's speech. Other authors (Rosenbek and LaPointe, 1985; Yorkston, Beukelman, & Bell, 1988) echo the importance of environmental management, reminding us to maximize the effectiveness, efficiency, and naturalness of communication.

68

How Do You Know What to Work On?

Physiologic Support: Which physiologic processes are necessary to support the problems you have described with the patient? For instance, if the patient has an abnormally soft voice, consider that the impaired physiology is probably decreased respiratory support. Therefore, you may want to work on increasing the strength of the respiratory muscles first.

Intelligibility: What would help intelligibility the most? More than one physiologic process is often impaired. What can you do that will yield the most immediate results for better intelligibility?

Stimulability: During your diagnostic evaluation, determine if any of the symptoms are amenable to change. It's frustrating to work hard on a symptom that probably won't change.

Optimizing the System

Another way to look at the organization of dysarthria management is the description given by Netsell (1983) who states that with adult dysarthrics, the two general goals of therapy are:

1. maximize the functional integrity of the musculoskeletal system

2. require the nervous system to selectively engage its speech motor systems

Netsell indicates methods to optimize the expression of the speech motor system:

- posturing to minimize the influence of pathologic reflexes

- musculoskeletal alterations such as surgery, palatal lifts, bite blocks, and abdominal binding

- orofacial stimulation and passive range of motion. Orofacial stimulation

maintains sensorimotor integrity. Passive range of motion maintains neuromuscular integrity.

- minimal strengthening exercises to maintain muscle mass

Netsell also states that orofacial stimulation, passive range of motion, and strengthening exercises to maintain muscle mass are of little value once minimal speech movement can be elicited from the vocal tract. For instance, if the patient is moving his tongue enough for chewing, it is probably sufficient activity to maintain nerve-muscle and sensorimotor integrity.

Instrumentation and Augmentative Information

There are many clinical settings where SLPs do not have easy access to instrumentation for use with patients with dysarthria, but there are some applications of instrumentation that can be very beneficial to patients. Most of these applications provide some form of biofeedback to the patient, allowing him to more accurately monitor his performance. If you have access to such instrumentation, keep in mind areas in which instrumentation can be helpful when assessing a patient's physiological deficits.

Augmentative and alternative systems are defined as "an integrated group of components, including the symbols, aids, strategies, and techniques used by individuals to enhance communication," (ASHA, 1991). It is beyond the scope of this book to describe alternative communication systems in detail, but a summary is provided below.

Alternative communication systems can range from a simple printed alphabet board to highly sophisticated computer-based electronic devices for communication that are designed to serve as alternatives to verbal speech. Augmentative devices might include something as simple as a personal voice amplifier or the Speech Enhancer™ which clarifies speech electronically. Specific augmentative aids will be described as needed throughout the remainder of this book. For example, the pacing board to help augment a rate disorder will be described in Chapter 8.

Augmentative communication may be used for individuals with non-progressive and degenerative dysarthrias. In an acute non-progressive dysarthria, augmentative and alternative communication (AAC) may be used early on until the patient regains enough function to communicate intelligibly via verbal speech. In a chronic non-progressive disorder, the patient may rely on an AAC system long term. With degenerative disorders, the patient may start using the system to augment verbal speech, but may end up using it as his only means of communication.

Where Are Patients with Dysarthria Treated?

Patients with dysarthria are treated in all settings by SLPs. In addition, dysarthrias of all types may be seen in any of these settings:

1. **Acute Care**

   (Note: These descriptions may also apply to sub-acute care, in-patient rehabilitation, skilled nursing facilities, and home health.)

   Acute Non-Progressive — Clinicians working in acute care may see acute onset of non-progressive dysarthria in the very early stages such as the result of a stroke. It is usually advisable to wait until the patient's condition is med-

ically stable before treating the patient. Also, if the patient is to undergo a medical procedure, treatment should generally not begin before the surgery. The exception might be to provide a way to help the patient augment his speech for increased intelligibility before the surgery. For instance, you might provide a letter board or picture board if the patient's dysarthria is so severe that it is interfering with his ability to communicate about his care.

If the doctor orders a consult for you, you might indicate:

Thank you for consulting us concerning Mr. Coleman's significant dysarthria. Since the dysarthria is indeed impairing his ability to communicate with staff and family at this time, we have initiated short-term treatment to teach the patient how to use an alphabet board to augment his intelligibility until his surgery can take place. We will be happy to fully evaluate the patient following surgery.

If the patient is able to communicate verbally:

Thank you so much for consulting us concerning Mr. Brook's mild dysarthria. Since surgery is planned for excision of the tumor which is the etiology of his dysarthria, we would prefer to assess his skills following surgery. We look forward to a consult at that time.

Patients with unilateral strokes may have a very mild dysarthria immediately after the stroke. If it is not interfering with intelligibility, it may be advisable to give the patient a few days to see if the dysarthria resolves itself.

Some patients may also present with mild facial droop that is a problem for them aesthetically, but does not interfere with speech. Typically, SLPs demonstrate labial strengthening exercises to the patient and then let him practice on his own and with his family rather than initiate active treatment. In response to a consult, you might reply:

Thank you for the consult concerning Mr. Thompson's complaint of "lip droop." Since the etiology is unilateral stroke, we expect good recovery. The labial weakness is not interfering with speech, but has mild impact on eating. We will show the patient some labial strengthening exercises and some compensation techniques to use when eating until function returns. Thank you for this consult.

Chronic Non-Progressive — Patients with chronic disorders of dysarthria such as those caused by a CVA in the past often return for multiple in-patient hospitalizations related to other medical conditions. If the patient has stabilized and has an effective way to communicate, then it is probably contraindicated for the acute care SLP to initiate treatment if there has been no change in dysarthria symptoms.

A physician will often order a speech consult simply because she notes that the patient's speech is slurred or slightly difficult to understand. It is important to obtain a history from the patient and family. Determine how long post-onset the patient is and whether he received any treatment immediately after the onset of the disorder which caused the dysarthria. If the patient is communicating effectively, although with noticeable dysarthria, and it has been a significant amount of time since onset, then

treatment is probably contraindicated. You might note for the physician who consults you:

Thank you for the order on Mrs. Kelly. Review of her medical record and discussion with patient and family revealed that her mild/moderate flaccid dysarthria is long-standing in nature. She communicates effectively as long as she over-exaggerates her speech.

She has received previous treatment for this disorder, therefore, it doesn't appear that further treatment at this time is indicated. We have counseled staff to encourage the patient to over-articulate and have posted this reminder sign in her room. Please let us know if there is any other reason we should initiate active treatment.

Degenerative — SLPs in acute care settings are typically in a position to see a patient who has first been diagnosed with a degenerative disorder which can cause or is causing dysarthria. If dysarthria is one of the early symptoms of the degenerative disorder, the neurologist is likely to consult you at that time. The symptoms may be very mild and your role may be one of demonstrating strengthening exercises (if appropriate for that particular disorder) that the patient can begin after discharge.

Your most important role may be that of counseling the patient and family about what to expect from this disorder. Be sure you speak with the neurologist (or other physician who has made this diagnosis) to find out exactly what he has told the patient about the course of the disease. Depending on how much the patient knows and understands about the course of the disease, be sure the patient and family understand the probable changes in the patient's ability to communicate and the rate at which the changes will occur. In response to a consult, you might reply:

Thank you for the consult on Mr. Travis. Although his speech symptoms are mild at this point, he and his family are understandably concerned about the symptoms. Evaluation revealed that he presents with a flaccid dysarthria, consistent with the diagnosis of progressive bulbar palsy.

I provided extensive counseling to the patient and family about the course of dysarthria associated with this disease. I initiated treatment to teach this patient strengthening exercises and some compensatory techniques to help him cope with the expected changes in speech. I have also counseled the patient that he will want to seek intervention at various points in the course of this disease as different techniques will be helpful at different periods of time.

If the patient is diagnosed with a degenerative disorder but still has no dysarthria symptoms, it is unlikely that the neurologist will consult speech-language pathology. This is an area which should challenge SLPs to meet with the neurologists on staff and educate them about the importance of a consult even before speech symptoms are visible. Then, when the patient begins to notice a degeneration in speech, she will know who to contact and perhaps even have learned some exercises and activities.

Patients with degenerative disorders resulting in dysarthria often return to acute care for periods of intervention. Carefully review the patient's history.

Talk with the patient and family to determine which techniques they have been taught in the past concerning management of the patient's dysarthria.

If there has been a significant change since the last episode of intervention by an SLP, then it may be entirely appropriate to re-evaluate the patient and make new recommendations. These may be short term in nature. For instance, a patient may return with an exacerbation of multiple sclerosis with a worsening of speech symptoms. It may be appropriate at that time to intervene with the patient and significant others to try and help the patient compensate for lost function and to improve environmental conditions for communication.

However, if the patient has a degenerative disorder and is using the techniques that are appropriate at the time for compensation for reduced intelligibility, then it is probably not appropriate to initiate any new treatment. The note to the doctor might read:

Thank you for the consult on Mrs. Zerga. She is known to us from her previous admits. At the present time, she is using a voice amplifier effectively. When she pairs this with over-articulation, her speech is understandable to staff and family.

At this point in the course of her disease, we do not have anything new to offer her. Exercises for return of function are not appropriate and she is using compensatory strategies quite nicely. As the disease progresses, we expect we may have to move the patient entirely to an alternative system of communication. Should that need arise in the future, we would be happy to see this patient.

2. **Skilled Nursing Facility**

    Chronic Non-Progressive — One pattern sometimes observed in skilled nursing facilities is that each time there is a change in speech-language pathology staff, the new SLP screens all patients in the facility to build a caseload and finds patients there with chronic non-progressive dysarthria. The same cautions stated above should be applied when considering whether to take these patients into the caseload.

    Carefully review the patient's medical record to determine if she has had appropriate treatment in the past and reached a plateau. If so, it is not appropriate to re-evaluate the patient and initiate more treatment simply because it has been a while since the patient has received any intervention.

    However, there are several studies that document the improvement patients have made many years post onset. Simpson, Till, and Goff (1988) describe a 58-year-old patient who received intermittent periods of therapy for almost four years post onset after a basilar artery thrombosis that resulted in quadriplegia. The patient improved from anarthric (totally without verbal speech) to producing 3 - 5 syllables and augmenting verbal speech attempts (i.e., using an alphabet board with verbal speech).

    Keatley and Wirz (1994) describe treatment of a client with dystonia who had been virtually speechless for 20 years because of a severe dysarthria. Therapy improved the client's intelligibility and increased his confidence and functional use of speech.

A particular challenge when working with patients with dysarthria in a skilled nursing facility is increasing the knowledge of nursing staff about dysarthria and its treatment. Sarvela, Sarvela, and Odulana (1989) examined the knowledge level of communication disorders among nursing home employees. Results showed that knowledge was particularly low on the causes and characteristics of dysarthria. It is important to provide training and education to staff so everyone who comes in contact with the patient uses appropriate techniques to help improve the patient's communication.

3. **Home Health**

    Chronic Non-Progressive — The restrictions described above also apply to home health situations. In this situation, it is sometimes difficult to obtain a full and complete medical history. Often times you appear at the patient's home for the assessment and have to get a complete history from the family.

    Sometimes the patient is referred to home health for another service (such as nursing or PT) and a member of the home health staff notices the patient's speech disorder. They may not consider the fact that the patient has already received intervention in the past and reached maximum potential. It is important to try to obtain information about past intervention before going to see this patient through home health.

4. **Schools**

    Congenital (Chronic Non-Progressive) — SLPs working in school settings are most likely to see congenital dysarthrias, such as those resulting from cerebral palsy. It is important to try to determine appropriate prognosis. Nothing can be more frustrating for the student, family, teacher, and others than for an SLP to spend months or even years trying to improve the child's verbal speech when the prognosis is poor.

A vivid case example is a nine-year-old with severe spastic cerebral palsy who had been treated since he entered first grade in a rural school setting. The goal established by the SLP was for the child to produce bilabials. This child did not have any potential for obtaining functional verbal speech even at the single word level and yet he had never been provided with an augmentative/alternative system for communication. A complete assessment revealed his cognitive skills to be within functional limits and, after appropriate intervention, the child communicated quite adequately with an augmentative system and participated fully in regular classrooms.

Environmental Modifications

Compensations for Unintelligibility

Berry and Sanders (1983) have adapted teaching principals involved in aural rehabilitation and applied them to other aspects of verbal communication. They dub this environmental education. "Environmental education is the process of providing pertinent information that, if applied by the dysarthric adult and those in the environment, will facilitate an improvement in the patient's intelligibility. Even if the patient resists teaching, verbal communication can be improved if significant persons who interact with the patient know more about their loved one's communication."

Berry and Sanders state that even though individual therapy may not be appropriate with some clients, environmental education can be implemented with almost every adult with dysarthria. Environmental education can involve working with listeners as much as with the patient. Berry and Sanders describe the variables that need to be controlled to help improve intelligibility. (See Appendix A, page 99, for family handout.)

1. Situation: The situation is the who, what, when, where, and why of the message. In controlling the situation, speakers with dysarthria can be taught to set the context for a listener. For example, the speaker can indicate that he wants to talk about his doctor's appointment. Listeners can also be taught to anticipate the message.

2. Noise: Most speakers speak louder to overcome noise. This rarely works with an individual who has dysarthria, as the extra effort tends to send the speech mechanism into overdrive and distort the speech even more. Instead, the individual should learn strategies such as:

   a. If the noise is variable, turn it down.

   b. If the noise cannot be controlled, try to move away from the noise.

   c. Learn to get visual attention of the listener.

   d. Do not use louder speech, but move closer to the listener, speaking slowly and precisely.

3. Lighting: Try to speak in a well-lit area.

4. Distance: Reduce the distance between the speaker and the listener.

5. Resonance/Acoustics: Modify situations if possible to dampen background noise. For example, speaking in a room with carpet and drapes provides better resonance than a bare room.

6. Posture: The speaker and listener should be standing or seated so that they are looking directly at one another.

7. External aids: Use devices like an amplifier to increase loudness. Augmentative systems can also enhance communication.

Ansel, McNeil, Hunker, and Bless (1983) describe 10 basic strategies speakers can use to clarify when they are not understood by their listener. (See Appendix B, page 100, for patient handout.)

1. Total repetition: Repeat the entire utterance.

2. Partial repetition/word: Repeat one word of the utterance.

3. Partial repetition/phrase: Repeat a segment of the utterance.

4. Elaboration: Use greater complexity and more detail.

5. Spelling of a word: Spell any words that are unclear.

6. Convergent phrase: Use a phrase where information is preserved, but with fewer syllable units. For example, the patient might change "This guy and I both went," to "We both went."

7. Synonym and word convergence: Use a single word that has almost the same meaning.

8. Syntactic revision: Change the structure of the original utterance by word reordering, changing from passive to active, or changing from negative to affirmative.

9. Simplification: Abbreviate a word or phrase such as using "OT" for occupational therapist.

10. Semantic specification: Express the utterance with greater complexity, fullness of detail, and fewer number of syllable units. For example, the patient might change "We talk about our problems," to "It's a support group."

The Ansel, McNeil, Hunker, and Bless study found that adult speakers with cerebral palsy used four of the verbal adjustments substantially more frequently than others. They were:

- total repetition
- partial repetition of a phrase
- partial repetition of a phrase with elaboration
- total repetition with elaboration

Environmental Modifications Goal and Treatment Objectives

These environmental modification treatment objectives will appear in each chapter.

Goal (EM): Speaker and listener will improve environment in which communication takes place.

Treatment Objectives:

EM 1: Speaker will give context of message before beginning to communicate.

EM 2: Listener will ask for clarification of context as needed.

EM 3: Speaker and/or listener will eliminate or reduce background noise.

EM 4: Speaker will gain visual attention of the listener before speaking.

EM 5: Speaker or listener will make sure area in which communication is taking place is well lighted.

EM 6: Speaker and/or listener will make sure that they are sitting/standing close to one another and looking at each other before communication begins.

EM 7: Speaker and/or listener will try to make sure that communication takes place in a room with dampened background noise.

EM 8: Speaker will use external aid for communication: _____ (Fill in as appropriate with voice amplifier, alphabet board, pacing board, etc.)

Treatment Planning from Physiologic System Approach

Although this book is organized around the perceptual characteristics as related to each physiologic component (respiration, phonation, etc.), it is critical to remember the relationship between these systems and processes. For instance, pitch and loudness variations may be listed under disorders of phonation, but they result in inappropriate emphasis which would be a problem described under prosody. Another example of interaction between components includes a patient who has a disordered rate, particularly too rapid a rate. This may be due to poor respiratory support and the patient trying to talk on inadequate breath support.

Therefore, when selecting treatment objectives and therapy activities, keep in mind the interrelationships between the physiologic components and the need to determine all possible causes for the symptoms. Remember that problems in specific physiologic components don't necessarily equal the sum of the parts. Each component may have a small deficiency which, when combined, yields very

poor intelligibility. Conversely, some patients whose components appear severely involved compensate nicely and present with functional speech. Make use of the charts to select goals and objectives, but don't lose sight of the long term goal of intelligibility. The following pages provide descriptions of different types of dysarthrias. The descriptions include:

- possible medical diagnoses
- neurological system affected (see Chapter 1)
- any associated neurological symptoms
- patient complaints
- reflexes involved
- helpful tasks to distinguish the particular dysarthria

The descriptions also include checklists of perceptual symptoms that list characteristics typically observed with each disorder and includes some suggested goals/treatment objectives to address the symptoms.

It may seem that the characteristics of one dysarthria run together with the characteristics of others. The most useful way to distinguish one type of dysarthria from another is not just by listening to the perceptual symptoms, but by looking at the entire picture of the patient (accompanying symptoms, complaints, etc.). The better you understand the physiologic cause of the problem, the more sense it makes.

Spastic dysarthria (may be called pseudobulbar palsy)

Possible Medical Diagnoses:	CVA (bilateral lesions to internal carotid, middle and posterior cerebral arteries, multiple lacunar strokes or single brainstem stroke); trauma (neurosurgical: TBI, pediatric: cerebral palsy); degenerative (Primary Lateral Sclerosis, Progressive Supranuclear Palsy); toxic/metabolic; inflammatory disease (leukoencephalitis)
Neurological system affected:	bilateral upper motor neuron lesions (pyramidal and extrapyramidal)
Associated neurological symptoms:	excessive muscle tone; weakness of distal muscles; loss of fine, skilled movement
Patient complaints:	slow speech rate, increased effort to speak, gets tired when speaking, poor control of emotions
Reflexes:	positive Babinski, suck, snout, jaw jerk, gag
Tasks most helpful to make diagnosis:	reading aloud and conversation (hypernasality; slow speech rate and imprecise articulation); speech AMRs (slow but regular); vowel prolongation (strained, strangled, or harsh voice; low pitch)

Checklist of Perceptual Symptoms

Physiologic	Characteristics Typically Seen With This Disorder	If Symptoms Observed, Consider These Goals/Treatment Objectives
Respiration	may have reduced vital capacity; difficult to separate from what is caused by poor laryngeal valving	RSP 9-20
Phonation	strained, strangled; low pitch; some pitch breaks; little loudness variation	PH 16-20
Resonance	hypernasality, but usually not nasal emission	RSN 1-10, 14
Articulation	imprecise consonants	AR 1-12, 29-43, 44-46, 47-50
Prosody	reduced stress; maybe excess and equal stress; slow rate	PR 11-16, 33-37, or 17-22 (excess and equal)

Flaccid dysarthria

Possible Medical Diagnoses: Neuropathy secondary to radiation; degenerative disease (progressive bulbar palsy); demyelinating disease (Guillain-Barre syndrome); infectious process (poliomyelitis); neurological complications of AIDS (cryptococcal meningitis); muscle disease (muscular dystrophy); vascular (brainstem stroke); Wallenberg's lateral medullary syndrome

Neurological system affected: pyramidal — lower motor neuron (cranial or spinal nerves)

Associated neurological symptoms: reflexive automatic and voluntary movements affected which leads to weakness, hypotonia, atrophy, and fasciculations (small spontaneous contractions of muscles) (Note: When several cranial nerves are damaged, it is called bulbar palsy.)

Patient complaints: speech sounds slurred; tongue feels thick

Reflexes: diminished

Tasks most helpful
to make diagnosis: tests of oral motor strength (decreased strength)

Checklist of Perceptual Symptoms

Physiologic	Characteristics Typically Seen With This Disorder	If Symptoms Observed, Consider These Goals/Treatment Objectives
Respiration	*decreased respiratory support secondary to muscle weakness (observed as monoloudness and short phrases)	RSP 1-20
Phonation	if unilateral damage in brainstem — voice will depend on where cord is (e.g. paramedian); if bilateral cord involvement; breathy; harsh voice; audible inspiration; decreased loudness	PH 1-15
Resonance	hypernasal and nasal emission	RSN 2-14
Articulation	imprecise articulation, especially tongue tip, plosives, and fricatives	AR 13-27, 28, 29-43, 44-46, 47-50
Prosody	prosodic insufficiency; monotone; monoloudness	PR 11-16, 23-32

*Note: Decreased respiratory support for speech is often manifested as problems with loudness (e.g. decreased overall loudness, monoloudness, inappropriate loudness changes). These characteristics are listed under Phonation as it is difficult to separate how much of the problem is respiratory vs. phonatory in nature.

Flaccid dysarthria

Medical Diagnosis: Myasthenia Gravis**

Neurological system affected: pyramidal — lower motor neuron, neuromuscular junction disease

Associated neurological symptoms: ptosis, weakness of facial muscle, dysphagia

Patient complaints: can speak better after resting

Reflexes: normal

Tasks most helpful
to make diagnosis: speech stress testing (if not already taking medications to lessen effect of fatigue)

Checklist of Perceptual Symptoms

Physiologic	Characteristics Typically Seen With This Disorder	If Symptoms Observed, Consider These Goals/Treatment Objectives
Respiration	*respiratory weakness (observed as short phrases; decreased intensity)	RSP 9-20
Phonation	progressively more breathy; decreased intensity	PH 10, 12
Resonance	hypernasal and nasal emission	RSN 2-8, 11-14
Articulation	imprecise articulation	AR 44-46, 47-50
Prosody	flat intonation (monotone)	PR 11-16, 23-32

*Decreased respiratory support for speech is often manifested as problems with loudness (decreased overall loudness, monoloudness, inappropriate loudness changes). These characteristics are listed under Phonation as it is difficult to separate how much of the problem is respiratory vs. phonatory in nature.

**Degenerative disorder — different goals and treatment objectives may be indicated at different stages of the disease. Environmental modification goals should be considered at all stages.

Flaccid dysarthria — Trigeminal (Vth) Nerve Lesions

(Note: Vth nerve has bilateral UMN innervation, so a unilateral lesion will have little effect)

Possible Medical Diagnoses:	stroke, infection, arteriovenous malformation, tumors, trauma to skull, trigeminal neuralgia
Neurological system affected:	Vth nerve rarely affected alone, usually with other cranial nerves; pyramidal — lower motor neuron (i.e., cranial nerve)
Associated neurological symptoms:	unilateral lesion: jaw deviates to weak side bilateral lesion: jaw may hang open at rest
Patient complaints:	chewing difficulty, drooling, decreased sensation to face and mouth
Reflexes:	not applicable
Tasks most helpful to make diagnosis:	reading aloud and conversation (reduced precision of lip and tongue movements for articulation); speech AMRs (imprecise and slow on /pʌ/, worse than for /tʌ/ or /kʌ/)

Checklist of Perceptual Symptoms

Physiologic	Characteristics Typically Seen With This Disorder	If Symptoms Observed, Consider These Goals/Treatment Objectives
Respiration	none	
Phonation	none	
Resonance	none	
Articulation	unilateral — none bilateral — imprecise bilabials labiodentals, linguadentals, lingual-alveolars, distorted vowels	AR 44-46
Prosody	unilateral — none bilateral — slow rate	don't address; will improve when articulation improves

Flaccid dysarthria — Facial (VIIth) Nerve Lesions

(Note: upper face has bilateral innervation; lower face mostly contralateral; unilateral lesions are more common)

Possible Medical Diagnoses:	Bell's Palsy, tumors (acoustic neuroma, cerebello pontine angle meningioma), infection (herpes zoster, mononucleosis, otitis media, meningitis, Lyme disease)
Neurological system affected:	pyramidal — lower motor neuron (i.e., cranial nerve)
Associated neurological symptoms:	forehead unwrinkled; eyebrow drooped; eye open and not blinking; drooling on affected side; nasolabial fold flattened; on smile, face retracts on unaffected side; fasciculations or atrophy on affected side
Patient complaints:	biting the cheek, difficulty keeping food in mouth
Reflexes:	normal
Tasks most helpful to make diagnosis:	reading aloud and conversation (flutter of cheeks, poor bilabial closure); speech AMRs (reduced precision and more slowness on /pʌ/ than /tʌ/ or /kʌ/)

Checklist of Perceptual Symptoms

Physiologic	Characteristics Typically Seen With This Disorder	If Symptoms Observed, Consider These Goals/Treatment Objectives
Respiration	none	
Phonation	none	
Resonance	none	
Articulation	unilateral — mild distortion bilabial and labiodentals, distortion of fricatives and affricates bilateral — distortion or inability to produce bilabials and labiodentals, possible vowel, lingual fricatives and affricates distorted	AR 44-46
Prosody	unilateral — none bilateral — slow rate	don't address; will improve when articulation improves

Flaccid dysarthria — Vagus (Xth) Nerve Lesions
Pharyngeal Branch Involvement

(Note: Xth nerve has bilateral innervation. Because the Xth nerve divides into three branches (pharyngeal branch, superior laryngeal branch, and recurrent laryngeal branch), the level of the lesion determines the symptoms. The higher the level of damage, the more muscle functions affected. Pharyngeal branch involvement indicates a high lesion which affects the superior and recurrent laryngeal branches.

- Pharyngeal branch: supplies muscles of pharynx, soft palate, and palatoglossus (responsible for pharyngeal constriction and palatal elevation and retraction)

- Superior laryngeal branch: sensory component (internal laryngeal nerve) sends sensation from larynx, epiglottis, base of tongue, and aryepiglottic folds; motor component (external laryngeal nerve) supplies inferior pharyngeal constrictors and cricothyroid

- Recurrent laryngeal branch: innervates all intrinsic laryngeal muscles except cricothyroid; sensory fibers carry sensation from vocal cords and larynx subglottally

Possible Medical Diagnoses: lesions can be intracranial (intramedullary - extramedullary) or extracranial; infection; stroke; polio; inflammatory and demyelinating (Guillain-Barré); surgery

Neurological system affected: pyramidal — lower motor neuron (i.e., cranial nerve)

Associated neurological symptoms: unilateral lesion: soft palate hangs lower on affected side and pulls toward unaffected side on phonation
bilateral lesions: palate hangs low at rest and moves minimally; nasal regurgitation when eating

Patient complaints: swallowing difficulties; listeners find it hard to hear voice

Reflexes: gag reflex diminished or absent

Tasks most helpful
to make diagnosis: conversational speech (breathy voice, reduced pitch)

Checklist of Perceptual Symptoms

Physiologic	Characteristics Typically Seen With This Disorder	If Symptoms Observed, Consider These Goals/Treatment Objectives
Respiration	none	
Phonation	unilateral — breathiness, hoarseness, diplophonia, reduced pitch and loudness bilateral — breathiness, aphonia, inhalatory stridor	PH 1-15
Resonance	unilateral — no affect to mild-moderate hypernasality and nasal emission bilateral — severe hypernasality, nasal emission, imprecise pressure consonants, short phrases secondary to nasal air wastage	RSN 2-14
Articulation	bilateral — weak pressure consonants	AR 44-46
Prosody		

Flaccid dysarthria — Vagus (Xth) Nerve Lesions

Superior and Recurrent Laryngeal Branch Involvement

Note: Xth nerve has bilateral innervation. Because the Xth nerve divides into three branches (pharyngeal branch, superior laryngeal branch, and recurrent laryngeal branch), the level of the lesion determines the symptoms. The higher the level of damage, the more muscle functions affected.

- **Superior laryngeal branch:** sensory component (internal laryngeal nerve) sends sensation from larynx, epiglottis, base of tongue, and aryepiglottic folds; motor component (external laryngeal nerve) supplies inferior pharyngeal constrictors and cricothyroid

- **Recurrent laryngeal branch:** innervates all intrinsic laryngeal muscles except cricothyroid; sensory fibers carry sensation from vocal cords and larynx subglottally

Possible Medical Diagnoses: lesions can be intracranial (intramedullary - extramedullary) or extracranial, Myasthenia Gravis, tumors in neck or thorax, aneurysm, surgery, stroke, Guillian-Barré

Neurological system: pyramidal — lower motor neuron (i.e., cranial nerve)

Associated neurological symptoms: vocal cords paralyzed in abducted position; weak cough; dysphagia

Patient complaints: voice weak and breathy

Reflexes: normal

Tasks most helpful to make diagnosis: vowel prolongation (breathy voice, diplophonia)

Checklist of Perceptual Symptoms

Physiologic	Characteristics Typically Seen With This Disorder	If Symptoms Observed, Consider These Goals/Treatment Objectives
Respiration	none	
Phonation	unilateral — breathiness or aphonia, reduced loudness, diplophonia, low pitch, rapid vocal flutter on vowel prolongation bilateral — all characteristics worse, monopitch	PH 1-15
Resonance	none	
Articulation	none	
Prosody	none	

Flaccid dysarthria — Vagus (Xth) Nerve Lesions

Superior laryngeal branch involvement (not recurrent)

Note: Xth nerve has bilateral innervation. Because the Xth nerve divides into three branches (pharyngeal branch, superior laryngeal branch, and recurrent laryngeal branch, the level of the lesion determines the symptoms. The higher the level of damage, the more muscle functions affected.

- **Superior laryngeal branch:**   sensory component (internal laryngeal nerve) sends sensation from larynx, epiglottis, base of tongue, and aryepiglottic folds; motor component (external laryngeal nerve) supplies inferior pharyngeal constrictors and cricothyroid)

Possible Medical Diagnosis: lesions can be intracranial (intramedullary-extramedullary) or extracranial, Myasthenia Gravis, tumors in neck or thorax, aneurysm

Neurological system affected: pyramidal — lower motor neuron (i.e., cranial nerve)

Associated neurological symptoms: unilateral: both vocal cords adduct, affected cord looks shorter, epiglottis and anterior larynx shift to affected side
bilateral: both cords appear short and bowed, epiglottis overhangs anterior portion of vocal cords

Patient complaints: inability to sing

Reflexes: normal

Tasks most helpful to make diagnosis: vowel prolongation (breathy voice)

Checklist of Perceptual Symptoms

Physiologic	Characteristics Typically Seen With This Disorder	If Symptoms Observed, Consider These Goals/Treatment Objectives
Respiration	none	
Phonation	unilateral — breathiness or hoarseness, mild inability to change pitch, loudness mildly reduced
bilateral — mild to moderate breathiness and hoarseness, decreased loudness and inability to change pitch, low pitch, poor laryngeal valving results in short phrases secondary to poor laryngeal valving	PH 1-15
Resonance	none	
Articulation	none	
Prosody		

Flaccid dysarthria — Vagus Xth nerve lesions

Recurrent Laryngeal Branch Involvement

Note: Xth nerve has bilateral innervation. Because the Xth nerve divides into three branches (pharyngeal branch, superior laryngeal branch, and recurrent laryngeal branch, the level of the lesion determines the symptoms. The higher the level of damage, the more muscle functions affected.

- Recurrent laryngeal branch: innervates all intrinsic laryngeal muscles except cricothyroid; sensory fibers carry sensation from vocal cords and larynx subglottally

Possible Medical Diagnosis: trauma (e.g., cardiac surgery)

Neurological system affected: pyramidal — lower motor neuron (i.e., cranial nerve)

Associated neurological symptoms: unilateral: affected vocal cord fixed paramedian, dysphagia, weak cough
bilateral: both cords paramedian, inhalatory stridor and airway compromise

Patient complaints: weak voice

Reflexes: normal

Tasks most helpful
to make diagnosis: vowel prolongation (breathy or hoarse voice, inhalatory stridor)

Checklist of Perceptual Symptoms

Physiologic	Characteristics Typically Seen With This Disorder	If Symptoms Observed, Consider These Goals/Treatment Objectives
Respiration	none	
Phonation	unilateral — breathiness or hoarse vocal quality, decreased loudness, diplophonia, pitch breaks bilateral — inhalatory stridor with airway compromise; voice fairly good, poor laryngeal valving results in short phrases	PH 1-15
Resonance	none	
Articulation	none	
Prosody	none	

Flaccid dysarthria — Hypoglossal (XIIth) Nerve Lesions

(Note: The UMN supply may be bilateral, but it is more contralateral.   Often affected with other cranial nerves, but isolated lesions can damage only the XIIth.)

Possible Medical Diagnoses:	tumors, trauma, vascular (aneurysm, carotid endarterectomy), infection
Neurological system affected:	pyramidal, lower motor neurons (i.e., cranial nerve)
Associated neurological symptoms:	unilateral: tongue atrophied on affected side, tongue deviates to weak side, may be able to push tongue into cheek on weak side bilateral: bilateral atrophy and fasciculations; tongue protrudes symmetrically but with limited range, may not be able to lateralize or elevate
Patient complaints:	bilateral feels like excess saliva, can't move food in mouth, tongue feels thick, drooling
Reflexes:	normal
Tasks most helpful to make diagnosis:	conversation (lingual distortions); speech AMRs (slow and imprecise for /tʌ/ and /kʌ/; adequate for /pʌ/)

Checklist of Perceptual Symptoms

Physiologic	Characteristics Typically Seen With This Disorder	If Symptoms Observed, Consider These Goals/Treatment Objectives
Respiration	none	
Phonation	none	
Resonance	bilateral — may be perceived as abnormal secondary to tongue falling back in oral cavity	treat articulation and resonance will improve
Articulation	unilateral or bilateral — imprecise articulation of lingual phonemes	AR 44-46
Prosody	slow rate	don't address; will improve when articulation improves

Hypokinetic dysarthria

Possible Medical Diagnoses:	Parkinson's disease; degenerative*** (includes Parkinson's and some patients with Alzheimer's disease), vascular, traumatic (multiple or bilateral strokes affecting the basal ganglia), inflammatory, toxic/metabolic (caused by antipsychotic medications), neoplastic, infectious (viral encephalitis)
Neurological system affected:	extrapyramidal — basal ganglia pathology
Associated neurological symptoms:	decreased mobility or range of motion, resting tremor, rigidity, bradykinesa, face has mask-like expression, drooling
Patient complaints:	voice cannot be heard in noisy environments, speech is too fast, voice has no emotion, sound like they are stuttering, lips feeling very rigid and stiff
Reflexes:	loss of postural reflexes
Tasks most helpful to make diagnosis:	conversational speech or reading (rapid rate, short rushes of speech, articulatory imprecision); speech AMRs (sound like they run together, reduced range of motion, rapid rate); vowel prolongation (decreased loudness and breathiness)

Checklist of Perceptual Symptoms

Physiologic	Characteristics Typically Seen With This Disorder	If Symptoms Observed, Consider These Goals/Treatment Objectives**
Respiration	*decreased support (results in mono-loudness and short rushes; decreased loudness)	RSP 1-20
Phonation	hoarseness; breathiness; tremors; decreased loudness; monoloudness	PH 1-15
Resonance	some hypernasality	RSN 3-12, 14
Articulation	changes in manner of production with undershooting on articulatory targets	AR 1-12, 29-43, 44-46, 47-50
Prosody	increased rate; monotone; short rushes of speech	PR 1-10, 11-16, 23-32

*Decreased respiratory support for speech is often manifested as problems with loudness (decreased overall loudness, monoloudness, inappropriate loudness changes). These characteristics are listed under Phonation as it is difficult to separate how much of the problem is respiratory vs. phonatory in nature.

**Although individual treatment goals are suggested for each physiologic component with symptoms, you'll find more information on the Lee Silverman Voice Therapy Approach (page 116).

***Degenerative disorder — different goals and treatment objectives may be indicated at different stages of the disease. Environmental modification goals should be considered at all stages.

Hyperkinetic dysarthria — Tremor

Possible Medical Diagnoses:	autosomal dominant condition, focal dystonia, spasmodic torticollis
Neurological system affected:	extrapyramidal (basal ganglia and related portions), possibly cerebellar control circuit
Neurological symptoms:	can occur in isolation but is often accompanied by tremors of the head or extremities, lingual tremor, tremors of jaw/ lips apparent at rest and sometimes during vowel prolongation
Patient complaints:	voice sounds tight, short of breath, some patients not aware if it is mild, others complain that it worsens with fatigue or stress and improves with alcohol
Reflexes:	normal
Tasks most helpful to make diagnosis:	vowel prolongation (should sound rhythmic but if severe, may have abrupt voice arrests)

Checklist of Perceptual Symptoms

Physiologic	Characteristics Typically Seen With This Disorder	If Symptoms Observed, Consider These Goals/Treatment Objectives
Respiration	none	
Phonation	regular tremor with alternating pitch and loudness; low pitch; pitch breaks	PH 16-20, 21-25
Resonance	none	
Articulation	none	
Prosody	rate may be slowed; monotone	PR 11-16, 23-32

Hyperkinetic dysarthria — Chorea

Possible Medical Diagnoses: infectious process (Syndenham's chorea), neoplasm (tumor in basal ganglia and thalamus), degenerative disease (Huntington's disease/Huntington's chorea)*

Neurological system affected: extrapyramidal (basal ganglia and related portions), possible cerebellar control circuit

Associated neurological symptoms: chewing and swallowing difficulties, occasional drooling, motor unsteadiness, choreiform movements (quick, unpredictable involuntary movements)

Patient complaints: speech sounds slurred and slow, hard to talk, difficulty chewing and swallowing

Reflexes: normal

Tasks most helpful
to make diagnosis: conversation, reading, and speech AMRs (unpredictable breakdown of articulation, abnormal rate, abnormal prosody); vowel prolongation (fluctuations caused by the choreiform movements)

Checklist of Perceptual Symptoms

Physiologic	Characteristics Typically Seen With This Disorder	If Symptoms Observed, Consider These Goals/Treatment Objectives
Respiration	sudden forced inspiration/expiration	cannot treat due to involuntary movements
Phonation	strained, strangled; excess loudness variation; voice stoppages/errors	PH 16-20, 21-25
Resonance	hypernasality	RSN 3-10, 14
Articulation	imprecise consonants; distorted vowels; irregular articulatory breakdown	AR 29-43, 44-46
Prosody	decreased or variable stress; prolonged intervals; variable rate; inappropriate silences	PR 11-16, 23-32, 33-37

*Degenerative disorder — different goals and treatment objectives may be indicated at different stages of the disease. Environmental modification goals should be considered at all stages.

Hyperkinetic dysarthria — Dystonia** and Athetosis

Possible Medical Diagnoses:

dystonia musculorum deformans; Meige's syndrome; vascular disorder (stroke and AVM); neoplasm (tumor in basal ganglia and thalamus); toxic/metabolic (neuroleptic and antipsychotic); cerebral palsy

Neurological system affected:

extrapyramidal (basal ganglia and related portions), possible cerebellar control circuit

Associated neurological symptoms:

drooling, dysphagia, dystonic movements (slower than choreiform movements with waxing and waning)

Patient complaints:

speech sounds slurred, slow, hard to talk, difficulty chewing and swallowing, voice sounds tight, short of breath, food may feel as if it gets stuck in the throat

Reflexes:

normal

Tasks most helpful to make diagnosis:

conversational speech or reading (watch the patient carefully to observe the involuntary movements during speech); speech AMRs (rate is generally slow); vowel prolongation (voice stoppages, strained quality)

Checklist of Perceptual Symptoms

Physiologic	Characteristics Typically Seen With This Disorder	If Symptoms Observed, Consider These Goals/Treatment Objectives*
Respiration	*poor respiratory support (athetosis) (observed as short phrases, monoloudness)	RSP 9-16
Phonation	harsh, strained, strangled quality; possible intermittent breathiness; voice stoppages secondary to involuntary movements and excess loudness variations; audible inspiration; monoloudness	PH 16-20, 21-25
Resonance	hypernasality	RSN 3-10, 14
Articulation	variable articulation; imprecise consonants; vowel distortions	AR 29-43, 44-46, 47-50
Prosody	short phrases with prolonged intervals and variable rate; monotone; monoloudness	PR 11-16, 23-32, 33-37

*Decreased respiratory support for speech is often manifested as problems with loudness (decreased overall loudness, monoloudness, inappropriate loudness changes). These characteristics are listed under phonation as it is difficult to separate how much of the problem is respiratory vs. phonatory in nature.

**Most dystonias are degenerative disorders — different goals and treatment objectives may be indicated at different stages of the disease. Environmental modification goals should be considered at all stages.

Mixed: Spastic/Flaccid

(Note: Initially patients with ALS may present with flaccid dysarthria since LMNs (multiple cranial nerves) may be affected first)

Possible Medical Diagnoses:	ALS; spinal muscle atrophy; progressive bulbar palsy**
Neurological system affected:	pyramidal system — upper motor neurons and lower motor neurons
Associated neurological symptoms:	fatigue, cramping, fasciculations, weakness, muscle atrophy (Note: 30% of patients show initial symptoms in speech and swallowing)
Reflexes:	positive jaw jerk, suck, hyperactive gag (if spastic)
Patient complaints:	trouble swallowing
Tasks most helpful to make diagnosis:	conversational speech and reading (disturbed prosody)

Checklist of Perceptual Symptoms

Physiologic	Characteristics Typically Seen With This Disorder	If Symptoms Observed, Consider These Goals/Treatment Objectives
Respiration	*decreased support (observed as monoloudness, prolonged intervals)	RSP 9-20
Phonation	UMN damage: low pitch; harsh strained, strangled with wet vocal quality; LMN damage: breathy; monoloudness	PH 10-12 (LMN damage) PH 16-20 (UMN damage)
Resonance	hypernasality (not nasal emission)	RSN 1-8
Articulation	imprecise consonants	AR 44-46, 47-50
Prosody	reduced stress, reduced rate; prosodic insufficiency; prolonged intervals; prolonged phonemes; monotone	PR 11-16, 23-32, 33-37

*Decreased respiratory support for speech is often manifested as problems with loudness (decreased overall loudness, monoloudness, inappropriate loudness changes). These characteristics are listed under Phonation as it is difficult to separate how much of the problem is respiratory vs. phonatory in nature.

Mixed dysarthria — Spastic/Ataxic

(Note: Mixed dysarthrias are often the result of more than one neurological event. They often occur in a number of degenerative diseases that affect more than one part of the nervous system.)

Medical Diagnosis: Multiple Sclerosis (demyelinating disease)**

Neurological system affected: pyramidal system (upper motor neuron) and cerebellum

Associated neurological symptoms: variety of symptoms because lesions occur in multiple places: gait and sphincter control problems, visual and other sensory deficits, cerebellar dysfunction, dysarthria, intention tremor, cognitive deficits

Patient complaints: can't control loudness, voice sounds harsh

Reflexes: increased deep tendon reflexes

Tasks most helpful
to make diagnosis: conversation/reading (sudden articulatory breakdowns, impaired loudness and pitch controls)

Checklist of Perceptual Symptoms

Physiologic	Characteristics Typically Seen With This Disorder	If Symptoms Observed, Consider These Goals/Treatment Objectives
Respiration	*decreased breath support (observed as impaired loudness control)	RSP 9-20
Phonation	impaired loudness control; harsh; breathy	PH 6-20, 21-25
Resonance	hypernasality	RSN 1-12, 14
Articulation	imprecise articulation	AR 1-12, 29-43, 44-46, 47-50
Prosody	impaired emphasis; impaired pitch control	PR 11-16, 23-32

*Decreased respiratory support for speech is often manifested as problems with loudness (decreased overall loudness, monoloudness, inappropriate loudness changes). These characteristics are listed under Phonation as it is difficult to separate how much of the problem is respiratory vs. phonatory in nature

**Degenerative disorder — different goals and treatment objectives may be indicated at different stages of the disease. Environmental modification goals should be considered at all stages.

Mixed dysarthria — Hypokinetic - Spastic - Ataxic

(Note: Mixed dysarthrias are often the result of more than one neurological event. They often occur in a number of degenerative diseases that affect more than one part of the nervous system.)

Medical Diagnosis: Progressive Supranuclear Palsy (PSP)**

Neurological system affected: extrapyramidal, pyramidal (upper motor neuron), and cerebellum

Associated neurological symptoms: ophthalmoparesis (paralysis of vertical gaze), gait difficulty, postural instability, falling, dysphagia; drooling, hypotonia, pseudobulbar affect

Patient complaints: speech seems slow

Reflexes: hyperactive jaw jerk

Tasks most helpful
to make diagnosis: conversation/reading (abnormal prosodic characteristics, imprecise articulation); vowel prolongation (hoarseness, hypernasality)

Checklist of Perceptual Symptoms

Physiologic	Characteristics Typically Seen With This Disorder*	If Symptoms Observed, Consider These Goals/Treatment Objectives
Respiration	none	RSP 9-20
Phonation	hoarseness	PH 16-20
Resonance	nasal emission; hypernasality	RSN 1-14
Articulation	imprecise articulation	AR 1-12, 29-43, 44-46, 47-50
Prosody	excess and equal stress; slow rate; monotone	PR 17-22, 33-37

*These characteristics were found more frequently in patients with PSP than Parkinson's disease (patients with PSP are often misdiagnosed with Parkinson's disease).

**Degenerative disorder — different goals and treatment objectives may be indicated at different stages of the disease. Environmental modification goals should be considered at all stages.

Mixed: Unilateral UMN (but most like Flaccid)

(Note: This dysarthria has been described by Duffy as often mild, short in duration and co-occurring with other deficits that may mask it. Although it is an UMN disorder, it is most like a flaccid dysarthria.)

Probable Medical Diagnosis:	vascular (right or left carotid or middle cerebral artery stroke, posterior cerebral and basilar stroke, lacunar stroke)
Neurological system affected:	pyramidal UMN and extrapyramidal UMN
Associated neurological symptoms:	often co-occurs with aphasia or apraxia if lesion in left hemisphere or with cognitive deficits or dysprosody if lesion in right hemisphere; weakness and incoordination of tongue and face on side opposite lesion (central facial weakness), hemiplegia, weakness and hypotonia after acute lesion with spasticity, increased tone emerging later
Reflexes:	positive Babinski on affected side
Patient complaints:	slurred speech, thick tongue, drooling, face feels heavy on affected side, chewing and swallowing problems
Tasks most helpful to make diagnosis:	speech and reading (imprecise consonants); speech AMRs (slow, irregular)

Checklist of Perceptual Symptoms

Physiologic	Characteristics Typically Seen With This Disorder	If Symptoms Observed, Consider These Goals/Treatment Objectives
Respiration	none	
Phonation	harshness	PH 16-20
Resonance	none	
Articulation	imprecise consonants, irregular articulatory breakdowns	AR 13-27, 29-43, 44-46, 47-50
Prosody	slow rate	PR 33-37

Ataxic dysarthria

Possible Medical Diagnoses:

degenerative (Friedreich's Ataxia; signs of spasticity, lower motor neuron weakness and extrapyramidal features including dystonia, chorea, and other movement disorders; Shy-Drager); Paroxysmal Ataxic Dysarthria (PAD); vascular disorders (aneurysm, arteriovenous malformations, cerebellar hemorrhage, occlusion in the vertibrobasilar system); tumors (acoustic neuroma; tumors in the cerebellar often involve multicranial nerves and may yield a mixed dysarthria); trauma; toxic/metabolic conditions (acute/chronic alcohol abuse, severe malnutrition, neurotoxic affects of drugs like Dilantin®, lithium, and Valium®); hypothyroidism

Neurological system affected:

cerebellum

Associated neurological symptoms:

broad-based stance and gait, instability of the trunk, tilted or rotated head posture, tremor, cognitive deficits

Patient complaints:

sound as if they are drunk, feel as if they are stumbling over words, bite tongue or cheek when eating, speech deteriorates significantly with alcohol intake

Reflexes:

gag and reflexive swallow normal

Tasks most helpful
to make diagnosis:

conversational speech or reading (prosody abnormalities and breakdowns in articulation, excess and equal stress, distorted vowels, and prolonged phonemes); speech AMRs (irregular speed); repetition of sentences containing multisyllabic words (irregular articulatory breakdowns and abnormalities in prosody)

Checklist of Perceptual Symptoms

Physiologic	Characteristics Typically Seen With This Disorder	If Symptoms Observed, Consider These Goals/Treatment Objectives
Respiration	may speak on low air	RSP 17-20
Phonation	excessive loudness variations; harshness; monoloudness	PH 21-25
Resonance	none	
Articulation	imprecise consonants; vowel distortions; irregular articulatory breakdowns	AR 29-43, 44-46, 47-50
Prosody	excess and equal stress; phoneme and pause prolongations; bursts of increased intensity after pauses; slow rate; monotone	PR 17-22, 33-37

Aprosodic dysarthria*

Possible Medical Diagnosis:	right hemisphere CVA
Neurological system affected:	pyramidal (upper motor neuron)
Associated neurological symptoms:	left-sided neglect, visuoperceptual problems, attentional deficits
Patient complaints:	voice cannot convey emotions; pitch doesn't sound right
Reflexes:	increased deep tendon reflex on (L); positive on (L)
Tasks most helpful to make diagnosis:	conversation in which patient is likely to generate a range of feelings; contrastive stress

Checklist of Perceptual Symptoms

Physiologic	Characteristics Typically Seen With This Disorder	If Symptoms Observed, Consider These Goals/Treatment Objectives
Respiration	none	
Phonation	none	
Resonance	none	
Articulation	none	
Prosody	flat intonation, monotone, reduced pitch and loudness variation, reduced or abnormal intonation, poor expression of irony and sarcasm, lack of emphasis, reduced affect and emotion	PR 11-16, 23-32, 38-47

*a deficit in the ability to interpret or produce distinctions of duration, amplitude, or pitch variations that convey emotional tone, emphasis, and other linguistic information

Helping to Improve Communication with the Patient who has Dysarthria

Situation

Have the patient give you the context for the message rather than just start talking without giving you a point of reference. You can ask questions such as "Are you telling me about your daughter?" or "Are you trying to ask me about paying the bills?"

Noise

If possible, turn down televisions or radios or even ask others who are speaking in the vicinity to speak quietly. You can also try to move away from the noise. Be sure you are standing where you can see the speaker's face when talking.

Lighting

Make sure the lights are turned on in the room so you can see each other's faces when communicating.

Distance

Stand or sit close to the speaker to help you hear what is said. Sit where the speaker and you can look at each other directly.

Noisy Rooms

Some rooms are much harder to hear a person in than others. For instance, very large rooms where speech can echo are harder to listen in than in rooms with carpeting and drapes where some of the sound is dampened.

Using External Aids

The speaker should use these aids/techniques to help improve intelligibility. _____

_____

_____

Adapted from: Berry, W. and Sanders, F. "Environmental Education: The Universal Management Approach for Adults with Dysarthria." *Clinical Dysarthria,* San Diego: College Hill Press, 1983.

The Source for Dysarthria   99

These are strategies you may use to clarify your message if your listener does not understand the first time you say something. Those marked with a star are used more frequently.

★   1.   Total repetition: Repeat the entire message again exactly as you said it the first time.

      2.   Partial repetition/word: Repeat the one word that you think was hard for your listener to understand.

★   3.   Partial repetition/phrase: Repeat the part of the message that you think your listener did not understand. Use the exact same words.

★   4.   Elaboration: Try giving more detail about what you just said. For instance, if you said "Is it time to eat yet?," you might elaborate by saying "I'm hungry and it's six o'clock. Is it time for us to have dinner yet?"

      5.   Spelling the word: If you can tell which word in your message caused your listener difficulty, try spelling the word. It is a good idea to introduce this by saying "I'll spell it for you."

      6.   Semantic specification: Try using simpler words to say the same thing. For instance, if you said "My friends in the women's circle," you could just say "the women's group."

Adapted from: Ansel, B., McNeil, M., Hunker, C., & Bless, D. "The Frequency of Verbal and Acoustic Adjustments Used by Cerebral Palsied Dysarthric Adults When Faced With Communicative Failure." *Clinical Dysarthria*, San Diego: College Hill Press, 1983.

Chapter 4
Respiration

Should you work on improving respiration with all patients? No.
Most authors agree that if the patient cannot maintain consistent air
pressure to produce more than one word per breath group, it should be
addressed. Yorkston, Beukelman, and Bell (1988) point out that some
individuals whose respiratory function is severely compromised are
able to do very well during speech. On the other hand, patients who
appear to have less impairment may have unusual or bizarre respiratory patterns that significantly affect their ability to speak.

In addition, most problems with respiration can be traced to weak
muscles. (Keep in mind that strengthening exercises are contra-indi-
cated for some patients, such as those with Myasthenia Gravis or ALS.)
Other problems with respiration are caused by abnormal tone (either
hypotonia or hypertonia). Physical therapists rather than SLPs
generally address abnormal tone. The chart on page 108 lists respiratory problems and their causes.

As is typical of our approach in therapy, some of our activities will
be designed to improve the actual physiology of respiration of speech
(f = facilitation techniques). Other times intervention will focus on
helping the patient compensate for decreased functions (c = compensatory techniques). Each treatment objective is marked with an (f)
or (c) to indicate if it is facilitation or compensation.

Perceptual problems noted under prosody (e.g., prolonged intervals,
monoloudness) may be caused by respiratory problems and/or problems
with the laryngeal and respiratory components. Therefore, you may
want to read about the perceptual effects of some respiratory deficits in
more detail in Chapter 8, Prosody.

What may sound like poor respiratory control or reduced vital capacity
is usually a problem caused by the patient wasting air because of poor
valving. This poor valving can occur either at the larynx (heard as a
breathy voice) or at the velopharyngeal port (heard as hypernasality or
nasal emission). In addition, some speakers with strained, strangled
vocal quality use so much pressure to start phonation that they cannot
maintain it. This may be perceived as reduced respiratory support.

In Chapters 4-8, the short-term goal is written in functional terms.
Treatment objectives are the smaller, measurable steps to achieve
the goal. Whenever possible, use target percentages with treatment
objectives.

Respiration (RSP) Goal and Treatment Objectives

Short Term Goal: Patient will improve respiratory support and the use of respiration for speech.

Treatment Objectives:

RSP 1: Patient will blow into a water glass/water bottle manometer and maintain 5cm of H_2O pressure for 5 seconds. (f)

RSP 2: Patient will use diaphragmatic breathing and prolong phonation of a vowel sound for ___ seconds.* (f)

RSP 3: Patient will produce a vowel sound while pushing and will maintain phonation for ___ seconds.* (f)

RSP 4: Patient will produce a vowel sound while pulling and will maintain phonation for ___ seconds.* (f)

RSP 5: Patient will control exhalation on slow blowing tasks for ___ seconds.* (f)

RSP 6: Patient will use abdominal girdling during supervised situations for increased intelligibility. (c)

RSP 7: Patient will use external pressure to the abdominal cavity to increase force of expiration. (c)

RSP 8: Patient will modify position/posture to enhance expiration (e.g., speaking when supine). (c)

RSP 9: Patient will respond to verbal/visual cues to "inhale more deeply" before beginning an utterance on phrase/sentence imitation.* (c)

RSP 10: Patient will respond to verbal/visual cues to "inhale more deeply" on phrases and sentence level responses.* (c)

RSP 11: Patient will respond to verbal/visual cues to "inhale more deeply" during conversational speech attempts.* (c)

RSP 12: Patient will "inhale more deeply" without cues during conversational speech.* (c)

RSP 13: Patient will respond to verbal/visual cues to "let the air out slowly" when imitating a phrase level utterance.* (c)

RSP 14: Patient will respond to verbal/visual cues to "let the air out slowly" on phrase/sentence level responses.* (c)

RSP 15: Patient will respond to verbal/visual cues to "let the air out slowly" during conversational speech attempts.* (c)

RSP 16: Patient will "let the air out slowly" without cues during conversational speech.* (c)

RSP 17: Patient will respond to verbal/visual cues to begin speaking at onset of exhalation on phrase level imitation.* (c)

RSP 18: Patient will respond to verbal/visual cues to begin speaking at the onset of exhalation using phrase/sentence level responses.* (c)

RSP 19: Patient will respond to verbal/visual cues to begin speaking at onset of exhalation in conversation.* (c)

RSP 20: Patient will begin speaking at onset of exhalation and conversation without cues.* (c)

* Appendix A describes these activities for the patient.

The Source for Dysarthria   102

Environmental Modification (EM) Goals and Treatment Objectives

Short Term Goal: Speaker and listener will improve environment in which communication takes place.

Treatment Objectives:

EM 1: Speaker will give context of message before beginning to communicate.

EM 2: Listener will ask for clarification of context as needed.

EM 3: Speaker and/or listener will eliminate or reduce background noise.

EM 4: Speaker will gain visual attention of the listener before speaking.

EM 5: Speaker or listener will make sure area in which communication is taking place is well lit.

EM 6: Speaker and/or listener will make sure that they are sitting/standing close to one another and looking at each other before communication begins.

EM 7: Speaker and/or listener will try to make sure that communication takes place in a room with dampened background noise.

EM 8: Speaker will use external aid for communication (e.g., girdling):

_____

Treatment Techniques to Achieve Treatment Objectives

The following are brief descriptions of activities for improving respiration. Noted in () after the name of each activity is the treatment objective or objectives related to the activity.

Blowing (RSP 1)

Netsell and Hixon (1978) were the first to describe a device using a U-tube water manometer for determining the pressure-generating capability of their clients. Hixon, Holly, and Wilson (1982) describe a simplification of this device. Although they describe the device for use as a diagnostic procedure, it certainly could be used to provide feedback to the patient about his ability to generate respiratory pressure. Hixon, Holly, and Wilson explain that at rest, liquids in a standing glass exert pressure in all directions. The magnitude of that pressure depends on how dense the liquid is and the depth of the liquid (for individuals who scuba dive, you are well aware of increased pressures at greater depths of water).

For those of us who are non-scientists, we appreciate Hixon, Holly, and Wilson's explanation that the pressure exerted when the straw is placed to 5cm below the surface is 5cm of H_2O. At 7.5cm down it is 7.5cm H_2O, etc.

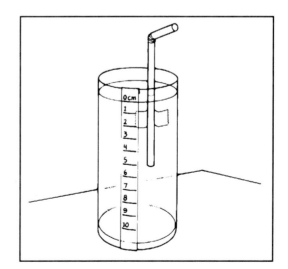

The patient is instructed to blow into the straw only as hard as necessary to create a bubble that will rise to the surface of the water. If the patient is unable to generate enough pressure to have a bubble rise to the surface when the straw is inserted at a certain level, then the straw can be backed out of the water until you reach a baseline. A therapeutic activity is to try to generate greater pressures over sequential sessions (or when practicing at home) when the straw is inserted at deeper and deeper levels.

Dworkin indicates that there is no good reason to push the patient beyond the threshold of maintaining 5cm H_2O over 5 seconds in duration. He indicates this is adequate for speech purposes. Dworkin uses the See-Scape™ device extensively for many of the breathing exercises described below.

Yorkston, Beukelman, and Bell (1988) have modified the Netsell & Hixon design. They use a plastic bottle with a hole in the cover. They insert a tube through the hole into the water. They like this approach because it keeps the water from being expelled when patients blow with too much pressure.

Diaphragmatic/Deep Breathing (RSP 2, 9 - 12)

It is easiest to begin this activity by having the patient lie on his back (supine). Have the patient place one hand on his abdomen and one on his upper chest. Rest your hands on top of the patient's hands.

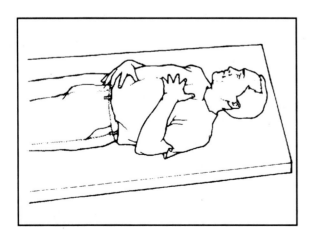

Instruct the patient to take a breath in and make the hand on his abdomen come up. Explain that when the diaphragm descends, it pushes into the abdominal cavity and pushes the contents of the abdominal cavity out. You are teaching the patient to use his diaphragm to pull more air into his lungs.

Ask the patient to watch and feel for movement of the hand on his abdomen and to have no movement of the hand on his upper chest. Ask the patient to watch the hand on his abdomen descend slowly on exhalation. For speech breathing, count to 2 for inspiration and encourage the patient to extend the exhalation for longer and longer counts. You can place a heavy book on the abdomen to actually make this more of a strengthening exercise. That way the patient has to exert more pressure to lift the book.

After the patient has mastered the appropriate breathing technique in supine, have the patient try the same technique standing or sitting as straight up as possible (Appendix A).

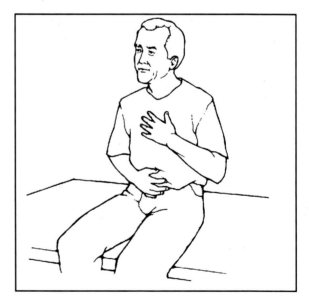

If the patient is having a hard time understanding the concept of breathing deeper, you may want to consult with a respiratory therapist concerning incentive spirometry. Spirometry is the measurement of breathing capacity of the lungs.

Incentive spirometer devices such as the Voldyne® Volumetric Exerciser are designed to encourage the patient to improve his inspiratory volume. Respiratory therapists are interested in this because it improves gas exchange when the patients inhale more deeply and utilize all the alveoli in their lungs. SLPs are interested in having the patient breathe more deeply so he will increase respiratory support for his speech. A device such as the Voldyne will provide the patient with visual input showing how deeply he is breathing.

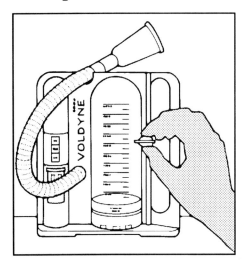

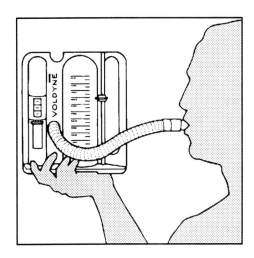

Increased Tone Through Pushing & Pulling (RSP 3 and 4)

Sometimes a patient can exhibit better respiratory control when he increases tone in the muscles of his diaphragm and chest wall.

Pushing and pulling are well-known techniques to increase vocal fold closure, but may also work to increase the overall tone in the abdomen and chest. This exercise is best paired with appropriate diaphragmatic breathing. Ask the patient to either push or pull and maintain phonation of a vowel sound while slowly exhaling. If the patient is successful, he should be able to continue for an increasing number of seconds (Appendix A).

Exhale Slowly (RSP 5, 13-16)

Have the patient inhale, then purse his lips and slowly blow the air out while you count the seconds. Each time, ask the patient to try and extend the exhalation a little longer. Provide these same instructions for the patient to use when speaking. The patient can slow his airflow by controlling the upward movement of the diaphragm, by better valving at the larynx, velopharynx, or a combination (Appendix A).

The incentive spirometer can also be inverted and used to help the patient see how to exhale more slowly. Ask the patient to place his lips around the mouthpiece and to keep the piston elevated in the tube for longer periods of time while you count aloud.

Abdominal Girdling (RSP 6)

Rosenbek and LaPointe (1985) describe the use of a band or girdle around the abdominal muscles. This helps provide a more normal posture for speech and allows the patient to exhibit stronger exhalation. This can be done using an elastic bandage or a Posey girdle.

It is not certain whether this girdling influences the amount of air the patient can inhale or helps him control his exhalation. Girdling can only be used for short periods of time as it can cause pneumonia and must be permitted and supervised by the physicians. It is best used when increased intelligibility is important to the patient.

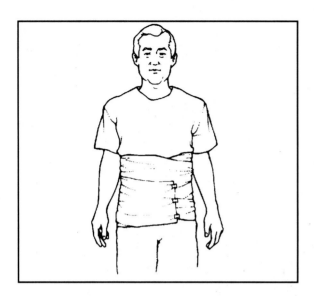

External Pressure to Abdominal Cavity (RSP 7)

Teach patients to lean against the edge of a table or even push their hands against the abdominal cavity. Patients can lean into the surface when they breathe in or out or only at the end of an utterance when they run out of breath.

If a patient is in a wheelchair, provide a lap tray with some padding for him to lean against. Ask the physical therapist to help you determine if the patient needs these modifications.

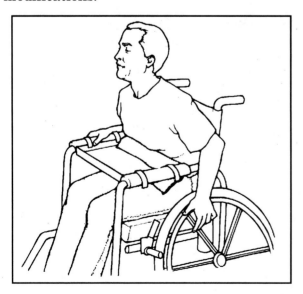

Supine vs. Upright Position (RSP 8)

Some patients do better in the supine position because it helps them stabilize their muscles so gravity will help push the abdominal contents up against the lungs for exhalation. This may help them increase loudness and to work less hard during speech attempts. Other patients, particularly those with ALS, don't do as well in the supine position because they have great difficulty on inspiration. These patients may do better in an upright position because gravity may help pull the diaphragm down. Patients who are weak and sit in a slumped position in a wheelchair may gain better respiratory support if a wooden seat is put into the wheelchair to help them straighten up. They may also benefit from a firm back in the chair (such as a board behind them). Better posture will allow them to maximize the use of their respiratory system.

Breathe Deeply (RSP 9 - 12)

Have the patient sit upright (unless supine is indicated for this patient) and purse his lips. This creates some noise on inspiration and allows you to better monitor the length of inspiration.

Ask the patient to take in as deep a breath as possible and hold it. While the patient is holding his breath, provide light pressure to his abdomen and ask the patient to push against your external pressure. Remind the patient to keep the air in his lungs.

Hammen et al (1994) and McHenry et al (1994) indicate that just telling the patient to breathe more deeply may result in better expiration because if there is more air in the lungs, more air can be forced out. Caution: if the patient breathes in too deeply, he will have excessive bursts when he breathes out. Netsell (1992) points out that you may have to tell the patients to slow down the exhalation (Appendix A).

Begin Speaking at Onset of Exhalation

(RSP 17 - 20)

With the patient in a supine or upright position, have him place one hand on his abdomen. Practice slow exhalation a few times. Remind the patient that he should feel his hand moving out on inhalation and in on exhalation.

Then, ask the patient to produce /m/ as soon as he starts to exhale. Tell the patient that phonation should begin as soon as he feels his hand start to fall back toward his spine. Place your hand lightly on the patient's hand to cue him by saying "now" when you feel exhalation begin. That is when the patient should begin phonation (Appendix A).

Respiratory Problems and Causes

What you hear	What could be causing the problem	SP	FL	FL Mya	V	VII	X PH	X S&R	X Sup	X Rec	Hypo	Hyper Trmr	Hyper Chorea	Dys & Ath	Mxd SP/FL	Mxd SP/AT	Mxd Hypo/SP/AT	UUMN	AT	AP
decreased loudness	weak muscles		★	★																
	abnormal tone										★									
monoloudness	weak muscles		★												★					
	abnormal tone										★									
	incoordination													★						
impaired control	abnormal tone	★														★				
short phrases	weak muscles		★	★																
	abnormal tone	★																		
	incoordinated muscles													★						
sudden inspiration/ expiration	incoordinated muscles												★	★						
short rushes of speech	abnormal tone										★									

Key

SP	Spastic dysarthria	X Sup	Flaccid dysarthria - Vagus (Xth) Nerve Lesions - Superior Laryngeal Branch Involvement
FL	Flaccid dysarthria		
FL Mya	Flaccid dysarthria- Mysathenia Gravis	X Rec	Flaccid dysarthria - Vagus (Xth) Nerve Lesions - Recurrent Laryngeal Branch Involvement
V	Flaccid dysarthria - Trigeminal (Vth) Nerve Lesions	Hypo	Flaccid dysarthria - Hypoglossal (XIIth) Nerve Lesions
VII	Flaccid dysarthria - Facial (VIIth) Nerve Lesions	Hyper Trmr	Hyperkinetic dysarthria - Tremor
X PH	Flaccid dysarthria - Vagus (Xth) Nerve Lesions - Pharyngeal Branch Involvement	Hyper Chorea	Hyperkinetic dysarthria - Chorea
X S&R	Flaccid dysarthria - Vagus (Xth) Nerve Lesions - Superior and Recurrent Laryngeal Branch Involvement	Dys & Ath	Hyperkinetic dysarthria - Dystonia and Athetosis

Mxd SP/FL	Mixed dysarthria - Spastic and Flaccid
Mxd SP/AT	Mixed dysarthria - Spastic and Ataxic
Mxd Hypo/SP/AT	Mixed dysarthria - Progressive Supranuclear Palsy (Hypokinetic Spastic/Ataxic)
UUMN	Mixed dysarthria - Unilateral UMN
AT	Ataxic dysarthria
AP	Aprosodic dysarthria

Breathing Exercises Appendix A

These exercises will help you improve the coordination of your breathing and strengthen your diaphragm. The diaphragm is the main muscle used for breathing.

Breathing while lying on your back

Lie on a firm surface without a pillow under your head. Put one hand on your abdomen and one hand on your upper chest.

Breathe in so that you feel the hand on your abdomen lift up when you breathe in. You should not feel the hand on your upper chest move.

As you slowly breathe out, you should feel the hand on your abdomen fall down toward your spine. Try to slow down the breathing-out phase.

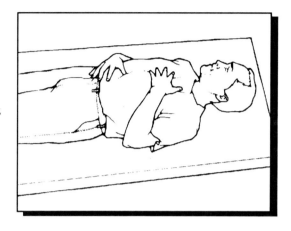

Breathing while sitting up

Sit up in a comfortable position. Put one hand on your abdomen and one hand on your upper chest.

Breathe in so that you feel the hand on your abdomen move out when you breathe in. You should not feel the hand on your upper chest move.

As you slowly breathe out, you should feel the hand on your abdomen move back toward your spine. Try to slow down the breathing-out phase.

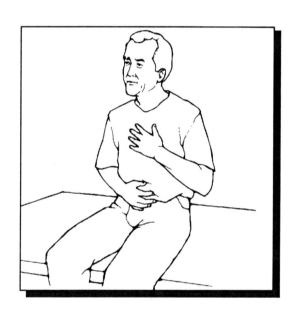

Variations

(Your speech-language pathologist may have you add any or all of these variations to your exercises.)

1. Time your voice to turn on as you begin to exhale. As soon as you feel your hand on your abdomen moving back towards your spine, begin producing the target sound.

2. Increase muscle tone through pushing/pulling. Put your hands under the chair you are sitting on. As soon as you start to exhale, pull up as if trying to lift the chair. Produce your target sound as you pull up.

3. Exhale slowly. As soon as your hand starts to move back towards your spine, start counting in your head. Try to extend your breathing for longer and longer counts.

4. Breathe in more deeply. Purse your lips so you can hear yourself breathe in through your mouth. Take in as deep a breath as possible. When your lungs are full, hold the air and press downward on your stomach. Resist the pressure, keeping the air in your lungs.

Chapter 5
Phonation

Disorders of phonation can be found in most types of dysarthria and can be helpful in making a differential diagnosis. Problems with pitch, loudness, and quality as well as incoordination between those parameters are observed in patients with dysarthria. Typical disorders of phonation seen in patients with dysarthria are:

- over-adduction of vocal folds (associated with increased tone)
- under-adduction of vocal folds (associated with decreased tone, weakness, decreased range of motion)
- poorly-coordinated laryngeal movements (associated with incoordination of laryngeal muscles or unpredictable movements)

The chart at the end of this chapter (page 118) lists the many kinds of phonatory problems you may hear. Over-adduction does not usually have a significant impact on intelligibility and may not warrant treatment. Weak, breathy phonation associated with under-adduction can interfere with intelligibility. Vocal incoordination usually doesn't interfere with intelligibility, but can interfere with naturalness. Phonatory characteristics are often treated with problems in other components (e.g., respiratory). If the phonatory disorder is not interfering with intelligibility and there are other physiologic components which are, you may not want to address phonation in therapy. Voice characteristics are often hard to modify. If, on the other hand, the phonation disorders are the primary problem making speech sound unnatural, you may need to address it. The treatment objectives are described as facilitation (f) or compensation (c) techniques, depending if you want the patient to improve function or to compensate for lost function.

Dworkin (1991) discusses the importance of appropriate timing of intervention. He usually treats respiration and resonance disorders first. Then, if phonation deficits remain, he addresses them. For patients who do not have deficits in respiration and resonance, he puts more of a priority on treating phonation.

Treatment Alternatives

I. Surgical Treatment

Some laryngeal disorders can be treated medically and surgically. When a patient has a paralyzed vocal cord and no return is expected, the patient may undergo a laryngoplasty. This surgery involves the surgeon cutting a window in the side of the thyroid cartilage on the same side as the paralyzed cord. The surgeon pushes implant material between the layers of the thyroid cartilage. This pushes the paralyzed cord toward midline, allowing the functioning cord to meet it. The advantage to this kind of surgery over using Teflon® or collagen (described below) is that the natural surface of the vocal cord is not disturbed, maintaining a smooth surface for closure against the other cord. Patients with unilateral paralysis may show good improvement in pitch, loudness, and intonation, but may still complain of a breathy quality and a voice that tires easily.

Teflon® or collagen can be injected into the surface of the paralyzed vocal cord. This increases the bulk of the cord and helps to create a surface for the good cord to contact. Teflon® cannot be removed, so otolaryngologists will usually not consider such a procedure until one year post-onset to allow maximum time for return of function.

2. Augmentative Devices

If the patient cannot produce adequate loudness, a portable amplification system may be helpful. This is crucial when the patient's spouse or other family member has a hearing loss. The patient's quiet voice and the spouse's decreased hearing make it almost impossible for them to communicate effectively. Remember that if the patient's speech is too quiet and unintelligible, use of an amplifier will only make his speech louder, not more intelligible. Patients may be reluctant to use an amplifier, especially when out in public. Counseling and reinforcement about the benefits of improved communication may be necessary.

Some patients cannot produce any audible voice. If so, you may try an artificial larynx. Patients may get confused as they think the electrolarynx is going to "talk"

for them. Explain to the patient that he still has to move his mouth and articulate the words. Have him practice using the electrolarynx, not only to understand how it works, but to get used to the sound it makes.

3. Treatment with Medication

Many different diseases/disorders cause dysarthria. Medication is not prescribed to treat the phonatory disorders associated with these diseases, but is prescribed for the disease itself. Some medications may have an impact on the phonatory characteristics (and other speech components as well). The following summary is offered as a reminder to discuss with the physician, nursing staff, or pharmacist what pharmacological intervention is being used with the patient, and what effect the medication may have on the patient's neuromotor symptoms.

- *Parkinson's disease:* treated with dopaminergic drugs such as Sinemet® and Parlodel®

- *Huntington's disease* (and other hyperkinetic disorders): treated with drugs that change the effects dopamine has on the body, such as Lithobid®, Mitoman®, Haldol®, Thorazine®, and Klonopin®

- *Dystonia:* treated with anticholinergic agents (i.e., block the passage of impulses through the parasympathetic nerves) such as Artane®, Parsidol®, and Cognetin®

- *Essential tremor:* treated with Inderal® which seems to have little effect on speech

- *Spasticity:* may be treated with muscle relaxants

- *Myasthenia Gravis:* treated with anticholinesterase drug, Mestinon®

112

We were taught in graduate school not to treat a patient with a voice disorder without medical clearance. The same holds true for patients with dysarthria. It is a good idea to discuss with the referring physician your observation of a phonatory component to the patient's dysarthria, and perhaps to ask if an exam by an otolaryngologist is indicated. The referring physician (usually a neurologist) will most likely tell you it's medically alright for you to proceed with your treatment. In 20 years of practice, I have had only one patient with dysarthria whose severely hoarse voice worried me enough (it sounded like smoker's hoarseness) that I insisted on an ENT consult with the primary physician's consent.

Efficacy

Do we know if treatment for disorders of phonation works? For more detailed information about efficacy, you might read "Summary of Treatment Efficacy for Dysarthria," (Yorkston, 1996). Two highlights from Yorkston's summary include:

1. Green and Watson (1968) studied 20 patients with Parkinson's disease. They used a portable amplifier and found that when loudness was the only symptom presented by the patient, intelligibility improved.

2. Ramig et al (1992, 1994, 1995) plus numerous other studies cite improvement in intelligibility for patients with Parkinson's disease after intensive work using the Lee Silverman Voice Treatment Approach. Ramig et al are currently investigating the efficacy of this approach with other neurologically-based dysarthrias. (Note: Ramig recommends taking an intensive training course before using the Lee Silverman Voice Treatment Approach.)

Phonation (PH) Goal and Treatment Objectives

Short Term Goal: Patient will maximize use of phonation to improve communication skills.

Treatment Objectives

PH-1 through PH-15 are indicated for patients with problems caused by weakness or decreased tone (e.g., breathiness, hoarseness, decreased loudness, low pitch, monopitch, diplophonia). They can also be used for phonatory instability (tremor) and with ataxia.

PH 1: Patient will complete breath hold and maintain pressure for ___ seconds.* (f)

PH 2: Patient will repeat vowel sounds using hard glottal attack.* (f)

PH 3: Patient will repeat vowel-initiate words using hard glottal attack (Appendix C).* (f)

PH 4: Patient will repeat vowel-initiate phrases/sentences using hard glottal attack (Appendix C).* (f)

PH 5: Patient will produce /a/ while pulling to increase resistance.* (f)

PH 6: Patient will produce /a/ while pushing to increase resistance.* (f)

PH 7: Patient will produce continuous tone from bottom of pitch range to top of range. (f)

PH 8: Patient will produce continuous tone from top of pitch range to bottom of range. (f)

PH 9: Patient will sustain phonation of vowel for ___ seconds at highest/lowest pitch. (f)

PH 10: Patient will speak at a higher pitch to increase loudness. (c)

PH 11: Patient will practice speaking over background noise. (c)

PH 12: Patient will start talking at the beginning of exhalation with/without cues. (c)

PH 13: Patient will turn head toward affected side when speaking with/without cues.* (c)

PH 14: Patient will push on thyroid cartilage on affected side when speaking.* (c)

PH 15: Patient will use high phonatory effort level when speaking. (c) (Note: There are many more sub-steps to this treatment objective when using the Lee Silverman Voice Therapy Approach.)

Treatment objectives PH-16 through PH-20 are indicated for patients with problems caused by increased tone (e.g., harshness, strained/strangled vocal quality, pitch breaks, low pitch, monoloudness). Note that the strained/strangled vocal quality associated with spastic dysarthria is not very amenable to treatment.

PH 16: Patient will use yawn-sigh to reduce tension in vocal mechanism.* (f)

PH 17: Patient will complete head rolls to reduce extrinsic laryngeal muscle tension.* (f)

PH 18: Patient will use easy onset to produce vowels.* (f)

PH 19: Patient will use easy onset to produce VCV sequences or vowel-initiate words.* (f) (Appendix B)

PH 20: Patient will speak with easy onset in conversation with/without cues.* (c)

Treatment objectives PH 21 through PH 25 are indicated for patients with incoordination of laryngeal movements (e.g., pitch irregularities, loudness irregularities), phonatory instability (tremor), and ataxia.

PH 21: Patient will sustain phonation of single vowels for ___ seconds with constant intensity and stability. (f)

PH 22: Patient will use continuous phonation on a series of vowel sounds and maintain steady pitch and/or loudness.* (f)

PH 23: Patient will use continuous phonation when repeating VCV sequences and maintain steady pitch and/or loudness.* (f) (Appendix B)

PH 24: Patient will use continuous phonation when repeating phrases and maintain steady pitch and/or loudness.* (f) (Appendix C)

PH 25: Patient will use continuous phonation in conversational level speech with/without cues.* (c)

* Appendix A describes these treatment techniques for the patient)

Environmental Modification (EM) Goals and Treatment Objectives

Short Term Goal: Speaker and listener will improve environment in which communication takes place.

Treatment Objectives:

EM 1:   Speaker will give context of message before beginning to communicate.

EM 2:   Listener will ask for clarification of context as needed.

EM 3:   Speaker and/or listener will eliminate or reduce background noise.

EM 4:   Speaker will gain visual attention of the listener before speaking.

EM 5:   Speaker or listener will make sure area in which communication is taking place is well lit.

EM 6:   Speaker and/or listener will make sure that they are sitting/standing close to one another and looking at each other before communication begins.

EM 7:   Speaker and/or listener will try to make sure that communication takes place in a room with dampened background noise.

EM 8:   Speaker will use external aid for communication (e.g., personal amplifier): _____

Treatment Techniques to Achieve Treatment Objectives

The following are brief descriptions of activities for improving phonation. Noted in () after the name of each activity is the treatment objective or objectives related to the activity.

Breath Hold (PH 1)

Instruct the patient to take a breath, bear down with the muscles in his throat, and hold for a count of ___ number of seconds. You can tell if the patient is holding his breath in one of two ways. You can either place a small mirror under the patient's nose to see if any exhalation is occurring or place your hand on the patient's upper chest to feel for chest wall movement (Appendix A).

Hard Glottal Attack (PH 2 - 4)

Ask the patient to bear down, hold his breath, and repeat vowels, vowel-initiate words, or vowel-initiate phrases/sentences (Appendices A and C).

Phonation with Pulling (PH 5)

Have the patient hold onto your hand, a bedrail, the chair seat, or the arm of his wheelchair and pull up while saying /a/. Have the patient produce the sound for longer periods of time. This technique can also be used for short utterances as a compensatory strategy (Appendix A).

Phonation with Pushing (PH 6)

If the patient can stand, have him put his hand(s) against the wall and attempt to push the wall away while saying /a/. If the patient is non-ambulatory, but has movement of at least one arm, have him lift his arm(s) with clenched fists to chest level and then push his arms down to his sides quickly while phonating. This technique can also be used for short utterances as a compensatory strategy (Appendix A).

Continuous Tone Scale (PH 7, 8)

Have the patient produce a continuous tone as if singing up or down the scale. Patients with weak, breathy voices often have restricted pitch range.

Sustained Phonation with Pitch (PH 9)

Once you have established the highest and lowest pitch the patient can produce, have him practice sustaining phonation at the highest and lowest pitch.

Speaking at Higher Pitch (PH 10)

Speaking at a higher pitch makes use of the adductory function of the cricothryoid muscles. Typical voice therapy procedures (Boone, 1988) are helpful in establishing a new pitch. Enhanced auditory and visual feedback (tape recorder, Visi-Pitch®) are often needed to assist the patient in monitoring pitch.

Background Noise (PH 11)

Have the patient practice speaking over background noise (music, TV) to help him carry-over use of a louder voice.

Timing Phonation with Exhalation (PH 12)

Sometimes patients fail to begin phonation until well into the exhalation phase. Review some of the breathing techniques (page 109) with the patient. Have the patient hold his hand on his abdomen. Place your hand lightly on the patient's hand to cue him by saying "now" when you feel exhalation begin. Have the patient start talking when exhalation begins.

Head Turn (PH 13)

If there is unilateral paralysis of a vocal cord through vagus nerve involvement, the patient may be able to achieve a louder voice by turning his head toward the affected side. This brings the stronger cord closer to the paralyzed cord (Appendix A).

External Pressure to Thyroid Cartilage (PH 14)

You or the patient can put some external pressure on the patient's thyroid cartilage on the affected side to push the weaker cord toward the stronger cord. This facilitates closure (Appendix A).

High Phonatory Effort Level (PH 15)

The traditional speech treatment approach for patients with Parkinson's disease focuses on improving articulation, reducing the rate, and sometimes improving intonation. However, there are no studies that demonstrate long-term effects from this treatment approach. In 1987, Ramig and Mead developed a program for patients with Parkinson's disease that focused on voice therapy. They call their approach the Lee Silverman Voice Training for Patients with Parkinson's Disease, as named for one of their patients.* Their approach was based on information in the literature that highlighted the high incidence of voice problems in patients with Parkinson's disease. Two earlier studies (Scott & Caird, 1968 and Robertson & Thompson, 1984) reported the success of intensive speech therapy focused on phonation in working with patients with Parkinson's disease.

Ramig and Mead's treatment program was designed to improve perceptual characteristics of voice and the patient's functional communication by addressing the laryngeal pathophysiology related to the voice disorder. Ramig summarizes this by stating that they addressed the breathy, weak voice of patients with Parkinson's disease by trying to increase loudness and decrease breathiness by increasing vocal fold adduction. They addressed the monotonous voice that patients with Parkinson's disease present (due to rigidity in the cricothyroid muscles) by increasing cricothyroid muscle activity. Another goal was to improve voice quality by increasing the stability of vocal fold vibration. The references listed on pages 255-256 will provide details about the Lee Silverman Voice Treatment for Parkinson's Disease approach. Note that this approach must be administered in an intensive program, with individual daily treatment for at least the first 16 sessions.

*This approach was developed at the University of Colorado-Boulder, Wilbur James Gould Voice Research Center at the Denver Center for the Performing Arts.

Yawn/Sigh (PH 16)

Best described by Boone, the Yawn/Sigh is designed to reduce tension in the vocal mechanism. Ask the patient to open his mouth very wide and try to yawn. The patient doesn't necessarily have to yawn, but does have to approximate this very open mouth/open pharynx position. Have the patient produce a very quiet sigh when the yawn is ending and exhalation is beginning (Appendix A).

Head Rolls (PH 17)

Head rolls should be done with slow, easy movements. Have the patient sit upright with his chin on his chest. Tell the patient to slowly rotate his head so he is looking over his right shoulder. He should then rotate his head so he is looking straight up to the ceiling. From there, have the patient rotate his head to look over his left shoulder and then drop his chin back onto his chest (Appendix A).

Easy Onset (PH 18 - 20)

Easy onset is a technique that is often used in fluency therapy. Since disfluency is characterized by spasms of the vocal cords, it makes sense that this technique would work with individuals with dysarthria as well.

Have the patient imagine that he is turning the volume knob on a radio all the way down before turning the radio on. Then, once the radio is on, he gradually adjusts the volume.

Have the patient start his vocal cords vibrating easily. You may need to model the difference between easy onset and hard glottal attack. Begin with vowel sounds and work up to trying VCV sequences, vowel-initiate phrases, and then to conversation (Appendices A, B, and C).

Continuous Phonation (PH 21-25)

Explain to the patient that some consonants in the English language are voiceless and that we stop vocal cord vibration briefly for these sounds. However, for patients experiencing incoordination of laryngeal muscles, it is very difficult for them to allow their vocal cords to stop vibrating and to start smoothly again.

Ask the patient to imagine a steady hum. You want the patient's voice to continually be "on." Contrast this for the client by repeating a phrase with many voiceless consonants like "puppet show," "clock tower," or "toss it up." Have the patient place a finger lightly on your larynx so he can feel the vibrations. As you produce the phrase, lengthen the duration of the voiceless segment so he can feel the vibration stop and start (Appendices A, B, and C). Then, model continuous phonation so the patient can feel the vibrations. This means that you are changing voiceless phonemes to their voiced cognates (e.g., "Pop ate it" becomes "Bob aid id.")

Phonation Problems and Causes

What you hear	What could be causing the problem	SP	FL	FL Mya	VII	X PH	X S&R	X Sup	X Rec	XII	Hypo	Hyper Trmr	Hyper Chorea	Dys & Ath	Mxd SP/FL	Mxd SP/AT	Mxd Hypo/SP/AT	U U M N	AT	AP
diplophonia	weakness		★			★	★	★	★											
breathy	weakness		★	★		★	★	★	★						★					
	decreased ROM										★									
	decreased tone		★	★																
	unpredictable movement													★						
hoarse	weakness					★	★	★	★								★			
	decreased ROM										★									
harsh	weakness		★																	
	increased tone														★	★		★		
	decreased tone		★															★	★	
decreased loudness	decreased tone		★	★											★					
	weakness		★	★		★	★	★	★											
	decreased ROM										★									
strained/strangled	increased tone	★													★					
	unpredictable movement												★	★						
low pitch/reduced pitch	increased tone	★													★					
	weakness					★	★	★	★											
pitch breaks	increased tone	★										★								
inconsistent pitch breaks	incoordination																			
voice errors	incoordination												★	★	★					
tremors	incoordination										★	★								
audible inspiration	weakness		★																	
	unpredictable movement													★						
inhalatory stridor	weakness					★	★		★											

See Key on the following page.

Key

SP	Spastic dysarthria
FL	Flaccid dysarthria
FL Mya	Flaccid dysarthria- Mysathenia Gravis
V	Flaccid dysarthria - Trigeminal (Vth) Nerve Lesions
VII	Flaccid dysarthria - Facial (VIIth) Nerve Lesions
X PH	Flaccid dysarthria - Vagus (Xth) Nerve Lesions - Pharyngeal Branch Involvement
X S&R	Flaccid dysarthria - Vagus (Xth) Nerve Lesions - Superior and Recurrent Laryngeal Branch Involvement
X Sup	Flaccid dysarthria - Vagus (Xth) Nerve Lesions - Superior Laryngeal Branch Involvement
X Rec	Flaccid dysarthria - Vagus (Xth) Nerve Lesions - Recurrent Laryngeal Branch Involvement
Hypo	Flaccid dysarthria - Hypoglossal (XIIth) Nerve Lesions
Hyper Trmr	Hyperkinetic dysarthria - Tremor
Hyper Chorea	Hyperkinetic dysarthria - Chorea
Dys & Ath	Hyperkinetic dysarthria - Dystonia and Athetosis
Mxd SP/FL	Mixed dysarthria - Spastic and Flaccid
Mxd SP/AT	Mixed dysarthria - Spastic and Ataxic
Mxd Hypo/SP/AT	Mixed dysarthria - Progressive Supranuclear Palsy (Hypokinetic Spastic/Ataxic)
UUMN	Mixed dysarthria - Unilateral UMN
AT	Ataxic dysarthria
AP	Aprosodic dysarthria

These exercises are designed to help you relax your vocal cords so your voice doesn't sound tight and tense.

_____ **Yawn/Sigh:** Open your mouth and throat very wide and start to yawn. At the end of the yawn as you are breathing out, make a very quiet sighing sound.

_____ **Head Rolls:** Drop your chin slowly to your chest. Slowly turn your head so you are looking over your right shoulder. Slowly rotate your head back to the middle so you are looking straight up at the ceiling. Slowly drop your head so you are looking over your left shoulder. Then let your head roll back down to your chest.

_____ **Easy Onset:** Read the nonsense syllables on Appendix B while you gradually turn your voice "on." Remember to think about this as turning up the volume on a radio very slowly.

This exercise is designed to help improve coordination of the movements of the larynx.

_____ **Continuous Phonation:** The English language contains some consonants that are produced with the vocal cords vibrating. These are called voiced consonants and include consonants such as *b, d, g, l, m,* and *z.* Other consonants are produced only with air and are called voiceless consonants. They include *f, k, s,* and *t.*

Sometimes the stopping and starting of the vocal cords is very difficult when your dysarthria causes incoordination of the muscles in your larynx. Keeping your vocal cords vibrating evenly and constantly may help your speech sound smoother. This means that you will produce all consonants as if they were voiced.

Read the column on the left on Appendix B. These are vowel-consonant-vowel sequences with a voiced consonant which will make it easier for you to keep your voice "on" the whole time. Then, try reading the column on the right. These contain voiceless consonants in the middle. Try to make each one sound like its match on the left.

These exercises are designed to help strengthen your vocal cords.

_____ **Holding your breath:** Take a deep breath and squeeze all the muscles in your throat, pretending you are trying to lift something very heavy. Hold your breath for ___ seconds.

_____ **Starting your voice hard:** Hold your breath as described above, then release your breath and read the words or phrases/sentences listed on Appendix C.

_____ **Pushing and pulling:** Hold onto the seat of your chair, a bedrail, or someone's hand and pull while saying "ah." You can also push against a wall or other solid surface while saying "ah."

These exercises may help if one of your vocal cords is weak.

_____ **Turning your head:** Turn your head toward the weak (left / right) side while talking.
 circle one

_____ **Pushing on the larynx:** Use your fingers to push lightly on the weak (left / right) side of your larynx while trying to talk.
 circle one

Use these for voice practice with the activity indicated on Appendix A.

aba	apa
ebe	epe
ibi	ipi
obo	opo
ubu	upu
aday	atay
ede	ete
idi	iti
odo	oto
udu	utu
aga	aka
ege	eke
igi	iki
ogo	oko
ugu	uku
aza	asa
eze	ese
izi	isi
ozo	oso
uzu	usu

able	able-bodied	enough	enough sugar for today
above	above and beyond	eye	eye for an eye
abrupt	abrupt ending	iced	Iced tea is delicious.
accidents	Accidents happen.	icy	icy cold ice cream
ache	ache in my neck	if	If you need me, just shout.
aching	aching back hurts	igloos	Igloos are not found here.
adhesive	adhesive tape	ignore	Ignore his tantrums.
adopt	adopt the kitten	incline	incline is steep
adore	adores his grandson	infant	infant in the crib
after	after dinner	iron	Iron this shirt.
age	Age is not important.	oatmeal	Oatmeal is good for you.
aging	Aging is part of life.	oats	Oats are good for horses.
aid	Aid the patient.	object	object in the distance
aim	Aim the camera.	oboes	Oboes are loud.
aisle	Aisle seats are the best.	observe	observe for a day
all	all the time	odor	odor from the skunk
amount	amount due	offer	Offer to help her.
any	any day now	ointment	Ointment is sticky.
anybody	Anybody know how?	old	Old shoes are worn out.
apple	Apple juice is tasty.	only	only you can go
April	April showers	open	Open your eyes.
arm	arm in a sling	over	over the bridge
around	around the house	ulcers	Ulcers are dangerous.
asleep	asleep at the wheel	umbrella	umbrella stand
away	away from here	undo	Undo this snap.
each	Each will get a cookie.	uneasy	uneasy stomach
eager	eager to fly	unit	unit of time
eagle	eagle flying high	united	United we stand, divided we fall.
east	east and west	up	up, up, and away
eat	Eat your vegetables.	upbeat	Upbeat music makes me happy.
edge	edge of the pool	uplift	Uplift my spirits.
eel	eel in the water	upper	upper-level bedroom
eggs	eggs and toast for breakfast	upset	upset stomach
enclose	Enclose in an envelope.	ushers	Ushers are helpful.
engage	engage in conversation	utter	Utter bad words.

Chapter 6
Resonance

Patients with dysarthria may present with disorders of resonance. The most common problem is hypernasality, but some patients may have nasal emission. The chart on page 129 lists the possible causes for hypernasality and nasal emission in a variety of types of dysarthrias. Hypernasality is associated with primarily two types of dysarthria: flaccid and spastic.

Flaccid Dysarthria

This is usually caused by either a unilateral or bilateral Xth cranial nerve lesion. A less likely cause is a lesion to the IXth or XIth nerve. The IX, X, and XI nerves are called the *pharyngeal plexus*. In these patients, you will observe unilateral or bilateral weakness or paralysis of the velum with hypotonicity and a hypoactive gag reflex. Treatment for velopharyngeal incompetence associated with flaccid dysarthria might include activities to improve velopharyngeal valving competence and activities to help the patient distinguish normal from hypernasal resonance. Some patients may also need a palatal lift, and in some instances, surgical intervention.

Spastic Dysarthria

Patients with spastic dysarthria who have velopharyngeal incompetence (VPI) must have bilateral corticobulbar lesions. They will show bilateral weakness and paralysis, hypertonicity, and in some cases, a hyperactive gag reflex. Behavioral techniques to treat this include normalizing the reflex and normalizing tone through touch pressure and massage and improving VPI through non-speech and speech exercises. These patients may also need a palatal lift or surgical intervention.

Dworkin (1991) points out that hypernasality rarely occurs in isolation, but usually occurs with disturbances in other physiologic systems. He points out that when the patient has a VPI, not only does he have resonance problems, but he places a burden on respiration, phonation, and articulation subsystems.

In most patients with hypernasality, it's usually not severe enough to warrant a lot of attention in therapy. Determine how much the hypernasality is interfering with intelligibility as compared to other factors such as impaired articulation or prosody. Hypernasality observed in patients with dysarthria may be inconsistent. Some patients only have assimilation nasality. This occurs when a sentence contains several nasal phonemes that cause the rest of the sentence to sound too nasal.

The hypernasality associated with dysarthrias usually doesn't have accompanying nasal emission.

Resonance (RSN) Goal and Treatment Objectives

Short Term Goal: Patient will reduce the amount of perceived hypernasality/nasal emission to increase intelligibility of speech.

Treatment Objectives:

RSN 1:   Patient will decrease hyperactive gag in preparation for placement of palatal lift. (f)

RSN 2:   Patient will tolerate placement of palatal lift for increasing periods of time. (c)

RSN 3:   Patient will repeat phrases/sentences beginning with open vowels (Appendix A) with exaggerated mouth openings while looking in the mirror. (c)

RSN 4:   Patient will repeat phrases with a balance of phoneme types (Appendix B) with exaggerated mouth openings while looking in the mirror. (c)

RSN 5:   Patient will repeat phrases/sentences with many nasal phonemes (Appendix C) or with pressure consonants (Appendix D) with exaggerated mouth openings while looking in the mirror. (c)

RSN 6:   Patient will repeat phrases/sentences with a balance of phoneme types (Appendix B) with exaggerated mouth openings without visual feedback from a mirror. (c)

RSN 7:   Patient will repeat phrases/sentences with many nasal phonemes (Appendix C) or with pressure conso-nants (Appendix D) with exaggerated mouth openings without visual feedback from a mirror. (c)

RSN 8:   Patient will transfer exaggerated mouth openings to conversational speech. (c)

RSN 9:   Patient will speak with increased loudness to reduce the perception of hypernasality at the phrase/sentence level with cues. (c)

RSN 10:   Patient will speak with increased loudness to reduce the perception of hypernasality at the phrase/sentence level without cues. (c)

RSN 11:   Patient will speak with decreased rate to reduce the perception of hypernasality with cues. (c)

RSN 12:   Patient will speak with decreased rate to reduce the perception of hypernasality without cues. (c)

RSN 13:   Patient will decrease nasal emission on phrases with pressure consonants with visual feedback provided by a mirror held under the nose (Appendix D). (c)

RSN 14:   Speaker will use the supine position for improving selected communicative messages. (c)

Environmental Modification (EM) Goals and Treatment Objectives

Short Term Goal: Speaker and listener will improve environment in which communication takes place.

Treatment Objectives:

EM 1:   Speaker will give context of message before beginning to communicate.

124

EM 2: Listener will ask for clarification of context as needed.

EM 3: Speaker and/or listener will eliminate or reduce background noise.

EM 4: Speaker will gain visual attention of the listener before speaking.

EM 5: Speaker or listener will make sure area in which communication is taking place is well lit.

EM 6: Speaker and/or listener will make sure that they are sitting/standing close to one another and looking at each other before communication begins.

EM 7: Speaker and/or listener will try to make sure that communication takes place in a room with dampened background noise.

EM 8: Speaker will use external aid (palatal lift, nares occlusion, nose clip) for improved communication.

Treatment Techniques to Achieve Treatment Objectives

The following are brief descriptions of activities for improving phonation. Noted in () after the name of each activity is the treatment objective or objectives related to the activity.

Prosthetic Management (RSN 1, 2; EM 8)
Palatal lifts may be indicated in severe velopharyngeal paralysis with resulting severe hypernasality which greatly interferes with intelligibility. Many patients cannot tolerate a palatal lift, so be cautious about recommending one. Consider doing so only if the hypernasality is a major factor in the patient's decreased intelligibility.

A palatal lift is constructed by a prosthodontist out of material similar to that which is formed into the plate which holds dentures. It usually has a portion that hooks onto the patient's back teeth with a part that extends against the soft palate to help elevate it toward the posterior pharyngeal wall. Patients with dentures can have the palatal lift built right onto the top denture.

Even if the hypernasality is severe and a palatal lift may improve it, if the patient's other symptoms of dysarthria are also severe and not expected to improve (e.g., severe unintelligibility secondary to paralysis of tongue and lips which precludes any approximation of normal articulation), then it is probably not worth it to put the patient through the fitting of the prosthesis. If the patient has intact sensation, he may experience gagging and discomfort with the palatal lift. This can be greatly eliminated by starting with a shorter palatal lift and having it gradually lengthened as the patient becomes accustomed to it.

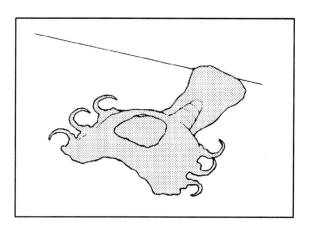

A systematic approach may desensitize a patient's gag reflex. Explain to the patient that you are going to "walk back" on his tongue with a tongue blade. Have him close his mouth when you reach the point where he feels like he is about to gag. Closing his mouth should stop the gag from happening. Patients usually feel much more comfortable knowing they have some control.

Use the tip of the tongue blade and provide firm pressure at midline at the front of the tongue. Move the tongue blade approximately one centimeter back from your starting position and hold steady pressure. Continue moving back until the patient closes his mouth to stop the activity. Repeat the exercise 10 - 15 times per session. The patient can also practice this himself several times a day when not in therapy.

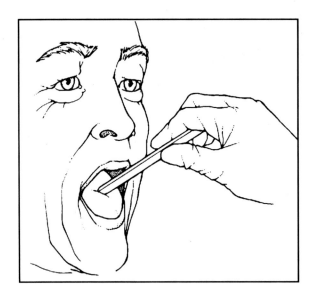

To find a prosthodontist, check in your region to see if there is a specialized cleft palate team. This team typically consists of a plastic surgeon, speech-language pathologist, audiologist, otolaryngologist, dentist, and prosthodontist. If there is a medical school nearby, check with the college of dentistry for help locating a prosthodontist. Keep in mind that not all prosthodontists are experienced in constructing palatal lift prostheses.

Rosenbek and LaPointe (1985) provide guidelines if you are considering recommending a palatal lift for a patient.

- Fit the patient as soon as he can tolerate the evaluation, fitting, and use of the lift. Some prosthodontists aren't willing to fit a palatal lift in a neurologically-impaired patient immediately, preferring to wait for any neurological

return. Speak with the prosthodontist about using the palatal lift while waiting since it wouldn't impede any possible neurological return.

- Help the patient have realistic expectations for what the prosthesis can do. If hypernasality is only one of the factors decreasing intelligibility, make sure the patient knows that the lift will decrease the hypernasality but his speech may continue to be difficult to understand. Note, however, that sometimes getting an appropriate palatal lift fitted will help improve all speech dimensions.

- Palatal lifts may not work well with patients with severe spastic dysarthria.

- If the patient has a degenerative disorder, and the course of degeneration is expected to be fairly quick, then the patient may lose all gains obtained from the lift.

- Work closely with the prosthodontist for multiple adjustments and fittings in order to get a prosthesis to work and to be accepted by the patient.

Linebaugh (1983) states that all patients who have been fitted with palatal lift prostheses, or have undergone pharyngoplasty, should receive a period of training.

Efficacy of Palatal Lifts

The success of palatal lifts are typically measured by increased intelligibility and improved articulation as well as a decrease in perception of hypernasality. Success has been reported by many authors: (Gonzalez and Aronson (1970); Hardy et al (1969); McHenry, Wilson, and Menton (1994); and Yorkston et al (1989). Patients who have flaccid, spastic, and mixed flaccid-spastic dysarthrias have benefitted from palatal lifts. The disorders causing the dysarthrias have ranged from stroke to traumatic brain injury to ALS.

Problems reported with palatal lifts typically include patients unable to become accustomed to wearing the lift despite attempts to desensitize a hyperactive gag or poor dental support to hold the lift in place.

Surgical Management
Some patients with severe hypernasality may benefit from surgical management of the VPI. Superiorly-based pharyngeal flaps are the method used most often to manage VPI. This surgery has yielded mixed results. There is more evidence that palatal lifts are more effective for a patient with dysarthria than surgery. However, Johns (1985) indicated his experience with many patients whose nasality was reduced through surgical management.

Facilitation Techniques
Facilitation techniques for improving velopharyngeal function are not described here in detail. Clinical experience leads me to agree with Johns (1985) who concluded that "the general consensus seems to be that these exercises are disappointing and generally ineffective."

Some clinicians use facilitation techniques such as icing and brushing to stimulate velopharyngeal function for flaccid dysarthria. They also use inhibition techniques such as prolonged icing, pressure to muscles, and slow stroking for individuals with spastic dysarthria. There are no significant studies in the literature to demonstrate the efficacy of these techniques in reducing hypernasality.

A recent study by Kuehn and Wachtel (1994) reported significant reduction in hypernasality in a patient treated with Continuous Positive Airway Pressure (CPAP). CPAP is often used in patients with sleep apnea. It delivers a positive airflow into the nasal cavities. Kuehn and Wachtel used the device and expected the patient to increase his velopharyngeal movement against the resistance provided by the airflow.

Dworkin (1991) recommends that hypernasal resonance and nasal air emission caused by VPI should receive top priority in treatment planning. He tries 10 hours of concentrated work on behavioral techniques even with moderate to severely hypernasal patients before recommending alternative approaches such as a palatal lift. Dworkin indicates that when the condition is mild, the prognosis is much better for improving velopharyngeal functioning through clinical exercises. He argues that delaying treatment for VPI allows the patient to establish abnormal resonance and articulation behaviors.

Linebaugh (1983) describes a method he uses with patients with flaccid dysarthria who have hypernasality. Linebaugh's method incorporates visual feedback of intraoral pressure where the patient puffs out his cheeks and maintains the pressure before releasing the air through his nose. However, Linebaugh states that this technique fails on a regular basis with patients with flaccid dysarthria.

Compensation Techniques

The following techniques are designed to compensate for velopharyngeal incompetence.

Exaggerate Mouth Opening (RSN 3-8)
The perception of hypernasality can be reduced by having the patient use a more open-mouth posture. Help the patient see that if he opens his mouth wider while speaking, there will be a mild change in the perception of the amount of nasality.

It is helpful to some patients if you provide a model of what they are listening for when you are describing their hypernasality, especially for patients with assimilation nasality only. Help them begin to recognize what nasal phonemes are and how the appearance of a nasal phoneme in an utterance can cause their speech to sound more nasal. Read sentences with nasal phonemes and no nasal phonemes and point out the differences (Appendices C and D). It is also helpful to read sentences with balanced phonemes (some nasal/some non-nasal) either producing the sentences in a hypernasal manner or with adequate resonance (Appendix B). Ask the patient to identify those sentences with appropriate resonance.

When asking the patient to produce sentences with a more wide-open mouth, start with phrases that begin with more open vowels such as /æ, ɑ, ɔ, oʊ, ʌ, ɛ/ (Appendix A). Have the patient look in the mirror and imitate productions of phrases and sentences with little mouth opening vs. exaggerated mouth opening.

It might help to try a technique called *negative practice*. Have the patient purposefully keep his mouth almost closed as he repeats sentences after you. This will make the nasality more significant.

Note: It may be particularly difficult to use an exaggerated mouth opening in sentences with many nasal phonemes (Appendix C).

Using increased loudness (RSN 9 and 10)

Having the patient increase volume may make it easier for listeners to perceive what is said. Model phrases for the patient using increased loudness. Combine this with other techniques such as exaggerated mouth opening. Increase difficulty by starting with phrases and sentences with balanced phonemes (Appendix B) and moving to those with more nasal phonemes (Appendix C).

Reducing the rate (RSN 11 and 12)

Having the patient reduce his rate may increase intelligibility and reduce the perception of hypernasality. For more information on reducing rate, see Chapter 8, Prosody.

Providing visual feedback to decrease nasal emission (RSN 13)

Some dysarthrias have nasal emission associated with the hypernasality. If so, it may be helpful to provide visual feedback to the patient to help him understand what nasal emission is and to encourage him to decrease it.

Hold a small mirror under your nares and repeat a sentence with no nasal phonemes. Show the patient that the mirror doesn't become clouded. Ask the patient to repeat words from the same sentence or the entire sentence and to try not to fog up the mirror. To increase difficulty, have patients produce sentences loaded with pressure consonants (Appendix D).

Using supine position (RSN 14)

Some patients can reduce the perception of hypernasality by speaking when lying on their backs (supine). This position allows the velum to fall backward and to contact the posterior pharyngeal wall more easily. This may help compensate for decreased velopharyngeal movement.

Resonance Problems and Causes

What you hear	What could be causing the problem	SP	FL	FL Mya	V	VII	X PH	X S&R	X Sup	X Rec	Hypo XII	Hyper Trmr	Hyper Chorea	Dys & Ath	Mxd SP/FL	Mxd SP/AT	Mxd Hypo/ SP/AT	UUMN	AT	AP
hypernasality	incoordinated/ unpredictable movement												★	★						
	vp weak		★	★			★								★					
	decrease ROM										★									
	increased tone	★														★	★			
	decreased tone		★												★					
nasal emission	vp weak		★	★			★													
	decrease tone		★														★			

Key

SP	Spastic dysarthria	
FL	Flaccid dysarthria	
FL Mya	Flaccid dysarthria- Mysathenia Gravis	
V	Flaccid dysarthria - Trigeminal (Vth) Nerve Lesions	
VII	Flaccid dysarthria - Facial (VIIth) Nerve Lesions	
X PH	Flaccid dysarthria - Vagus (Xth) Nerve Lesions - Pharyngeal Branch Involvement	
X S&R	Flaccid dysarthria - Vagus (Xth) Nerve Lesions - Superior and Recurrent Laryngeal Branch Involvement	
X Sup	Flaccid dysarthria - Vagus (Xth) Nerve Lesions - Superior Laryngeal Branch Involvement	Mxd SP/FL — Mixed dysarthria - Spastic and Flaccid
X Rec	Flaccid dysarthria - Vagus (Xth) Nerve Lesions - Recurrent Laryngeal Branch Involvement	Mxd SP/AT — Mixed dysarthria - Spastic and Ataxic
Hypo	Flaccid dysarthria - Hypoglossal (XIIth) Nerve Lesions	Mxd Hypo/ SP/AT — Mixed dysarthria - Progressive Supranuclear Palsy (Hypokinetic Spastic/Ataxic)
Hyper Trmr	Hyperkinetic dysarthria - Tremor	UUMN — Mixed dysarthria - Unilateral UMN
Hyper Chorea	Hyperkinetic dysarthria - Chorea	AT — Ataxic dysarthria
Dys & Ath	Hyperkinetic dysarthria - Dystonia and Athetosis	AP — Aprosodic dysarthria

These phrases and sentences will encourage an exaggerated mouth opening to reduce nasality.

You should produce these phrases/sentences with:

_____ exaggerated mouth opening

_____ increased loudness

_____ decreased rate

1. Apple pie is good.
2. at the front door
3. attitude adjustment
4. alley behind the store
5. asters and geraniums
6. able-bodied workers
7. often enough
8. off the wall
9. awful tasting
10. all right with me
11. August 8th
12. awkward situation
13. odd couple
14. Amish community
15. awning over the window
16. honest opinion
17. awful situation
18. oboe player
19. okra and tomatoes
20. end of the line
21. ebb and flow
22. extra mustard
23. eggs and toast
24. electric guitar
25. emery board
26. Ensign in the Navy
27. elbow room
28. energy-saving device
29. Ever seen one?
30. Ellie is ticklish.
31. elbow macaroni
32. only a little late
33. Open the door.
34. oatmeal for breakfast
35. oats for the horse
36. over the rainbow
37. ozone layer
38. up and down
39. under the steps
40. utter a word
41. ugly costume
42. upper hand
43. utmost importance
44. oven cleaner
45. ankle-length dress
46. ad in the paper
47. after you
48. agriculture class
49. acting school
50. at school all day

These sentences contain nasal and non-nasal phonemes. These sentences have balanced phonemes and they may be easier to produce than sentences with many nasal phonemes.

You should produce these phrases/sentences with:

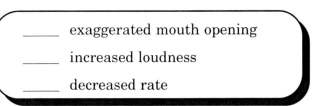

_____ exaggerated mouth opening

_____ increased loudness

_____ decreased rate

1. I don't feel well.
2. It's hot in here.
3. Is it lunch time?
4. Where's the new doctor?
5. Call the nurse.
6. My daughter called me.
7. It's not time yet.
8. Do you know her?
9. I took my medicine.
10. I didn't sleep well.
11. I've never been there.
12. I'm retired now.
13. Our children don't live here.
14. Can you reach that?
15. Don't open the window.
16. Please turn on the TV.
17. I want to go outside.
18. Is it raining today?
19. I think I caught a cold.
20. The new blanket is warm.
21. The police captured him.
22. The man was very helpful.
23. We asked for directions.
24. We took a long car trip.
25. The cat climbed the tree.
26. The dogs enjoy running.
27. He's a vegetarian.
28. I'm not sure what time it is.
29. Did he go to the dining room?
30. The light is too dim to see.
31. The timing was perfect.
32. She bought a vegetarian cookbook.
33. He ran around the lake.
34. The ivy climbs up the post.
35. It's been a long day.
36. The teacher gave directions.
37. There were two men there.
38. Give the book to him.
39. It was very warm in May.
40. Do you think it will rain?
41. I want another cup of coffee.
42. Turn off the lights.
43. Open the big present first.
44. Can you help me?
45. The children made lots of noise.
46. I'm going to bed early.
47. Have you been here long?
48. I didn't have dessert.
49. The medicine is bitter.
50. Don't you want a cup?

Phrases/Sentences with Nasal Phonemes

These sentences contain many nasal phonemes.

You should produce these phrases/sentences with:

> _____ exaggerated mouth opening
>
> _____ increased loudness
>
> _____ decreased rate

1. Make mine mint.
2. The number was 919.
3. Manny's mom meant it.
4. Many names come to mind.
5. Newman knew nineteen nouns.
6. Mom made Mark maintain his manners.
7. The gnome's name was not known.
8. Norman's nanny never knows his name.
9. My mom was marooned on Monday.
10. Many men named Newman came.
11. Nancy's not a minor, she's nineteen.
12. Ninety members climbed the mountain.
13. Manny saw the moonbeam on the mountain.
14. The mime and the nun knew one another.
15. Madeline married the mechanic on Monday.
16. Manuel was the musicians' manager.
17. The noodles made Natalie nauseous.
18. Never mind what Nancy named him.
19. Mack has a misconception about Montana.
20. There were many mannequins in Mary's window.
21. Martin said the scenery in Vietnam was stunning.
22. Meredith was amazed to find her motorbike missing.
23. The mammals on the mountain were known to have mange.
24. Gina frowned when the dry cleaner ruined her linen napkins.
25. Now Norman says he never meant it.

The Source for Dysarthria   132   Copyright © 1997 LinguiSystems

Sentences with non-nasal pressure consonants require you to build up air pressure in your mouth. If you have nasal emission, pressure consonants will be more difficult for you to say.

You should produce these phrases/sentences with:

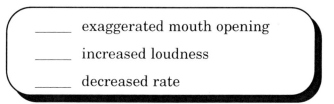

_____ exaggerated mouth opening

_____ increased loudness

_____ decreased rate

1. Keri told her to do it.
2. Beth was by the boat.
3. Bob bought bagels for Robbie.
4. Paul was petrified by the pet parrot.
5. Pick up the paddles for the boat.
6. She bought paper flowers for the party.
7. Bob's passport was by the paperback book.
8. Pat parked the jeep by the pool.
9. Patty prefers papaya juice.
10. Please put the paper by the back door.
11. Pat was chopping peppers for the pasta.
12. Put the paper clips and paper towels in the paper bag.
13. Shelly said the floor was shaky.
14. Please pat the soft puppy.
15. Carol and Carl collided in the corridor.
16. Carrie cried on the courthouse steps.
17. The tourist plugged in the toaster.
18. Sue's soccer trip was delayed.
19. The singers liked to play softball.
20. Sherry shattered the glass with her voice.
21. He was awarded three wishes.
22. The girl in the photograph was pretty.
23. Do you still use a typewriter?
24. His picture was posted at the post office.
25. The cowboy covered his head with a hat.

Chapter 7
Articulation

One of the main differences in treating the articulation deficits of dysarthria as compared to articulation deficits in children is that you must be aware of the relationship of the articulation disorder to deficits in other physiologic systems.

- If respiratory support is decreased, it may be easier for the patient to work on stops and nasals.

- If the patient has better respiratory support, he can try fricatives and affricates.

- If the patient has velopharyngeal incompetence, he may be better able to produce nasals, vowels, and glides.

- If movement of the velopharyngeal mechanism has improved and needs to be carried over into speech, nasal/oral contrasts may be used such as *may/pay* or *my/pie*.

- If working on lingua-alveolar sounds, high front vowels (i, I) may be the easiest context.

The chart at the end of this chapter (page 147) lists Articulation problems and their causes.

Articulation (AR) Goal and Treatment Objectives

Short Term Goal: Patient will improve articulation to increase intelligibility.

Treatment Objectives
Treatment objectives AR 1 - 12 are designed to reduce spasticity and/or rigidity in the oral articulators.

AR 1:   Patient will maintain maximum stretch for ___ seconds on jaw opening with/without physical assist from the clinician. (f)

AR 2:   Patient will maintain maximum jaw lateralization for ___ seconds to the right/left with/without assistance from clinician. (f)

AR 3:   Patient will maintain maximum protrusion of the tongue for ___ seconds with/without physical assist from the clinician. (f)

AR 4:   Patient will maintain maximum retraction of the tongue into the oral cavity for ___ seconds. (f)

AR 5:   Patient will maintain maximum lateralization of the tongue for ___ seconds to the right/left with/without clinician physical assistance. (f)

AR 6:   Patient will sustain maximum pull on the lower lip for ___ seconds. (f)

AR 7:   Patient will sustain maximum pull on upper lip for ___ seconds. (f)

AR 8:   Patient will sustain maximum lip retraction for ___ seconds with/without assistance from clinician. (f)

AR 9:   Patient will maintain maximum lip pursing for ___ seconds with/without physical assistance from clinician. (f)

AR 10: Patient will use a bite block to decrease spasticity during speech. (c)

AR 11: Patient will complete jaw shaking. (f)

AR 12: Patient will use the Froeschels chewing method during speech attempts. (c)

Treatment objectives AR 13 - 27 are designed to increase strength of articulators for improved speech intelligibility.

AR 13: Patient will open jaw against resistance. (f)

AR 14: Patient will close jaw against resistance. (f)

AR 15: Patient will lateralize jaw right/left trials against resistance. (f)

AR 16: Patient will protrude lower jaw against resistance. (f)

AR 17: Patient will protrude tongue tip against tongue blade trials. (f)

AR 18: Patient will lateralize tongue right/left against resistance. (f)

AR 19: Patient will push tongue inside right/left cheek against resistance. (f)

AR 20: Patient will elevate tongue tip against resistance. (f)

AR 21: Patient will elevate tongue blade against resistance. (f)

AR 22: Patient will elevate tongue base against resistance. (f)

AR 23: Patient will maintain lip closure against the pull of a button. (f)

AR 24: Patient will maintain pucker against resistance. (f)

AR 25: Patient will maintain smile against resistance. (f)

AR 26: Patient will maintain placement of tongue blade between lips. (f)

AR 27: Patient will use bite block during repetition of words, phrases, and sentences with labial and lingual sounds (Word Lists, pages 148-186). (f)

Treatment objective AR 28 is designed to increase tone to improve speech intelligibility:

AR 28: Patient will use pushing or pulling to increase overall effort of speech. (c)

Treatment objectives AR 29 - 43 are designed to increase precision (accuracy, speed, range) of oral-motor movements to improve intelligibility.

AR 29: Patient will open/close jaw in smooth, precise manner with/without model. (f)

AR 30: Patient will protrude/retract lower jaw in smooth, precise manner with/without model. (f)

AR 31: Patient will round/relax lips in smooth, precise manner with/without physical assist. (f)

AR 32: Patient will round lips and then relax in smooth, precise manner with/without model. (f)

AR 33: Patient will alternate lip rounding/lip retraction with/without physical assist. (f)

AR 34: Patient will alternate lip rounding/lip retraction with/without model. (f)

AR 35: Patient will maintain jaw closure while opening and closing the lips with/without model. (f)

AR 36: Patient will pucker lips and then lateralize the puckered lips right/left with/without physical assist. (f)

AR 37: Patient will pucker lips and then lateralize the puckered lips right/left with/without a model. (f)

AR 38: Patient will protrude and retract tongue with/without model. (f)

AR 39: Patient will maintain jaw opening and elevate tip of tongue to alveolar ridge and to floor of mouth behind anterior/lower incisors with/without a model. (f)

AR 40: Patient will elevate blade of tongue to hard palate with/without a model. (f)

AR 41: Patient will elevate back of tongue to velum with/without a model. (f)

AR 42: Patient will lateralize tongue right/left into corners of the lip with/without a model. (f)

AR 43: Patient will lateralize tongue into right/left buccal cavity with/without a model. (f)

Treatment objectives AR 44 - 46 are designed to improve patient's point of articulation for improved ability to produce specific phonemes/classes of phonemes to improve intelligibility. Appendices A-D may be helpful. The chart on page 139 provides a reminder of consonant classification.

AR 44: Patient will improve production of the following manner/place of phonemes/specific phonemes in initial/medial/final position of syllables: ____ (f)

AR 45: Patient will improve production of the following manner/place of phonemes/specific phonemes in initial/medial/final position of words: ____ (f) (Word Lists, pages 148-186)

AR 46: Patient will improve production of the following manner/place of phonemes/specific phonemes in initial/medial/final positions of phrases and sentences: ____ (f) (Word Lists, pages 148-186)

Treatment objectives AR 47 - 50 are designed to improve overall articulatory intelligibility through compensatory techniques. These techniques work for most dysarthria types.

AR 47: Patient will increase the number of intelligible word/phrase/sentence level utterances on intelligibility drills. (c)

AR 48: Patient will over-articulate consistently when imitating multi-syllabic words, phrases, or sentences (Word Lists, pages 148-186). (c)

AR 49: Patient will over-articulate consistently when responding to questions with words, phrases, or sentences. (c)

AR 50: Patient will over-articulate consistently in spontaneous speech. (c)

Environmental Modification (EM) Goal and Treatment Objectives

Short Term Goal: Speaker and listener will improve environment in which communication takes place.

Treatment Objectives:

EM 1: Speaker will give context of message before beginning to communicate.

EM 2: Listener will ask for clarification of context as needed.

EM 3: Speaker and/or listener will eliminate or reduce background noise.

EM 4: Speaker will gain visual attention of the listener before speaking.

EM 5: Speaker or listener will make sure area in which communication is taking place is well lit.

EM 6: Speaker and/or listener will make sure that they are sitting/standing close to one another and looking at each other before communication begins.

EM 7: Speaker and/or listener will try to make sure that communication takes place in a room with dampened background noise.

EM 8: Speaker will use external aid (bite block) for improved communication.

138

*Consonants Classified by Manner, Place, and Voicing

Manner	Place	Voiced	Voiceless
Stop	Bilabial	b	p
	Alveolar	d	t
	Velar	g	k
	Glottal	_____ ʔ	_____
Fricative	Labiodental	v	f
	Linguadental	ð	θ
	Alveolar	z	s
	Palatal	ʒ	ʃ
	Glottal		h
Affricate	Palatal	dʒ	tʃ
Nasal	Bilabial	m	
	Alveolar	n	
	Velar	ŋ	
Lateral	Alveolar	l	
Rhotic	Palatal	r	
Glide	Palatal	j	
	Labial/Velar	w	hw

Treatment Techniques to Achieve Treatment Objectives

The following are brief descriptions of activities for improving phonation. Noted in () after the name of each activity is the treatment objective or objectives related to the activity.

Treating Hypertonicity (AR 1 - 12)

Hypertonicity (increase in tone) can be one of two types:

- *spasticity* (caused from damage to the pyramidal tract). Spasticity is more dramatic during the initial part of a movement.

- *rigidity* (damage to the extrapyramidal tract). This affects the full range of motion.

Stretching is indicated for patients with spasticity and rigidity. It's a technique used by physical therapists for treatment of spasticity in the limbs. They use a steady prolonged directional stretch on the limb to reduce the spasticity or rigidity. These same principles may be applied to reducing tongue, lip, and jaw hypertonicity or rigidity.

Jaw (AR 1, 2)

Pull the patient's jaw into maximal opening and have him sustain it. Push the patient's mandible to the left/right and maintain that posture.

Tongue (AR 3-5)

Have the patient protrude, retract, or lateralize the tongue and maintain it in that position for several seconds. If the patient has difficulty performing this activity, wrap the end of the tongue in gauze and pull the tongue into the stretched position. This may be the best way to achieve the full stretch.

Lips (AR 6 - 9)

Using gauze, grasp the patient's lower lip and pull it down. You can also grasp the upper lip and pull it up. Stretching can also be done with lip retraction and pursing. You may need to help the patient pull the lips into full retraction and hold it for several seconds. You may also need to physically assist the patient in achieving lip pursing and holding for several seconds.

Bite Block (AR 10)

A bite block can be used to maintain slight jaw opening (stretching) to decrease spasticity during speech attempts.

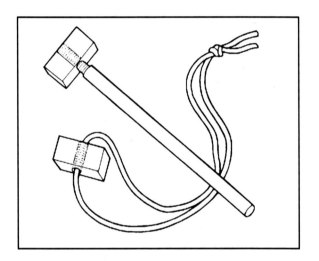

Jaw Shaking (AR 11)

Patients who are spastic may have spasticity in the articulatory muscles such as the jaw, lips, and tongue. One technique that Froeschels (1943) describes is called jaw shaking. This should only be used with patients who have significant spasticity. Have the patient let his jaw hang open and shake his head sideways to help relax his jaw.

Chewing (AR 12)

You may be also familiar with Froeschels chewing method in which he has the patient simulate chewing motions during speech.

Muscle Strengthening (AR 13 - 27)

There is not sufficient evidence in the literature to indicate that muscle strengthening will have a significant impact on articulation. Different authors suggest different timelines as to when to institute the strengthening exercises. Darley, Aronson, and Brown (1975) recommend holding muscle strengthening exercises until other methods are proved unsuccessful. In contrast, Froeschels would work on muscle strengthening first.

Patients with spastic or flaccid dysarthria or a mixed dysarthria with a combination of the two usually need strengthening exercises. Dworkin (1991) recommends reducing the hypertonicity in spastic patients before beginning strengthening exercises. He says that strengthening exercises should be initiated before the initiation of any other articulation exercises.

Duffy (1995) points out that "non-speech strengthening exercises should be used only after establishing the weakness is clearly related to impairment and disability." Yorkston, Beukelman, and Bell (1988) note the absence of data on the effect of strengthening exercises for articulatory adequacy. They indicate that there are probably only a small number of patients for whom strengthening exercises are appropriate.

Duffy summarizes the work of Barlow and Abb (1983) and DePaul and Brookes (1993) when he states that the articulators use very little of their maximum force (tongue 10%, lips 30%, and jaw 2%) for speech. Therefore, many authors agree that muscle strengthening exercises probably should only be continued until the patient can engage in speech activities.

Dworkin (1991) recommends trying muscle strengthening exercises for three to four intensive sessions. If significant change is going to occur, you should be able to tell after that time. Linebaugh (1983) suggests that strengthening exercises be done 3-5 times per session with 5-10 exercise periods per day.

It's important for you to decide whether the muscle weakness is really interfering with speech intelligibility. This is often found in patients at the two ends of the extreme. That is, patients with a severe flaccid dysarthria with extreme muscle weakness may need muscle strengthening to achieve any approximation of accurate articulation of phonemes. On the other hand, patients with very mild dysarthria (those patients who can tell that their speech doesn't sound the same to them but is only mildly distorted), will benefit from muscle strengthening exercises which they can complete independently after instruction. For instance, a patient with resection of a cranial-based tumor with removal of the hypoglossal nerve and resulting unilateral paralysis of the tongue may find strengthening exercises helpful to begin to compensate for decreased unilateral movement.

Note: Muscle strengthening exercises are contraindicated in patients with Myasthenia Gravis, ataxia, and ALS.

Resistance Exercises/Strengthening

These exercises are best done with the patient looking in a mirror to improve self-monitoring.

Jaw (AR 13 - 16)

Place your hand under the patient's chin and ask the patient to try to open his jaw while you provide resistance. Place your hand on the patient's lower jaw and give downward pressure. Ask the patient to try to close his jaw against resistance.

Provide resistance against the side of the patient's jaw and have him attempt to lateralize his jaw against resistance. Then, place your hand in front of the patient's mandible and ask him to jut his jaw forward against resistance.

Tongue

Anterior (AR 17)
Put a tongue blade in front of the patient's tongue. Ask the patient to push against the tongue blade with the tip of his tongue.

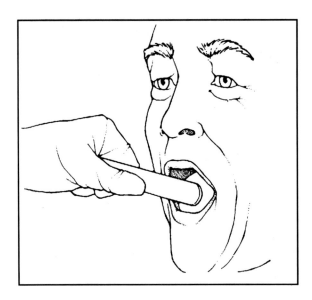

Lateral (AR 18, 19)
Have the patient stick out his tongue. Place the tongue blade alongside the left and/or right border of the patient's tongue and ask the patient to push against the tongue blade with his tongue. Place two fingers on the patient's cheek. Ask the patient to put his tongue inside his cheek and push against your fingers.

Elevation (AR 20, 21)
Place the tongue blade on top of the patient's tongue at the tip or near the front. Ask the patient to push up against the tongue blade toward the roof of his mouth.

Back of Tongue (AR 22)
If the patient doesn't have a hyperactive gag, place the tongue blade at the back of his tongue and ask the patient to push up against it. If the patient has a hard time doing this, cue him to say /k/. This will help the patient understand how to lift that part of his tongue.

Lips

Maintaining Closure (AR 23)
Tie a string or dental floss through a clean button or place the button in a finger cot. Ask the patient to put the button in front of his teeth behind his lips with his teeth closed. Gently pull on the string as the patient resists and keeps the button behind his lips.

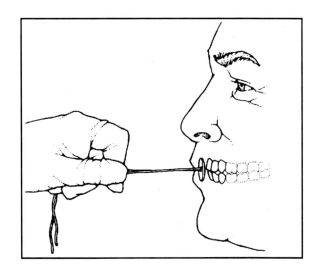

Maintaining Pucker (AR 24)
Ask the patient to pucker and protrude his lips as far as possible. Tell the patient to maintain the pucker while you place your forefinger on one side of his lips and your thumb on the other as you try to push his lips into a smile.

Maintaining Smile (AR 25)
Ask the patient to smile as broadly as possible. Have the patient maintain his smile while you place a forefinger on one side of the

lip and a thumb on the other and try to push his lips into a pucker.

Hold Tongue Blade (AR 26)
Place a tongue blade between the patient's lips (be careful that it is not going between the patient's teeth or that the patient is not curling his lips around his teeth). Ask the patient to press down hard on the tongue blade with his lips to the count you establish.

You can make this a bit easier by using two or three tongue blades for a thicker unit.

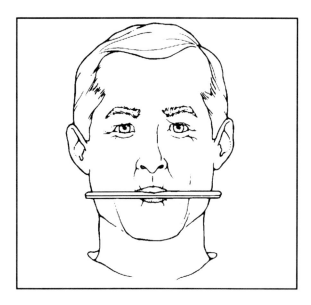

Bite Block (AR 27)
Have the patient put a bite block between his back teeth on one side or in the front of his mouth and repeat words, phrases, and sentences with lingual and labial phonemes (Word Lists, pages 148-186). The articulators will work harder to reach the point of articulation and therefore gain strength.

Increasing Tone (AR 28)

For patients with hypotonia, you may note some improvement by simply asking them to increase their effort when talking (see description of the Lee Silverman Voice Training Method in Chapter 5, page 116). It seems that when you ask the patient to use more energy and effort when speaking, it helps the patient compensate for the hypotonia. In order to help increase the speaking effort, have the patient use techniques he would use to increase phonatory effort such as pushing or pulling.

Improving Accuracy (AR 29 - 43)

These exercises are designed to improve the accuracy, speed, and range of oral-motor movements of the articulators including the jaw, lips, and tongue. They are best done with the patient seated in front of a mirror to provide visual feedback. These exercises may be done with or without your model. Some of them may also be done with a physical assist. That means you may actually place your hands on the patient's articulators and help him achieve the movement. Ask the patient to pay careful attention to performing these movements:
- accurately
- as quickly as possible while maintaining accuracy
- completely through the full range of motion

Jaw (AR 29, 30)
Ask the patient to open and close his jaw in a smooth, continuous motion. Also ask the patient to protrude (i.e., jut out) his lower jaw and then retract it into the relaxed position.

Lips (AR 31 - 37)
To encourage the patient to round his lips, ask him to say /u/. Then ask him to return his lips to a relaxed, closed position. To physically assist with this movement, place your forefinger on one side of the patient's lips and your thumb on the other to help the patient pull his lips forward into the rounded position.

The next movement is a little more difficult because the patient has to round his lips and, instead of relaxing his lips to a closed position at the end of the movement, the patient must pull his lips back into lip retraction. Ask the patient to say /u/ then /I/. To provide a physical assist for the lip retraction, keep your forefinger on one side of the patient's lips and your thumb on the other. After you help push the patient's lips into a rounded position, help retract the lips symmetrically. Ask the patient to pucker his lips forward and then, while keeping his lips puckered, lateralize his lips to the right and the left.

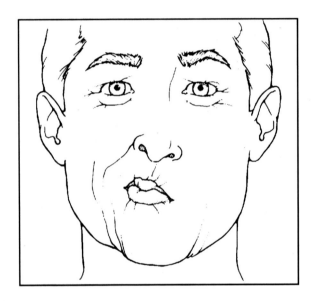

Tongue

Protrusion/Retraction (AR 38)
Ask the patient to protrude his tongue and try to maintain it at midline. Then have the patient retract his tongue.

Tongue Elevation (AR 39 - 41)
Ask the patient to stabilize his jaw (i.e., not to use the jaw to assist the tongue in its movement). If the patient cannot do this independently, use a bite block for stability. Then ask the patient to elevate either his tongue tip to the alveolar ridge, his blade to the alveolar ridge (it's easiest to see if this is being done if the patient keeps his tongue tip down), or the back of his tongue up towards the velum.

Tongue Lateralization (AR 42, 43)
Make sure the patient holds his jaw steady and does not use his jaw to assist in this movement. Ask the patient to lateralize the tip of his tongue to the left corner of his mouth and then to the right. Have the patient repeat this sequence. You can also ask the patient to repeatedly lateralize his tongue from the left buccal cavity to the right buccal cavity.

Stimulating Production of Individual Sounds (AR 44-46)

At times it may be helpful to teach a patient how to accurately produce an individual phoneme or class of phonemes. Standard articulation techniques used with children with articulation disorders can be helpful. Since those techniques are well-known to all SLPs, they won't be reiterated here. However, an excellent resource for very specific suggestions on how to achieve correct phonetic placement can be found in Dworkin (1991).

Too often SLPs focus on defective articulation (i.e., the production of sounds and syllables) when identifying goals for a patient with dysarthria. This is not surprising since many SLPs are most comfortable with treatment of articulation. It is critical to remember the inter-relationship between all the processes and the impact they have on intelligibility.

Rosenbek and LaPointe (1985) discuss the importance of traditional methods of articulation therapy for dysarthric speakers. Rosenbek and LaPointe describe three specific approaches:

- *Integral stimulation:* Watch me, listen to me, and imitate what I do.

- *Phonetic placement:* Use any and every model to help the patient achieve accurate placement. This therapy can include tongue and lip placement pictures, descriptions of the articulatory gestures, and physically moving the patient's articulators into the correct position for producing the sound.

- *Phonetic derivation:* This therapy involves using a speech sound the patient can produce correctly and helping him mold it into the production of a sound he is unable to make (e.g., shifting from production of /t/ to production of /s/).

Other Helpful Techniques

1. Use phonetic context to help the patient produce the sound. Remember that phonemes that come before or after a target phoneme can affect how easily the patient produces the target phoneme.

2. Use contrastive drills that require the patient to contrast the incorrect production with the correct production. Common contrasts include:

   - voiceless vs. voiced: Have the patient feel your larynx for vibration on voiced consonants. Have the patient extend vowel duration before a voiced sound (Appendix A).
   - errors of placement such as palatal vs. depalatal (Appendix B)
   - omission of consonants in blends (e.g., *fat/fast, boo/blue*) (Appendices C-1, C-2)
   - plosives vs. fricatives (e.g., *pay/fay, boat/vote*) (Appendices D-1, D-2)

3. It's important to analyze why the patient is exhibiting certain errors. For instance, if the patient's production of /p/ is more like /f/, it's probably because he doesn't have adequate lip strength to close his lips and may also have poor timing in learning how to open his lips. Therefore, you might work on muscle strengthening of the lips. If, on the other hand, the patient's /f/ sounds more like a /p/, it may be a problem with timing and accuracy of muscle movement. Sometimes slowing the rate can help correct this problem.

4. It's generally agreed that it is much better to work on movements and syllables rather than fixed positions of articulatory sounds.

5. It's also typical to use meaningful stimuli rather than nonsense syllables, but there are times when you may have to use nonsense syllables when contrasting correct vs. incorrect production.

6. Patients with dysarthria may have developed compensatory movements to help them achieve more accurate articulatory production. If these compensatory movements yield a closer approximation of the target sound, it's important to allow the patient to continue to use these compensatory strategies. For instance, patients often use mandibular movement to assist tongue tip elevation. If it's functional for the patient and you don't think he'll be able to achieve adequate production of the phoneme without the compensatory movement, then don't try to eliminate the compensation.

7. It's also important to remember when working with patients with dysarthria that you may have to accept approximations rather than precise productions of particular phonemes. Help the patient be realistic about whether an approximation is acceptable.

Compensatory Techniques (AR 47 - 50)

Intelligibility Drills

Provide the patient with a list of words, phrases, and/or sentences and ask the patient to read one without letting you see what he is reading (Word Lists, pages 148-186). Repeat the word, phrase, or sentence and keep score as to how many of the patient's utterances were intelligible to you. If the patient is a non-reader, use picture stimuli instead of written stimuli. Yorkston, Beukelman, and Bell (1988) state that intelligibility drills involve the production of a small set of words similar except for a single phoneme (Appendices A-D). For instance, they may have the patient read words beginning and ending with the same consonant and just changing the vowel sound. Or they might have the patient read a list of words with the same vowel final consonant combination and a different initial consonant. Yorkston, Beukelman, and Bell point out that these drills are helpful for several reasons:

- The drills don't require specific instructions to the patient on how to produce the sound. They depend on the patient to determine a way to compensate for his motor impairment to produce an acceptable sound.

- The difficulty of the task can be easily adjusted to meet the needs of the patient. The drills can even be used with the most severely-involved speaker by using very specific targets and short words.

- The drills allow you to train the patient early in how to use strategies when communication breaks down. If a listener is unable to accurately understand and repeat the word the patient has said, the patient must determine a way to change the production so that the message is understood. This might involve having the patient repeat the word with a more accurate production or use an augmentative device such as an alphabet board to help improve intelligibility.

Intelligibility drills are similar to barrier game activities used with children in which the sender of the message must determine a way to modify the message to ensure it is understood. It also bears some similarities to

pace therapy (Promoting Aphasics Communicative Effectiveness) in which the sender of the message is also responsible for assuring it is understood.

Over-articulation (AR 48 - 50)

Over-articulation is a compensatory technique used frequently with patients who have unintelligible speech related to their dysarthria. Explain to the patient that you want him to exaggerate all his speech movements as if he is trying to help someone read his lips from across the room. These directions usually result in a slower rate of speech which is necessary for over-articulation to be successful. Have the patient look in the mirror as you demonstrate speech articulated with little to no lip or tongue movement and speech with exaggerated lip and tongue movement. Have the patient try to exaggerate lip and tongue movements to match yours for words, phrases, and sentences (Word Lists, pages 148-186). The patient also needs to be able to perform this over-exaggeration in connected speech.

The lists on the following pages provide words, phrases, and sentences with selected phonemes that are often misarticulated by patients with dysarthria. The lists contain the target sound in a variety of positions within the word. The lists are prepared in large type with directions at the top of each page so you can copy them to leave with the patient for continued practice. Use the lists with any of the three methods to achieve accurate production of the phoneme:

- integral stimulation
- phonetic placement
- phonetic derivation

Some of the lists are designed to be used in contrastive drills. They can also be used for any other techniques you use for carryover.

Articulation Problems and Causes

What you hear	What could be causing the problem	SP	FL	FL Mya	V	VII	X PH	X S&R	X Sup	X Rec	Hypo XII	Hyper Trmr	Hyper Chorea	Dys & Ath	Mxd SP/FL	Mxd SP/AT	Mxd Hypo/SP/AT	UUMN	AT	AP
imprecise consonants	weakness		★	★	★	★	★			★								★		
	incoordination														★	★	★	★	★	
	unpredictable movement												★	★						
	decreased ROM	★									★						★			
	increased tone	★									★				★	★				
irregular breakdowns	incoordination														★	★			★	
	unpredictable												★	★						
vowel distortions	weakness					★												★		
	incoordination																	★	★	
	decreased ROM																			
	unpredictable												★	★						

Key

SP	Spastic dysarthria	X Sup	Flaccid dysarthria - Vagus (Xth) Nerve Lesions - Superior Laryngeal Branch Involvement
FL	Flaccid dysarthria	X Rec	Flaccid dysarthria - Vagus (Xth) Nerve Lesions - Recurrent Laryngeal Branch Involvement
FL Mya	Flaccid dysarthria- Mysathenia Gravis	Hypo	Flaccid dysarthria - Hypoglossal (XIIth) Nerve Lesions
V	Flaccid dysarthria - Trigeminal (Vth) Nerve Lesions	Hyper Trmr	Hyperkinetic dysarthria - Tremor
VII	Flaccid dysarthria - Facial (VIIth) Nerve Lesions	Hyper Chorea	Hyperkinetic dysarthria - Chorea
X PH	Flaccid dysarthria - Vagus (Xth) Nerve Lesions - Pharyngeal Branch Involvement	Dys & Ath	Hyperkinetic dysarthria - Dystonia and Athetosis
X S&R	Flaccid dysarthria - Vagus (Xth) Nerve Lesions - Superior and Recurrent Laryngeal Branch Involvement	Mxd SP/FL	Mixed dysarthria - Spastic and Flaccid
		Mxd SP/AT	Mixed dysarthria - Spastic and Ataxic
		Mxd Hypo/SP/AT	Mixed dysarthria - Progressive Supranuclear Palsy (Hypokinetic Spastic/Ataxic)
		UUMN	Mixed dysarthria - Unilateral UMN
		AT	Ataxic dysarthria
		AP	Aprosodic dysarthria

P at the beginning of words

The *p* sound is produced by maintaining tight lip closure, building up air pressure behind your lips, and releasing the air.

pack	peach	pine	paddle
page	peak	pink	painted
paid	peal	pint	panic
paint	pear	pipe	parade
pair	pearl	point	pardon
pale	peck	pool	parking
palm	Peg	porch	parrot
pan	pen	pound	payroll
pant	pet	puff	penny
park	pick	pull	pillow
part	pie	punch	pirate
pass	pig	pure	pizza
paste	pike	purse	polish
patch	pile	push	polite
pay	pill	put	punish

Phrases

pack of gum

page in the book

pail of water

paint on the door

palm of your hand

park full of trees

pat of butter

payment is late

pearl necklace

peck on the cheek

peeling paint

pen and ink

point of information

pool of water

porch swing

pound of nails

poor children

pushing hard

paddle in the boat

pancake breakfast

payroll department

peanut butter sandwich

pickles and tomatoes

pillow on the bed

panic attack

Sentences

Please pick up the paper.

Don't pack the pink shirt.

He paid all the bills.

Put it in the palm of your hand.

Part of it was left in the pan.

The puppy barked at the parrot.

The police were in the patrol car.

People in Pittsburgh are polite.

We can patch it with paste.

She peeled the peach.

I need a pen and paper.

Pick a piece of chocolate pie.

The pool was near the porch.

He paid the bills promptly.

Don't park near the pipe.

He painted the paddlewheel boat.

I drink a pint of water with my pills.

Pass the potatoes, please.

The payroll department makes us punch the clock.

He pointed to a pair of plaid pants.

P at the end of words

The *p* sound is produced by maintaining tight lip closure, building up air pressure behind your lips, and releasing the air.

cap	drop	shape	type
cape	heap	sheep	up
cheap	jump	ship	wrap
chip	keep	shop	zip
chop	lap	sleep	doorstop
clip	leap	soap	dust mop
crop	map	soup	landscape
cup	nap	step	makeup
deep	rip	stop	tulip
dip	ripe	trap	turnip
drape	rope	trip	workshop

Phrases

hungry ape	tomato soup
baseball cap	bar of soap
Superman's cape	ray of hope
not cheap	Scotch® tape
chocolate chip	car trip
loud clap	bus stop
paper clip	cough drop
soybean crop	round trip
seedless grape	toy shop
moan and gripe	jump rope
sore lip	baseball cap
road map	beauty sleep
dirty mop	masking tape
daily nap	shoulder strap
noisy pup	candy shop
woolly sheep	chimney sweep
sudden stop	soda pop

Sentences

He wore a cap and a cape.

Take a dip in the deep end.

Don't drip soap on the floor.

Those sheep are in good shape.

I skipped the movie so I could sleep.

Don't drop the grape.

The group had vegetable soup.

He bought a gumdrop in the candy shop.

He will gripe on a car trip.

The turnip burned my lip.

I can't sleep on a ship.

Cats can leap and jump.

Don't drop the dust mop.

The workshop is in terrible shape.

He spilled soy sauce on his cape.

The turnip is not ripe.

Fix the rip with tape.

Type a note about our trip.

The pup jumped into my lap.

Keep the children out of deep water.

K at the beginning of words

The *k* sound is made by lifting the back of your tongue up and quickly releasing it to let air flow out.

cab	coach	cow	camera
calf	coat	cuff	cancel
call	coin	cup	canoe
calm	cold	curb	canteen
can	comb	curve	capsule
cane	come	keep	carpet
cap	cool	key	carrot
car	cop	kid	cartoon
card	corn	kin	castle
care	cost	king	coffee
case	couch	kiss	color
cash	cough	kite	common
cat	could	cabin	copier
catch	count	cable	cushion
caught	court	camel	custom

Phrases

calling card

coming over

car in the driveway

case of soda

cat in the window

catching cold

coaching two teams

cold outside

combing hair

cooking breakfast

cool breeze

couch potato

cut it out

key in the lock

kiss goodnight

cable TV

cancel appointments

cardboard boxes

careless mistake

carton of milk

coloring pictures

coming for dinner

confiding in him

cowboy movie

cotton shirt

Sentences

Call him when the cake is ready.

She can't walk without the cane.

Do you care where I park the car?

He paid cash for the cake.

There was a couch in the cabin.

Wash the collar and the cuffs.

She got a cute haircut.

The castle was lit by candles.

She made a carrot cake.

What color was the capsule?

Put a coin in the meter by the curb.

There was coffee outside the courtroom.

The coach said it was too cold to practice.

The kitten curled up on the couch.

Help the kids fly the kite.

Do you care if I play cards?

They cancelled their cable TV.

The cop counted the money.

How much does the coat cost?

The cow was with her calf.

K at the end of words

The *k* sound is made by lifting the back of your tongue up and quickly releasing it to let air flow out.

back	hike	rake	weak
bake	hook	rock	wreck
bike	joke	sack	alike
block	knock	shake	attic
book	lake	sick	lipstick
brake	lick	soak	notebook
brick	like	sock	plastic
chalk	look	take	scrapbook
choke	make	talk	shamrock
fake	oak	truck	shipwreck
gawk	pack	wake	toothpick
hawk	rack	walk	unlock

Phrases

read a book	already sick
ride a bike	dirty sweatsock
on the hook	magic trick
made of brick	spiral notebook
piece of cake	kept him awake
funny joke	on a hike
will choke	in the lake
drink of Coke®	good luck
long look	grocery sack
on the deck	light snack
at the dock	private talk
sore neck	chocolate cupcake
pet duck	cotton fabric
ate a cornflake	

Sentences

Jack took a hike around the block.

Dick said he'd read the book.

Did you bring a cake to the bake sale?

Don't choke on that Coke®.

We saw a hawk by the brook.

I'd like to go to the lake.

We'll look for a flock of geese.

Mike makes a great milk shake.

The smoke made her sick.

He picked up a stick and a rock.

We can walk around the track.

Please don't wreck the truck.

The joke kept him awake.

She had a cupcake for a snack.

That was a real stroke of luck.

The bike needs a new hand brake.

Don't knock over the rake.

Should we take a hike or a walk?

Put the rock back in the sack.

I had to rake the oak leaves.

F at the beginning of words

The *f* sound is produced by placing your top teeth on your bottom lip and blowing an airstream out.

face	fat	fist	farmer
fade	fear	fold	fellow
fail	feed	food	fingerpaint
faint	feet	fool	fireman
fair	fell	foot	fireproof
fake	fence	fort	forehead
fall	field	four	forget
fan	fight	fudge	forgive
far	film	phone	fourteen
farm	fine	fancy	photo
fast	firm	farewell	phrases

Phrases

fad diet	fool and his money
fair decision	fork, knife, and spoon
fake fur	phone call
fame and fortune	famous actor
far away	farmyard animal
fear of heights	fever pitch
feeding pets	fireworks display
feel sick	fireside chat
feet on the ground	football field
field of dreams	fortune lost
fifth inning	Fort Wayne, Indiana
fine with me	Fort Worth, Texas
fire alarm	furry kitten
five o'clock	photo opportunity
food coloring	

Sentences

I'm feeling very faint.

Is it very far to the state fair?

Firefighters do not like false alarms.

The fawn cannot jump the fence.

There are ferns growing in the field.

Let's not fight about which film to see.

Help me find Fort Worth.

Can you fit five people in the car?

We couldn't find Fort Wayne because of the fog.

We found four kittens at the side of the road.

You need a fork to eat that food.

Phil will answer the phone.

Help me finish the fondue.

I forgot to fill the gas tank.

The foreman was quite fat.

The fullback plays football.

It's not your fault that the fan broke.

It's not the first time he's thrown a fit.

I'll never forget how foolish he was.

The famous actress said farewell.

F at the end of words

The *f* sound is produced by placing your top teeth on your bottom lip and blowing an airstream out.

chef	Jeff	reef
chief	knife	roof
cough	laugh	rough
cuff	leaf	safe
goof	life	staff
graph	loaf	thief
hoof	off	tough
huff	proof	whiff
if	puff	wife

Phrases

talented chef	maple leaf
police chief	long life
on the cliff	double loaf
bad cough	on and off
off-the-cuff	enough proof
piece of fluff	new roof
a nice graph	smooth and rough
not gruff	in the safe
horse's hoof	caught the thief
sharp knife	not too tough
loud laugh	husband and wife

Sentences

Jeff said the meeting would be brief.

The chef spilled sauce on his cuff.

I knew the puppy was deaf when he didn't hear the laugh.

Cut the loaf with a sharp knife.

Don't goof when making the graph.

I need proof she's the chief.

The water by the reef was very rough.

The thief climbed on the roof.

Jeff had a very rough life.

Joseph is a show-off.

Is it safe to ask for an autograph?

The sheriff has a bulletproof vest.

She read a paragraph to Jeff.

The chef took a whiff of the soup.

The staff wanted proof.

The chef preferred a sharp knife.

Joseph made an off-the-cuff remark.

He was very gruff with the staff.

Did the fire chief eat the whole loaf?

Do you have enough proof?

V at the beginning of words

The *v* sound is produced like *f* by placing your top teeth on your bottom lip and blowing an airstream out. Your voice is turned on for *v*.

vain	vest	vacuum
Val	vet	valley
valve	Vic	velvet
van	vice	Vermont
vane	view	victim
vase	vine	village
vat	vise	viper
vein	vote	vocal
vent	vacant	volley
verb	vaccine	vowel

Phrases

vase of flowers	vein in the leg
vault is locked	Vermont winter
veering right	vacuuming rugs
veil of tears	valet parking
venting anger	valley of the dolls
verb and noun	verb and noun
vise grips	varnish remover
view from the top	velvet dress
voting Tuesday	veto power
vain man	vital statistics
vat of iron	village leader
vowels and consonants	vacuum cleaner
victim of circumstance	vine on the railing
vice squad	vet's office

Sentences

Van helped him install the weather vane.

There are too many verbs in that verse.

I vow to vote every year.

Vince said the view was spectacular.

Vern seems very vain.

The dog was vaccinated by the vet.

There are vines growing all over the valley.

Vance promised to buy her a new vacuum.

That vacuum is a good value.

The vaccine vanished into thin air.

The victim was pleased with the verdict.

Vikings used to live in villages.

Was the villain in the vacant house?

The vulture circled the valley.

Vermont has very few vineyards.

He considered the verdict a victory.

The viper has poisonous venom.

Valerie wants to play the violin.

The villager was very verbal.

Vivian was a vegetarian.

V at the end of words

The *v* sound is produced like *f* by placing your top teeth on your bottom lip and blowing an airstream out. Your voice is turned on for *v*.

brave	give	wave
cave	glove	above
clove	hive	alive
cove	leave	arrive
Dave	live	believe
dive	love	forgive
dove	move	motive
drive	of	native
drove	shave	olive
five	shove	relive
gave	sleeve	remove

Phrases

Mammoth Cave	soft glove
quiet cove	can't move
scuba dive	close shave
mourning dove	long sleeve
Adam and Eve	over and above
high five	still alive
tight glove	won't behave
in the groove	green olive
not so brave	dark cave
cinnamon and clove	can't be Dave
scenic drive	high dive
can't give	four or five
never leave	mother's love
give a shove	on the move
crashing wave	torn sleeve

Sentences

Dave was brave to dive into the water.

Will you drive us to the cove?

Eve drove to her mother's house.

Did the glove prove anything?

Dave needs time to grieve.

We have a beehive in the grove of trees.

Let's leave the cave now.

We've learned how to weave.

You have to prove it to me.

I'll forgive you if you arrive on time.

The dove flew into the orange grove.

Help me move the beehive.

Does Dave love Eve?

Give me a long-sleeve shirt.

You've never been one to arrive on time.

I believe you can achieve it.

Help me heave it into the cave.

They've gone to the cove.

They've gone for a drive.

Please wave when they leave.

CH at the beginning of words

The *ch* sound is produced by placing your tongue tip tightly against the roof of your mouth, building up some air pressure behind it, and quickly releasing your tongue.

chain	cheese	chapter
chair	chess	checkerboard
chalk	chest	cheetah
chance	chief	cherry
change	chill	childhood
chant	choose	children
charge	chow	chilly
chase	churn	chipmunk
cheap	chamber	chopsticks
check	champion	chowder
cheer	channel	chuckle

Phrases

cheetah in the forest	chewing gum
chairs and table	chip the golf ball
cherry cobbler	chocolate candy
churning butter	chug of the engine
chopping onions	choosing sides
cheap jewelry	chores to do
cheering teams	charcoal grill
charge account	checking locks
chimes on door	chain on bike
change your mind	chief of police
chipped his tooth	chance of a lifetime
chopsticks or fork	chilly day
chest of drawers	children in school
chapter in a book	cheetah running

Sentences

Chilly days are good for a hot bowl of chili.

Please do not change the channel again!

That chain around your neck looks too chunky.

The children fed cheese to the chipmunk.

Using chopsticks is a real challenge.

The farmer chanted a song while he churned the butter.

Don't take a chance by getting too close to the cheetah.

My brother and Chuck like to play chess.

Please check if the charcoal is hot enough yet.

The champ chased his opponent.

I had a nice chat with Chet.

Help me chop up the cheese for the party.

The children seemed to like the chili.

Charles has many chores.

The chess champion gave his autograph.

He chipped his tooth on that chair.

It seems like he's always changing channels.

Did you choose chopsticks or a fork?

Chad was sitting in the cheap seats.

When the crowd cheered we all chimed in.

CH at the end of words

The *ch* sound is produced by placing your tongue tip tightly against the roof of your mouth, building up some air pressure behind it, and quickly releasing your tongue.

batch	French	perch
beach	grouch	porch
bench	hatch	punch
branch	hitch	ranch
breach	itch	search
bunch	lunch	speech
catch	march	starch
coach	match	teach
couch	much	touch
ditch	ouch	witch
each	peach	wretch

Phrases

on the beach	eating lunch
painting a bench	wooden match
using bleach	not much
broken branch	Georgia peach
having brunch	fast pitch
can't catch	bowl of punch
basketball coach	on a ranch
on the couch	cat scratch
on a crutch	inspiring speech
in the ditch	likes to teach
studying French	soft touch
a big grouch	digital watch
wagon hitch	wicked witch

Sentences

The ostrich ate the peach.

Please don't touch the bleach.

They each dug a ditch.

The chair should match the couch.

Put the batch of cookies on the bench.

There was a leech crawling on the branch.

I ate too much at lunch.

I'd like to munch on a peach.

Watch him sketch a picture.

Which French film did you like best?

The coach sat down on the couch.

You need a latch to hitch the wagon.

The coach called for a fast pitch.

Please don't touch the wrench.

Give your speech in French.

The ostrich gave a screech.

Mitch needs a patch on his sleeve.

Crouch down in the ditch.

Approach the pooch carefully.

I need to switch to another wrench.

J at the beginning of words

The *j* sound is produced the same as *ch*. Place your tongue tip tightly against the roof of your mouth, build up some air behind it, and release it. Your voice is turned on for *j*.

gem	joke	jelly
germ	joy	Jerry
jab	judge	jewel
jade	jug	jolly
jar	juice	journal
jerk	jump	journey
Jill	June	juicy
Jim	gentle	jungle
Joan	German	junior
job	giant	jury
jog	jacket	
join	jealous	

Phrases

gym class	German shepherd
jack of all trades	giant sunflower
jar of pickles	Jack Frost
jazz music	jealous person
heavy jar	jelly and peanut butter
Jack and Jill	jewelry box
joke book	juggling balls
joining hands	jumper cables
judge and jury	jury duty
jug of water	jerk the chain
jumping high	job hunting
jog in the morning	jungle animals
join hands	German chocolate cake
joy and sorrow	juice in a box

Sentences

George is a real gentleman.

He practices jabs at the gym.

Jade is jagged around the edge.

I like jam better than jelly.

Jane couldn't open the jar.

Jeff is part of a jazz band.

Joe is a real jerk.

Jack and Jill went up the hill.

John jogged around the track three times.

Joyce enjoys telling jokes.

The judge just sits there and listens.

We are going to take a journey through Germany.

The giraffe has strong jaws.

Jimmy worked a jigsaw puzzle.

I've got some jitters about this journey.

The jurors were intent on seeing justice done.

There are jaguars and giraffes at the zoo.

That's a giant jar of jelly.

They called him the gentle giant.

The janitor picked up the junk.

J at the end of words

The *j* sound is produced the same as *ch*. Place your tongue tip tightly against the roof of your mouth, build up some air behind it, and release it. Your voice is turned on for *j*.

age	lodge	garbage
badge	page	hostage
bridge	pledge	language
cage	rage	luggage
dodge	sage	marriage
edge	stage	mortgage
fudge	wage	package
grudge	baggage	passage
hedge	bandage	salvage
huge	cabbage	village
judge	carriage	wreckage

Phrases

over the bridge	blank page
in the cage	on the stage
at the edge	fair wage
chocolate fudge	carry baggage
gas gauge	cooked cabbage
hold a grudge	off to college
thorny hedge	major damage
too huge	propose marriage
fair judge	in the village
at the lodge	looks his age
wearing a badge	peanut butter fudge
covered bridge	rugged lodge
parsley and sage	torn page
go backstage	heavy baggage

Sentences

The judge took out the garbage.

He put the cage behind the hedge.

Nudge her onto the stage.

The hedge looks like sage.

The lodge is on the ridge.

Madge held a grudge against him.

The fudge was on the edge of the table.

The carriage wouldn't budge.

The judge took a pledge.

The carriage went over the drawbridge.

Throw the cabbage in the garbage.

The hostage didn't speak their language.

Can you salvage the porridge?

Can we manage the mortgage payment?

The hostage was held in the village.

Is there fudge in this package?

Midge went off to college.

What percentage will stay in the lodge?

Curly is only one Stooge.

The judge punished him for his rage.

L at the beginning of words

The *l* sound is produced with the tip of your tongue placed on the ridge behind your upper teeth. The words in the first and second columns may be easier to produce because they're followed by vowels that also require lifting the front of the tongue.

lead	leak	lace
leaf	lean	lake
league	led	lamb
leak	left	land
leap	lend	lap
ledge	lent	large
leech	less	lark
leg	lid	last
lens	lesson	late
lick	lettuce	laugh
licked		lawn
		like
		lime
		line
		look

Phrases

lease agreement	list of words
lunch time	license to drive
leash on the floor	lit the candle
lounge around	lettuce salad
least of all	leg cramp
loud music	loaning money
leaves to burn	less work
looking at him	lemonade on ice
leaves of grass	let her
Lake Cumberland	lost and found
limp around	led the parade
lame horse	last to arrive
lipstick on collar	lid on the bowl
large car	Long Island

Sentences

He put the lead dog on the leash.

She put lipstick on her lips.

Let him draw left handed.

I dropped the lettuce and the letters.

Listen to the leaves in the wind.

It's a little late for lunch.

Lucy was too loud in the lunchroom.

He ran a lap around the lake

Let's have lunch on the lawn.

She has a very loud laugh.

That plane is the last one to land.

The cat will leap from the ledge.

The league plays on the vacant lot.

Put the lid on so it doesn't leak.

He turned his lesson in late.

You need lessons to learn how to drive.

He loves looking in the mirror.

The lawyer loaned him the money.

The loaf of bread was cooling on the ledge.

Lend me a lemon.

173

L blends at the beginning of words

The *l* sound also occurs in blends. This means that another consonant appears right before the l. Be sure you carefully lift your tongue for the *l* when it appears. The first three columns have the vowels which require high tongue placement and may be easier to pronounce.

bleach	flesh	please	bloom
bleak	flint	pleat	blouse
bleat	flip	pledge	blow
bled	flit	sleek	clothes
bleed	gleam	sleep	clown
blimp	glean	sleet	club
blink	glee	sleeve	flies
bliss	glee club	slept	floor
clean	glib	slick	glasses
cleats	glimmer	slid	glove
flea	glisten	slim	glue
fleece	glitter	slip	plow
fled			plum
			slow

blimp in the sky	slept too late
flea on the dog	slick operation
flint arrowhead	slim down
glimmer of hope	slept well
cleats on shoes	blooms in the spring
pleats in the skirt	flood gates
fled the scene	floor tiles
slid sideways	flies away
slip on ice	glove box
bleach in the wash	glue and paste
blinking lights	glasses are gone
flipping pancakes	club soda
flesh and blood	clouds in the sky
glee club singing	plum pudding
pleasing attitude	plow in the barn
pledge of allegiance	slow down
sleeves rolled up	

Sentences

It was too cloudy for the blimp to fly.

Please pick out a nice blouse.

The sled ruined the hardwood floors.

Can you glue the glasses?

The boy slipped on the floor.

The birds flew through the clouds.

When he slipped, he tore his slacks.

The car slid on the sleet.

The clown wore funny clothes.

They pledged money to the glee club.

Where are my clean clothes?

Please don't wear cleats in the house.

The gymnast did flips on the floor.

Don't slam the door to the club.

That clown looks very sloppy.

This fly landed on my sleeve.

Don't pour bleach on the blouse.

The wind blew the door open while he slept.

Can you flip the top of the glue?

Those will be slow to bloom this spring.

S at the beginning of words

The *s* sound is produced by closing your teeth with your lips in a smile. Direct a thin stream of air through your teeth.

sack	seed	soft	salty
sad	sell	soon	senate
safe	send	sore	senior
said	sent	sound	service
saint	serve	soup	seven
sale	sick	sour	sewer
salt	side	such	soapy
Sam	sign	suds	soda
sand	sing	suit	softball
sang	sink	sum	sunlight
sank	sip	sun	sunny
sat	size	sung	support
save	soak	center	
seal	soap	saddle	
seam	sock	safety	

Phrases

sad face	serving dinner
sail the boat	setting the table
sale on sheets	sewing machine
salt and pepper	sick at heart
same old thing	side window
sand bag	sign in a window
sat on the couch	singing along
saw a bird	sinking ship
sea breeze	sitting down here
seed pack	soap and water
seems alright	soft bed
selling the house	some more please

son and daughter

sore throat

sound of music

sour candy

south of the border

suit and tie

cement mixer

saddle on a horse

salmon color

secret garden

senior class

service station

sidewalk sale

Sentences

She sang the first song.

Please save some salt for me.

The thief searched for the safe.

This seems like a good seat.

I'll sew the button on the side pocket.

We could see the sign from here.

Buy some soap at the store.

He wore a suit on Sunday.

That song sounds familiar.

We need to soak the socks in the suds.

The ceiling was sagging at the center.

She used the scissors to cut the silk.

Sea gulls like sandy beaches.

She serves dinner promptly at seven o'clock.

The juniors challenged the seniors to a softball game.

I'm talking softly because I have a sore throat.

Is the saddle for sale?

I can't see the sign from here.

He is serving soup for lunch.

We sat in the sun at the softball game.

S at the end of words

The *s* sound is produced by closing your teeth with your lips in a smile. Direct a thin stream of air through your teeth.

boss	ice	place
brace	juice	race
bus	kiss	rice
case	less	this
chase	mess	us
chess	mice	yes
class	miss	across
dice	moss	caboose
face	mouse	erase
gas	nice	furnace
grass	niece	lettuce
guess	pass	necklace
house	piece	office

Phrases

off base	bag of ice
silk blouse	cranberry juice
my boss	goodnight kiss
ride on the bus	big mess
carton or case	field mouse
give chase	nephew and niece
lucky dice	another piece
blue dress	fried rice
clean face	no or yes
premium gas	walk across
flock of geese	in the doghouse
Canadian goose	clean fireplace
in the house	gas furnace
cold as ice	picking lettuce

Sentences

Please put some ice in the juice.

Their house has lace curtains.

Bruce was safe at third base.

We live across the street from the firehouse.

The police chased the bus.

Take a chance and roll the dice.

There is a crease in this blouse.

Put the chess pieces in the case.

Don't put gas in a glass container.

They have a gas furnace.

There is no grass around that house.

This place has mice.

Those mice have lice.

His niece will erase it.

He will miss his niece.

The bus slid on the ice.

Their price is twice as much.

Pass the salt across the table.

The vase is made of glass.

Is that rice for us?

S blends at the beginning of words

These words have an *s* followed by another consonant. Be sure you pronounce the *s* clearly.

scar	slam	snoop	steam
scare	slip	snore	steeple
schedule	slow	snorkel	stew
school	slump	snow	stir
score	sly	spend	stock
Scott	smack	spice	stone
skate	smart	spill	stop
ski	smell	spin	store
skin	smile	spoon	stork
skip	smoke	sport	story
skirt	snail	spud	stranger
sky	snake	stamp	strike
slab	sneak	stare	stuffy
slack	sneakers	start	
slain	snip	state	

Phrases

Swiss cheese sandwich

swim in the pool

swallow the pill

stamp on the letter

stubborn boy

story at bedtime

state of the union

stalk of celery

space heater

skip and hop

schedule a meeting

skating on thin ice

spicy food

spool of thread

snooping around

smile or frown

slippery road

skim milk

Scarlet O'Hara

skin your knee

scoring touchdowns

spill the beans

stir the soup

snail's pace

Sentences

He swerved around the snake.

Stock car racing is a sport.

Stir the stew with a spoon.

There was smoke coming from the steeple.

People wear sneakers to play sports.

That stew was steaming hot.

We can swim or snorkel in the ocean.

We went sledding in the snow.

The store smells like fresh baked bread.

Scott wore a scarf to hide the scar.

She wore her new skirt to school.

Please don't stop telling the story.

He said he could smell the smoke.

He snores when he snoozes.

He'll clear the snow with the snowplow.

He spent too much money on the snowsuit.

There's a stain on his new sport shirt.

He started to swim early in the morning.

He likes to study the different stamps.

That sweatsuit really stinks.

S blends at the end of words

These words have an *s* blend at the end. That means there is a consonant followed by an *s*. Be sure you pronounce the *s* clearly.

chiefs	jacks	license	bats
coughs	lakes	chips	boats
cuffs	likes	cups	boots
proofs	socks	flops	dates
handcuffs	stakes	grapes	eats
backs	tacks	gripes	gates
blocks	bounce	hopes	mats
books	dance	hops	nuts
brakes	ounce	lips	oats
bricks	prince	maps	sheets
checks	rinse	raps	shorts
cooks	absence	ropes	sites
fix	advance	snaps	
fox	announce	tapes	
hawks	balance	types	

Phrases

great aunt's	red lips
wooden bats	daily naps
many boats	table scraps
dirty boots	seven weeks
hungry cats	broken sticks
never fights	city tax
never fits	grey slacks
wrought iron gates	dirty socks
flying kites	milk shakes
fast jets	on the hooks
never meets	door creaks
humming notes	building blocks
mixed nuts	cake mix
filling the cups	empty sacks

Sentences

The chief coughs because he smokes.

Her new slacks have cuffs.

Please put the books back in the library stacks.

He cooks without an ounce of salt.

There are hawks and a fox at the lakes.

She backs the truck up to load the bricks.

Can you fix those blocks he likes?

He rents an apartment and pays in advance.

Don't announce our balance to everyone!

Does he have a license to drive those big trucks?

He prints his checks on the computer.

Sally likes to dance in her socks.

He gripes about what the chef cooks.

He hopes the grapes weren't ruined by the frost.

His great aunt's hungry cats were sitting by the empty sacks.

The dog never fights with the cats over table scraps.

The books on the top shelves are full of maps of the lakes and rivers.

In the king's absence, the prince will announce the results.

The fast jets passed the high flying kites.

The sacks are empty except for the boxes of cake mix.

The little boy flops on his bed to take off his shoes and socks.

She is filling the cups with mixed nuts and mints.

He has been wearing those gray slacks for seven weeks.

The front door creaks and there are bats in the attic.

183

Z at the beginning of words

The *z* sound is made like *s* by closing your teeth with your lips in a smile. Direct a thin stream of air through your teeth. Your voice is turned on for *z*.

Xerox®	zillion	zipper
zap	zinc	zone
zeal	zip	zoo
zebra	Zip code	zoom

Phrases

zapping bugs

Zest® soap

zero balance

zinc oxide

zillion dollars

zipping up

zipper stuck

zoo animals

zoom lens

zoom around

Zip code is wrong

Sentences

That bug spray will zap the bug.

He has a real zest for life.

Don't forget to write your Zip code.

We live in a temperate zone.

He likes to visit the zoo.

He will zoom around in the car.

He owes me a zillion dollars.

The coat needs a new zipper.

The zebra is a beautiful animal.

The Xerox® machine is always broken.

Wear zinc oxide at the beach.

The camera has a zoom lens.

He won a zillion dollars.

The account has a zero balance.

The zipper on the coat is stuck.

Zip codes have five plus four digits.

The zoo has rare animals.

Our tickets were in the end zone.

They are mining for zinc.

The zebra has stripes, not spots.

Z at the end of words

The *z* sound is made like *s* by closing your teeth with your lips in a smile. Direct a thin stream of air through your teeth. Your voice is turned on for *z*.

as	ease	size
boys	eyes	sneeze
buys	fleas	snooze
cause	fuse	squeeze
cheese	fuzz	tease
chews	hose	ties
chose	lies	toes
close	noise	toys
cries	nose	twos
crows	paws	because
daze	peas	confuse
draws	please	pillows
dries	rise	surprise

Phrases

wasps and bees	cheddar cheese
blue eyes	too much noise
rhythm and blues	baby cries
purple haze	fruit pies
girls and boys	ocean cruise
garden hose	as you please
summer breeze	seven days
true lives	tight squeeze
just because	union dues
evening news	ten toes
broken toys	silk ties
will confuse	loud sneeze
blown fuse	a good cause

Sentences

I like the blues and jazz music.

What is the cause of that buzz?

Did he choose a cheese sandwich?

The cries of the crows kept him awake.

We took a cruise for ten days.

Does the breeze make it feel cooler?

How many days has he been gone?

Please pose for the picture.

His rose won a prize.

We cruise the seven seas.

These are not my size.

He says they are spies.

He tries not to sneeze in class.

Whose quiz is this?

Please give them some applause.

She grows rows of peas.

He has fleas on his paws.

These toys are in the way.

Is Liz very wise?

The boys doze on the couch.

Voiceless vs. Voiced Consonants in Words

The words in each column are exactly the same except that you need to turn your voice on for the first sound in the words in the second column.

Voiceless Initial Sounds   Voiced Initial Sounds

Voiceless Initial Sounds	Voiced Initial Sounds
pack	back
pad	bad
pail	bail
pear	bear
palm	balm
pan	ban
pang	bang
pea	bee
peach	beach
peak	beak
pear	bear
peat	beat
perch	birch
pet	bet
pie	by
pig	big
pill	bill
pike	bike
pen	Ben
pit	bit
post	boast
poor	bore
pun	bun
punch	bunch
push	bush
tab	dab
tale	Dale
tan	Dan
tear	dare
tell	dell
ten	den
tide	died
tie	die

Voiceless Initial Sounds   Voiced Initial Sounds

Voiceless Initial Sounds	Voiced Initial Sounds
till	dill
time	dime
tin	din
tip	dip
tire	dire
ton	done
two	do
town	down
tuck	duck
cab	gab
cage	gauge
came	game
cap	gap
card	guard
cash	gash
cause	gauze
coal	goal
coat	goat
cold	gold
cool	ghoul
cord	gourd
core	gore
cot	got
could	good
curl	girl
kale	Gale
sap	zap
seal	zeal
sink	zinc
sing	zing
sip	zip
Sue	zoo

The sounds *s* and *sh* can sometimes be hard to distinguish. The *s* sound is made with your flattened tongue tip behind your teeth. The *sh* sound is made with your tongue tip up towards the top of your mouth and a curled tongue. The following list of words contrast *s* and *sh*.

sell	shell
sack	shack
sag	shag
said	shed
sake	shake
Sam	sham
same	shame
sank	shank
save	shave
sea	she
seen	sheen
seep	sheep
self	shelf
sew	show
sick	Schick®
sign	shine
sin	shin
sip	ship
sock	shock
sun	shun
sore	shore
sort	short
sour	shower
suck	shuck

This list contrasts words without *l* blends to words with *l* blends.

words with no *l* blends	words with *l* blends
back	black
bade	blade
band	bland
bank	blank
bear	blare
beach	bleach
beak	bleak
beat	bleat
bed	bled
bead	bleed
bend	blend
boo	blue
bind	blind
boat	bloat
bob	blob
bond	blond
boom	bloom
bow	blow
buff	bluff
burr	blur
Burt	blurt
fair	flare
fake	flake
fame	flame
fat	flat
fee	flee
fed	fled
feet	fleet
fight	flight
fit	flit
four	floor
foe	flow
gas	glass
goat	gloat

words with no *l* blends   words with *l* blends

go	glow
gum	glum
came	claim
camp	clamp
can	clan
cap	clap
cash	clash
cause	clause
caw	claw
kick	click
caught	clot
cove	clove
cub	club
pace	place
pain	plain
pan	plan
pant	plant
pay	play
pea	plea
pop	plop
puck	pluck
pump	plump
sack	slack
sang	slang
sap	slap
sack	slack
save	slave
saw	slaw
said	sled
seek	sleek
say	slay
sick	slick
side	slide
sing	sling
sip	slip
soup	sloop
sew	slow
sir	slur

191

This list contrasts words without *s* blends to words with *s* blends.

words with no *s* blends	words with *s* blends
kale	scale
cat	scat
coop	scoop
cope	scope
core	score
cower	scour
come	scum
key	ski
kill	skill
kin	skin
lab	slab
lack	slack
lap	slap
late	slate
law	slaw
led	sled
leave	sleeve
lay	sleigh
leapt	slept
lick	slick
lid	slid
lied	slide
lime	slime
lip	slip
lot	slot
low	slow
lump	slump
Mack	smack
mash	smash

words with no _s_ blends   words with _s_ blends

words with no _s_ blends	words with _s_ blends
Mel	smell
mock	smock
nail	snail
nap	snap
knees	sneeze
knob	snob
nor	snore
no	snow
pat	spat
pent	spent
pill	spill
pin	spin
poke	spoke
purr	spur
tack	stack
tag	stag
take	stake
teal	steal
team	steam
teed	steed
two	stew
tick	stick
till	still
tore	store
toe	stow

Produce *p* by tightly closing your lips to build up air pressure, then release. Produce *f* by placing your top teeth on your bottom lip and blowing a continuous stream of air.

Plosive *p*	Fricative *f*
pace	face
pact	fact
pad	fad
paid	fade
pail	fail
paint	faint
pair	fair
pan	fan
pang	fang
par	far
past	fast
pat	fat
pawn	fawn
peat	feat
pea	fee
peel	feel
pain	feign
pelt	felt
pew	few
peeled	field
pierce	fierce
pig	fig
pile	file
pill	fill
pin	fin
pine	fine
purr	fur
pit	fit
pull	full
pour	four
port	fort
pudge	fudge
pull	full
pun	fun

Produce *b* by tightly closing your lips to build up air pressure, then release. Produce *v* by placing your top teeth on your bottom lip and blowing a continuous stream of air. Your voice is turned on for both *b* and *v*.

Plosive *b*	Fricative *v*
bane	vane
bail	veil
ban	van
base	vase
bat	vat
bend	vend
bent	vent
best	vest
bet	vet
bile	vile
by	vie
boat	vote
bowel	vowel
bow	vow

Chapter 8
Prosody

Prosody is described as those features which help speech sound smooth and natural. There are many ways to describe the aspects of prosody, but in this book, prosody includes:

- Rate/Rhythm: Rate is decided by the articulation time (how fast you produce the actual phonemes) and pause time (the spaces inserted between words and segments). Rhythm is the perception of time applied to phonetic events. The durational relationship between articulation time and pause time is what constitutes rhythm.

  For the purposes of setting goals and treatment objectives, rate and rhythm are considered to be interrelated and addressed as one component of prosody.

- Stress: Stress is the perception of syllable emphasis relative to the emphasis perceived on other syllables in the same sentence or phrase.

- Intonation: Intonation is the perception of changes in the fundamental frequency of vocal fold vibration during speech production.

The chart on page 209 lists prosody problems and their causes.

Understanding the Prosodic Features

Suprasegmentals are features of speech above the segmental (production of segments of sounds) level. Rosenbek and LaPointe (1978) list the suprasegmentals as:

- pitch
- loudness
- articulation time
- pause time

They define prosodic features as those features that are produced by the interaction of the suprasegmentals. It's easy to see how pitch (variation, level, quality), loudness (level and variation), and timing interact to produce stress, intonation, and the rate and rhythm of speech.

The type and degree of disordered prosody is associated with the site and extent of the related neurological disorder. Three patient populations who typically have problems with prosody are individuals with:

- ataxic dysarthria
- hypokinetic dysarthria
- right hemisphere aprosodic dysarthria

Individuals with ataxia lengthen segments in atypical proportion which disrupts the normal timing of speech. Individuals with hypokinetic dysarthria (mostly Parkinson's disease) reduce normal prosodic patterns so that everything sounds compressed together. Damage to the right hemisphere can result in deficits in both comprehension and production of prosody. Some studies have indicated that the aprosodic nature of right hemisphere disorders may occur in patients with anterior lesions in the right hemisphere. Some authors (Shapiro and Danly, 1985) have indicated that posterior right hemisphere lesions result in exaggerated use of fundamental frequency cues. This is described as hyperprosody.

A Closer Look

1. Rate and Rhythm

There are two parts that make up speaking rate: articulation time and pause time. We often attend to articulation time, or the time the patient spends producing the actual speech sounds. The use of pauses is equally important. Pauses may represent up to 50% of total talk time and are usually more easily modified than the actual production of speech sounds (Henderson, Goldman-Eisler, and Skarbek, 1966). Many authors have pointed out that pauses are more important in modifying rate than actually slowing down articulation time (Rosenbek and LaPointe, 1985; Yorkston, Beukelman, and Bell, 1988). Rate affects intelligibility. If the patient is talking too fast, the articulators do not have time to reach their targets.

Many patients benefit from a modification in rate. If no other techniques are chosen, modifying rate by itself may significantly improve intelligibility. It can be used with many different types of dysarthria because it facilitates articulatory movements. Duffy (1996) indicates that it may also be easier for patients with dysarthria to achieve a reduced rate than other motor goals.

Try to determine an optimal articulation rate for your patient. How fast can the patient move his articulators and still produce different phonetic segments? Because of the weakness of the muscles of articulation, many dysarthric speakers experience slow movements and tend to undershoot places of articulation which is then complicated by their use of a faster than optimal articulation rate. Determine the number of syllables the patient can produce comfortably on one breath. Help the patient learn to recognize the number of syllables. This is sometimes best done by beginning with reading passages and marking off the number of syllables until the patient becomes comfortable learning when to stop and take a breath.

Dworkin (1991) describes a method which can be used to determine the patient's speaking rate. These same techniques have often been used with patients who stutter. Tape record one-minute samples of reading, monologue, and conversation. It's helpful to tape record more than one sample for each condition. As you listen to the tape, count the number of words spoken during each sample. Take an average of the number of words.

You can also count the number of syllables per minute. An easy way to do this is to use a calculator and tap for each syllable you hear. Typically you hit the M + 1 and then =. Thereafter, tap the = button each time you hear a syllable. This should continue to add the number of syllables for a running total. If you practice this skill, you can do it while

198

the patient is speaking rather than listening to a taped sample. Most normal adults speak at a rate of 130-220 words per minute and use between 3 and 5 syllables per second. Oral reading rate tends to be slightly lower.

Rhythm is very related to the use of pause time. It's defined as the relationship between pause time and articulation time. Patients' speech can sound very disrupted if they present with a staccato rhythm or a rhythm with many abnormal pauses and short rushes of speech.

2. Stress

Stress can be defined as one unit of speech appearing more prominent than others. Stress can occur on a different syllable in a word and change the meaning of the word. For example, the word <u>contract</u> is a noun meaning a binding, legal document. *Contract* is a verb meaning to execute an agreement between two parties. These are forms of lexical stress.

Stress can also occur within a phrase or sentence and change the meaning. For example, "<u>Bill</u> ate blueberries" indicates it was Bill and no one else who ate those berries, but "Bill <u>ate</u> blueberries" indicates that Bill didn't grow them or pick the blueberries, he ate them. This is an example of contrastive stress, also known as emphatic stress.

It's difficult to choose a single acoustic parameter that indicates stress, but the perceived emphasis may result from fundamental frequency shifts, durational changes, intensity variations, changes in vowels, or any combination of parameters. However, stress is generally accomplished by increased loudness, increased pitch, or increased articulation or pause time. That is, the stressed

segment or syllable may be longer than the non-stressed segment or syllable, or a pause may be inserted before the stressed segment. Most normal speakers use pitch as the most important cue for indicating stress and use loudness the least (Rosenbek and LaPointe, 1985).

It seems that some patients can signal stress by changing their pitch or their loudness or their duration, but may not be able to use all of those parameters. Some patients use one parameter better than others. You may want the patient to first try indicating stress by reading phrases in which you have a target word in bold (Appendix A-1).

Listen to how the patient is attempting to indicate stress. You may hear the patient use a change in pitch or loudness, hold onto the word, or insert a pause. If you find a parameter the patient is able to change to indicate stress, use it to help improve stress marking in other situations. For example, Yorkston, Beukelman, and Bell (1988) indicate that patients with ataxia seem to do better by prolonging a syllable and inserting a pause at the appropriate time to signal stress.

3. Intonation

Intonation is the perception of changes in fundamental frequency of the vocal fold vibration during speech production.

Rosenbek and LaPointe (1985) indicate that we really don't understand intonation in normal speakers, and certainly have even less information on how intonation is used in patients with dysarthria. Helpful information can often be found in materials prepared for speakers of English as a second language. Craig and Sikorski (1985) describe intonation at the word and sentence level. They describe eight basic word-level intonation patterns in English (Appendix G). They indicate that these patterns combine pitch and stress to create the intonation for a given word.

Craig and Sikorski also describe sentence-level intonation. They point out that declarative messages usually have a falling inflection. If we use the sentence in a questioning way, it can have a slightly rising inflection. They also state that interrogative messages will have either a falling inflection or a slightly rising inflection.

They state that the choice of pattern depends on custom and grammatical construction, but that there should always be one major stressed word in each contour. Use Appendix B to practice some basic falling and rising inflections for both interrogative and declarative sentence types. These are very fine distinctions and may be somewhat difficult for patients with dysarthria. It certainly seems appropriate to start on stress and contrastive stress activities before having the patient try to approximate sentence-level intonation patterns.

Some SLPs approach dysarthria treatment by addressing all other aspects of the dysarthria (e.g., articulation, resonance) before prosody. Some investigators (Rosenbek, 1978; Yorkston and Beukelman, 1981) indicate that we shouldn't wait until the end of treatment to address prosody, but should instead address it immediately. They suggest that treatment of prosody may have a facilitory effect on segmental production. For example, when you teach a patient to reduce his rate, articulation may improve because the articulators have time to reach their targets.

Rosenbek and LaPointe (1985) also indicate that stress drills shouldn't be saved until the

end of therapy, but should be an early goal because stress drills might improve respiratory, resonatory, and articulatory performance. You may also find that working on prosody can have some effect on the rate control itself. Simmons (1983) found that working on pitch and loudness variation and word stress patterns in a patient with ataxia also resulted in the reduction of speaking rate.

Efficacy

Do we know if treatment for disorders of prosody works? For more detailed information, see the *Summary of Treatment Efficacy for Dysarthria* (Yorkston, 1996). Other important studies are summarized here.

Helm (1979) documented working with an individual who had encephalitic Parkinson's disease using a pacing board. The results indicated that the patient was able to speak slowly and control his rate independent of the clinician.

Several studies have demonstrated the effectiveness of rate control strategies. Such studies have been completed with individuals with ataxic dysarthria and are designed to decrease the bizarre sound of speech and to improve naturalness. Barry and Goeshorn (1983); Yorkston and Beukelman (1981); and Yorkston, Hammen, Beukelman, and Traynor (1990) all describe types of treatment designed to improve rate control with the results indicating improved speech intelligibility that are more natural sounding.

Yorkston et al (1990) compared different pacing strategies with four patients with severe ataxic dysarthria and four with severe hypokinetic dysarthria. They examined the effects of this rate control on sentence and phoneme intelligibility and speech naturalness. Sentence intelligibility improved for both groups. The technique of metered pacing showed the largest improvement, but metered rate control strategies were associated with the lowest ratings of naturalness.

Yorkston and Beukelman (1981) discussed the difficulty ataxic speakers have in achieving normal prosodic patterns. They used durational adjustments to signal stress and were able to achieve stress on targeted words consistently as well as minimize bizarreness.

Several other studies have investigated the use of an alphabet board in which the patient is asked to point to the first letter of each word on the alphabet board as the word is spoken. Beukelman and Yorkston (1977) reported that although the rate of communication remained below the typical speaking rate, using this approach allowed the patient to interact socially and to convey immediate needs.

Crow and Enderby (1989) examined whether the use of the aided technique described by Beukelman and Yorkston changed the auditory characteristics of speech, and thereby improved speech intelligibility. They found that when the speakers used the alphabet chart to aid their speech, intelligibility increased, speech and rate decreased, and the articulatory accuracy improved as compared with habitual speech.

Bellaire, Yorkston, and Beukelman (1986) described the importance of analyzing a patient's use of breath groups. They indicate that a patient's speech may sound monotonous because the patient uses short, uniform breath groups. They indicate that to better understand the dimension of naturalness, it may be necessary to consider the breath group as a unit of prosody.

McHenry and Wilson (1994) examined several techniques used to improve the intelligibility of a patient following traumatic brain injury. They document the successful use of a pacing

board indicating that speaking rates dropped considerably and were less variable when the pacing board was used.

Other attempts have been made to improve prosody. Scott and Caird (1983) described 26 subjects, some who received treatment with visual feedback, and some who had no visual feedback during treatment. Both groups showed gains in prosody and intelligibility with some of the treatment effects being maintained. Johnson and Pring (1990) worked with six subjects and compared them to six other subjects who did not receive treatment. Treatment focused on the prosodic features of pitch and intensity with visual feedback. Their studies showed that treatment improved prosody on a rating scale and with objective measures.

Prosody (PR) Goal and Treatment Objectives

Short Term Goal: Patient will improve use of prosody to increase intelligibility and make speech sound more natural.

Treatment Objectives
Treatment objectives PR 1 - 10 are designed to help the patient reduce rate of speech to improve intelligibility.

PR 1: Patient will be able to discriminate fast rate from appropriate rate from tape recorded samples. (f)

PR 2: Patient will use the following metered pacing technique to slow rate when reading/imitating multi-syllabic words: pacing board/window card/tapping/one word per index card (Appendix C-1). (c, f)

PR 3: Patient will use the following metered pacing technique to slow rate when reading/imitating phrases/sentences: pacing board/window card/tapping/one word per index card/alphabet board (Appendices C-2 and E). (c, f)

PR 4: Patient will use the following metered pacing technique to slow rate when answering questions requiring phrase/sentence-level responses: pacing board/window card/tapping/one word per index card/alphabet board (Appendices D, E). (c, f)

PR 5: Patient will use the following metered pacing technique to slow rate of structured conversational speech: pacing board/window card/tapping/one word per index card/alphabet board (Appendices D, E). (c, f)

PR 6: Patient will reduce rate of speech using a rhythmic pacing technique when reading phrases/sentences (Appendix C-2). (c, f)

PR 7: Patient will reduce rate of speech using a rhythmic pacing technique when reading paragraph level material. (c, f)

PR 8: Patient will reduce rate by inserting pauses at pre-marked locations when reading phrases/sentences. (c, f)

PR 9: Patient will reduce rate by inserting pauses when answering questions requiring phrase/sentence level responses. (c, f)

PR 10: Patient will reduce rate by inserting pauses in conversational speech. (c, f)

Treatment objectives PR 11 - 16 are designed to help the patient increase use of stress to convey meaning and reduce perception of monotone.

PR 11: Patient will use increased pitch/loudness/timing to indicate stress when reading/imitating words/phrases/sentences when stressed syllable/word is marked (Appendices A-1, F-1, and F-2). (f)

PR 12: Patient will use increased pitch/loudness/timing to indicate stress when reading/imitating words/phrases/sentences when stressed word is not marked (Appendix A-2). (f)

PR 13: Patient will use increased pitch/loudness/timing to indicate stress when reading phrase/sentence answers to questions when stressed word is marked (Appendix A-1). (f)

PR 14: Patient will use increased pitch/loudness/timing to indicate stress when reading phrase/sentence answers to questions when stressed word is not marked (Appendix A-2). (f)

PR 15: Patient will use increased pitch/loudness/timing to indicate stress when reading unmarked paragraph level material. (c, f)

PR 16: Patient will use increased pitch/loudness/timing to indicate stress appropriately in conversation (Appendix D). (c, f)

Treatment objectives PR 17 - 22 are designed to help patients who use excess and equal stress reduce the perception of too much stress by helping them reduce stress on all but the target word.

PR 17: Patient will reduce pitch/loudness on all but the target syllable/word to eliminate the perception of excess and equal stress when reading/imitating phrases/sentences when stressed word is marked (Appendices A-1, F-1, and F-2). (f)

PR 18: Patient will reduce pitch/loudness on all but the target word to eliminate the perception of excess and equal stress when reading/imitating phrases/sentences when stressed word is not marked (Appendix A-2). (f)

PR 19: Patient will reduce pitch/loudness on all but the target word to eliminate the perception of excess and equal stress when reading phrase/sentence answers to questions when stressed word is marked (Appendix A-1). (f)

PR 20: Patient will reduce pitch/loudness on all but the target word to eliminate the perception of excess and equal stress when reading phrase/sentence answers to questions when stressed word is not marked (Appendix A-2). (f)

PR 21: Patient will reduce pitch/loudness on all but the target word(s) to eliminate the perception of excess and equal stress when reading unmarked paragraph level material. (c, f)

PR 22: Patient will reduce pitch/loudness on all but the target word(s) to eliminate the perception of excess and equal stress appropriately in conversation. (c, f)

Treatment objectives PR 23 - 32 are designed to help the patient improve use of intonation to help speech sound more natural.

PR 23: Patient will imitate word level intonations patterns (Appendix G). (f)

PR 24: Patient will read word level intonation patterns appropriately (Appendix G). (f)

PR 25: Patient will imitate sentence level declarative intonation patterns (Appendix B). (f)

PR 26: Patient will imitate interrogative falling inflection patterns (Appendix B). (f)

PR 27: Patient will imitate rising inflection interrogative patterns (Appendix B). (c, f)

PR 28: Patient will read sentence level declarative intonation patterns (Appendix B). (c, f)

PR 29: Patient will read interrogative falling inflection patterns (Appendix B). (c, f)

PR 30: Patient will read interrogative rising inflection patterns (Appendix B). (c, f)

PR 31: Patient will use appropriate intonational patterns when answering questions requiring phrases/sentence level responses (Appendices D and H). (c, f)

PR 32: Patient will use appropriate intonation in conversational speech. (c, f)

Treatment objectives PR 33 - 37 are designed to help the patient increase rate or modulate irregular rate of speech to help speech sound more natural.

PR 33: Patient will read multisyllabic words at the rate tapped out by the clinician (Appendix C-1). (c, f)

PR 34:   Patient will read phrase/sentence level material syllable by syllable at the rate tapped out by the clinician (Appendix C-2). (c, f)

PR 35:   Patient will be able to read in unison with a taped sample of phrase/sentence level material. (c, f)

PR 36:   Patient will be able to read in unison with a taped sample of paragraph level material. (c, f)

PR 37:   Patient will increase or modulate rate of speech in conversation. (c, f)

Treatment objectives PR 38 - 42 are designed for patients with right hemisphere aprosodic dysarthria who have a reduced ability to comprehend prosody. If you have a patient like this, you may need to address these objectives before PR objectives 11 - 16 and 23 - 32.

PR 38:   Patient will indicate which syllable or word the clinician stressed when listening to words/phrases/sentences (Appendices A-1, A-2, F-1, and F-2). (f)

PR 39:   Patient will indicate if clinician used pitch/loudness/timing to indicate stress on words/phrases/sentences (Appendices A-1, A-2, F-1, and F-2). (f)

PR 40:   Patient will indicate if clinician used appropriate word-level intonation pattern (Appendix G). (f)

PR 41:   Patient will indicate if clinician used appropriate intonation patterns to indicate happiness, sadness, or surprise (Appendix H). (f)

PR 42:   Patient will discriminate between interrogative rising and falling inflection produced by clinician (Appendix B). (f)

Environmental Modification (EM) Goal and Treatment Objectives

Short Term Goal: Speaker and listener will improve environment in which communication takes place.

Treatment Objectives:

EM 1:   Speaker will give context of message before beginning to communicate.

EM 2:   Listener will ask for clarification of context as needed.

EM 3:   Speaker and/or listener will eliminate or reduce background noise.

EM 4:   Speaker will gain visual attention of the listener before speaking.

EM 5:   Speaker or listener will make sure area in which communication is taking place is well lit.

EM 6:   Speaker and/or listener will make sure that they are sitting/standing close to one another and looking at each other before communication begins.

EM 7:   Speaker and/or listener will try to make sure that communication takes place in a room with dampened background noise.

EM 8:   Speaker will use external aid (pacing board, DAF, alphabet board) to slow rate to improve speech intelligibility and communication.

Treatment Techniques to Achieve Treatment Objectives

The following are brief descriptions of activities for improving phonation. Noted in () after the name of each activity is the treatment objective or objectives related to the activity.

Awareness of rate (PR 1)

Increase the patient's awareness of rate by using a tape recorder. Tape record a spontaneous speech sample or a reading sample during one session and play it back for the patient during the next session. That way, the patient won't remember what he said or read and it may become more apparent to him how difficult it is to understand his speech because of his rate.

For a patient with a fast rate, using an analogy of a motor act can help him understand the need to slow down his speech. Ask the patient if he thinks people who are learning to ice skate can do so quickly or slowly at first. Explain that if they skate slowly enough, their muscles can keep up with their actions, but if they try to skate too fast, they are generally going to fall. For a patient using too slow a rate, use the analogy of learning to ride a two-wheel bicycle. If the child goes too slowly, the bike tips over.

Another technique is to increase a patient's ability to discriminate appropriate rate from slow or fast rate as modeled by you. Demonstrate appropriate rate vs. fast or slow rate and ask the patient to indicate when he understands or fails to understand because of the rate.

Metered Pacing (PR 2 - 5)

A variety of pacing techniques can be used to help the patient learn to pace his speech in order to slow his rate. The patient first needs to understand the concept of syllables. Ask the patient to tap his finger for each syllable produced. It may take a while for patients to understand this concept. They'll often start a phrase by tapping each syllable and then tap once for the remaining syllables. You can present written phrases with the syllables marked if a patient is having difficulty (Appendices C-1, C-2).

If a patient is having a particularly hard time understanding the concept of syllables, have him work on tapping for each word produced. This technique reduces rate, but not as effectively as the syllable technique. Helm (1979) designed a pacing board that is a rigid piece of plastic with raised ridges. The patient slides his finger along the board and is forced to pause between syllables because he has to lift his finger over each ridge.

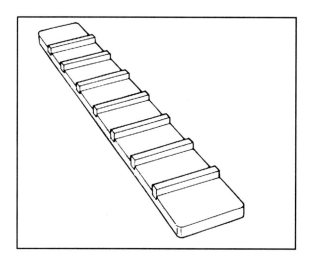

Beukelman and Yorkston (1977) modified this rate control/pacing technique by using an alphabet board. They describe this as alphabet board supplementation. They have the speaker point to the first letter of each spoken word on the alphabet board (Appendix E). Not only does this slow the rate, but it provides the listener with added information because the first letter of each word the patient is trying to say is pointed out.

Window cards can also be used to help control rate. A small window is cut in an index card. This card is then moved across a printed sentence so that only one word is revealed in the window at a time (Appendices C-1, C-2). You can also print each word from a sentence on individual cards and hand them to the patient one at a time to teach the concept of pacing.

Pacing can also be completed without the use of prosthetic devices. Patients can be taught to tap their finger or their hand on their leg or table. They may be able to generate this syllable-by-syllable tapping technique without having to carry along a pacing board or an alphabet board. It should be noted that some patients with Parkinson's disease tend to tap their hands faster and faster, eliminating any benefits from the technique.

Keep in mind that any of these rigid metered pacing techniques make the patient's speech sound very unnatural. Try to wean the patient from using these techniques if at all possible. Encourage the patient to concentrate on how speech feels when it is slower so they might carry over the technique without the use of external aids.

The Visi-Pitch® can be used to display rate. Have a patient say an utterance. Using the left and right cursor, determine how long it took the patient to say that utterance. Then clear the screen and move the right cursor farther to the right. Ask the patient to make the utterance last the distance between the cursors.

Rhythmic Cueing/Pacing (PR 6, 7)
Yorkston and Beukelman (1981) describe a technique they call rhythmic cueing. Rhythmic cueing uses written passages and the clinician points to each word in a rhythmic fashion. This means that the clinician stops at boundaries such as commas and periods and may give more time to words that should carry more meaning in the sentence. This rhythmic cueing approach has been computerized by B. V. Tice, 1988.

Duffy (1995) indicates that pacing may be more effective when it's metered (i.e., each syllable or word is given equal time, such as in the use of the pacing board and alphabet board or finger tapping) rather than rhythmic cueing where you try to approximate natural-sounding speech. Yorkston (1990) reported

that speakers with ataxic and hypokinetic dysarthria had more improvement in intelligibility using a metered technique.

Use of pauses (PR 8 - 10)
Use sentence or paragraph-level material and highlight the punctuation marks. Ask the patient to pause at these marks. Facilitate the pause by giving a visual signal such as holding up your hand when the patient reaches one of the natural pause marks. In a lengthy utterance, you may also want to insert another pause for the patient between syntactic boundaries. For example:

> The fans, // who were dressed in an assortment // of blue and white attire // of all sizes and shapes, // lined up outside the arena // to buy tickets for the basketball game.

Delayed Auditory Feedback (DAF) (EM 8)
DAF may be more well known in treating individuals who stutter. It uses instrumentation where the patient listens to her own speech through headphones after a delay which is set by the clinician.

Duffy (1995) suggests that DAF only be used when other rate control techniques fail. When using DAF, speech sounds very unnatural. It also doesn't work well with patients who speak in short utterances. Studies have found some success in using DAF for patients with hypokinetic dysarthria, but typically didn't find the patient able to wean from using the DAF (Adams, 1994; Hanson and Metter, 1995). Hanson and Metter suggest a delay of approximately 50 milliseconds, but they have used delays as great as 150 milliseconds. Patients with flaccid dysarthria reportedly do not benefit from DAF.

Stress (PR 11 — 15)
There are two basic types of stress: lexical and contrastive (or emphatic). Lexical stress is when we use stress on a different syllable to change the meaning of the word. Have the patient read (or imitate) the words and sentences (Appendices F-1, F-2) and use stress to change meaning.

Contrastive stress drills were probably first described by Fairbanks (1960). Short phrases and sentences are used and can change meaning if the stress on one word is changed to stress on another word (Appendices A-1, A-2). Have the patient read a phrase. Then ask the patient a question and have him say the phrase again to answer the question. Some patients will understand this concept quickly and easily, where others will be confused.

If the patient is unable to read, be sure to use short utterances so the patient can recite them from memory. Before having the patient attempt this activity, you might have the patient imitate your production of the phrases. It's not usually important if the patient achieves the change in stress by loudness, pitch, or duration. Normal speakers generally use pitch to change stress. Patients may need to be taught to use articulation time and pause time. Other patients seem to indicate stress by a loudness change.

Stress in conversation (PR 16)
Rosenbek and LaPointe (1985) discuss the importance of helping the patient generalize the use of stress into conversation. They describe what they call a pre-planning activity. They use biographical or high-interest stimuli (Appendix D) and ask the patient a question. After the patient answers the question, the clinician purposely mis-states the information so the patient has to repeat his answer to clarify. The patient is asked to pause and silently rehearse the answer before giving the corrected answer. Rosenbek and LaPointe ask the patient to wait until a signal is given before answering.

They then move into real dialogue where the patient uses appropriate stress.

Eliminating Excess and Equal Stress (PR 17 - 22)
Some patients, particularly those with ataxic dysarthria, use excess and equal stress. It's important to teach them how to reduce stress, maintaining the stress only on the appropriate syllable, word, etc. Show the patient how to reduce pitch/loudness to create the perception of no stress except on the word that should be stressed (Appendices A-1, A-2, F-1, F-2).

Intonation (PR 23 - 32)
Closely related to the inability to demonstrate stress is an overall flat intonation. Intonation is produced by a change in fundamental frequency and is therefore primarily controlled by pitch modulations.

Craig and Sikorski (1985) describe intonation at the word and sentence level. They describe eight basic word-level intonation patterns in English. They indicate that these patterns combine pitch and stress to create the intonation for a given word.

    I. one-syllable words with falling inflection
        eat
        go

    II. two-syllable words: stress on the second syllable, falling at the end
        balloon
        profound

    III. two-syllable words: stress on the first syllable, second syllable unstressed
        football
        crowded

    IV. three-syllable words with stress on the middle syllable
        dehydrate
        withdrawal

V. three-syllable words: stress on first syllable, secondary stress on third syllable

    butterscotch

    punctuate

VI. three-syllable words: stress on first syllable, no stress on other syllables

    lemonade

    actual

VII. three-syllable words: primary stress falling at the end of the third syllable

    overdrawn

    immature

VIII. four-syllable words with stress on third syllable

    transportation

    information

There are minimal differences between patterns V and VI, and most patients can't make the distinction, so they have been combined on Appendix G. Ask the patient to read the words and imitate the stress patterns. You can also ask a question that requires the patient to use the target word as an answer. For example, if the target word is *balloon*, you could ask "What is filled with helium?" or if the target word is *lemonade*, you could ask "What is made from lemons and is good to drink on a hot day?"

Sentence-level intonation patterns are sometimes subtle and hard for the patient to produce. The Visi-Pitch® is an excellent tool for providing the patient with a visual representation of intonation contours. If you don't have this type of instrumentation, draw an intonation curve on paper. Appendices B and H have sentence-level material for practice.

Increasing rate (PR 33 - 37)

Some types of dysarthria (flaccid, spastic, ataxic) cause patients to speak with too slow a rate. Try to increase the patient's rate if the rate is interfering with intelligibility or making speech sound unnatural. You must determine whether the rate can be modified without reducing intelligibility.

Dworkin (1991) uses a metronome and asks the patient to keep up with the beats per minute set on the metronome as he reads. Materials which are marked by syllables can be used with a metronome, having the patient speak each syllable to the beat of the metronome. You can also do this by tapping your hand on the table or holding the patient's hand as you tap to model a more appropriate rate. The goal is to increase the patient's rate somewhat, not to achieve a fast rate or even "normal" rate.

Tape record sentence or paragraph-level material. Give the patient a written copy of what you record. Have the patient read aloud and keep up with your taped model.

Improving comprehension of prosody (PR 38 - 42)

Patients who have suffered a right hemisphere cortical lesion may present with an aprosodic dysarthria. In addition to difficulty producing stress and intonation, they may have difficulty perceiving the differences. Read the materials from Appendices B and H to help patients learn to hear the differences.

Prosody Problems and Causes

What you hear	What could be causing the problem	SP	FL	FL Mya	V	VII	X PH	X S&R	X Sup	X III	Hypo	Hyper Trmr	Hyper Chorea	Dys & Ath	Mxd Sp/FL	Mxd Sp/At	Mxd hypo/Sp/At	UUMN	AT	AP
reduced stress or excess equal stress	increased tone	★															★			
	decreased tone														★	★			★	
	unpredictable/incoordinated movement												★						★	
monoloudness	decreased tone		★	★											★					
	increased tone	★																		
	decreased ROM										★									
	unpredictable movement													★						
slow rate	decreased strength				★	★									★					
	decreased tone																	★	★	
	incoordinated movement											★					★		★	
	decreased ROM	★																		
monotone or poor pitch control	weakness		★	★																
	decreased tone														★		★		★	
	decreased ROM										★									
	unpredictable/incoordinated movement											★		★						
	increased tone															★				★
prolonged intervals/variable rate	decreased respiration														★					
	decreased tone																		★	
	unpredictable movement													★						
increased rate/short rushes	decreased resp. support										★									

See Key on the following page.

Key

SP	Spastic dysarthria
FL	Flaccid dysarthria
FL Mya	Flaccid dysarthria - Mysathenia Gravis
V	Flaccid dysarthria - Trigeminal (Vth) Nerve Lesions
VII	Flaccid dysarthria - Facial (VIIth) Nerve Lesions
X PH	Flaccid dysarthria - Vagus (Xth) Nerve Lesions - Pharyngeal Branch Involvement
X S&R	Flaccid dysarthria - Vagus (Xth) Nerve Lesions - Superior and Recurrent Laryngeal Branch Involvement
X Sup	Flaccid dysarthria - Vagus (Xth) Nerve Lesions - Superior Laryngeal Branch Involvement
X Rec	Flaccid dysarthria - Vagus (Xth) Nerve Lesions - Recurrent Laryngeal Branch Involvement
Hypo	Flaccid dysarthria - Hypoglossal (XIIth) Nerve Lesions
Hyper Trmr	Hyperkinetic dysarthria - Tremor
Hyper Chorea	Hyperkinetic dysarthria - Chorea
Dys & Ath	Hyperkinetic dysarthria - Dystonia and Athetosis
Mxd SP/FL	Mixed dysarthria - Spastic and Flaccid
Mxd SP/AT	Mixed dysarthria - Spastic and Ataxic
Mxd Hypo/SP/AT	Mixed dysarthria - Progressive Supranuclear Palsy (Hypokinetic Spastic/Ataxic)
UUMN	Mixed dysarthria - Unilateral UMN
AT	Ataxic dysarthria
AP	Aprosodic dysarthria

By changing the word you stress in a sentence, you can change the meaning. First read the sentence normally. Then have someone ask you the question on the left. Read the answer again, but stress the bold word to change the meaning so you answer the question.

In Appendix A-2, there are several sentences without bold words. See if you can figure out which word to stress in each sentence.

You can also do this activity another way. Read one of your sentences, stressing the underlined word. Have whoever is helping you guess which word you are trying to stress.

(Note to SLP: You may want to copy only the right side of the page for the patient to read while you read from the book to avoid giving the patient extra cues.)

Clinician/Caregiver	**Client**
	I love a hot cup of coffee.
Do you love a <u>cold</u> cup of coffee?	I love a **hot** cup of coffee.
Do you love a hot cup of <u>tea</u>?	I love a hot cup of **coffee**.
Do you <u>hate</u> a hot cup of coffee?	I **love** a hot cup of coffee.
Do you love a hot <u>mug</u> of coffee?	I love a hot **cup** of coffee.
	Geri was late for the sales meeting Wednesday.
Was Geri <u>early</u> for the sales meeting Wednesday?	Geri was **late** for the sales meeting Wednesday.
Was Geri late for the sales meeting <u>Tuesday</u>?	Geri was late for the sales meeting **Wednesday**.
Was Geri late for the <u>marketing</u> meeting Wednesday?	Geri was late for the **sales** meeting Wednesday.
Was <u>Tom</u> late for the sales meeting Wednesday?	**Geri** was late for the sales meeting Wednesday.

Clinician/Caregiver	**Client**
	Sue wants spaghetti without tomato sauce.
Does <u>Mary</u> want spaghetti without tomato sauce?	**Sue** wants spaghetti without tomato sauce.
Does Sue want <u>rigatoni</u> without tomato sauce?	Sue wants **spaghetti** without tomato sauce.
Does Sue want spaghetti <u>with</u> tomato sauce?	Sue wants spaghetti **without** tomato sauce.
Does Sue want spaghetti without <u>mushrooms</u>?	Sue wants spaghetti without **tomato sauce**.
	His plane was late landing in Lexington.
Was <u>her</u> plane late landing in Lexington?	**His** plane was late landing in Lexington.
Was his plane <u>early</u> landing in Lexington?	His plane was **late** landing in Lexington.
Was his plane late <u>taking off</u> in Lexington?	His plane was late **landing** in Lexington.
Was his plane late landing in <u>Louisville</u>?	His plane was late landing in **Lexington**.
	Her family will visit on Sunday.
Will her family visit on <u>Monday</u>?	Her family will visit on **Sunday**.
Will her <u>friend</u> visit on Sunday?	Her **family** will visit on Sunday.
Will <u>his</u> family visit on Sunday?	**Her** family will visit on Sunday.
Will her family <u>call</u> on Sunday?	Her family will **visit** on Sunday.
	They cheer for the Kentucky Wildcats.
Do they cheer for the <u>Arizona</u> Wildcats?	They cheer for the **Kentucky** Wildcats.
Do they <u>boo</u> the Kentucky Wildcats?	They **cheer** for the Kentucky Wildcats.
Do they cheer for the Kentucky <u>Thoroughblades</u>?	They cheer for the Kentucky **Wildcats**.

Clinician/Caregiver

Client

The doctor ordered another test.

Did the <u>nurse</u> order another test?

The **doctor** ordered another test.

Did the doctor <u>ask</u> for another test?

The doctor **ordered** another test.

Did the doctor order another <u>x-ray</u>?

The doctor ordered another **test**.

The cat was in the window watching the birds.

Was the cat in the window watching the <u>dogs</u>?

The cat was in the window watching the **birds**.

Was the cat in the <u>doorway</u> watching the birds?

The cat was in the **window** watching the birds.

Was the cat in the window <u>listening</u> to the birds?

The cat was in the window **watching** the birds.

Was the <u>dog</u> in the window watching the birds?

The **cat** was in the window watching the birds.

The farmer planted corn and soybeans.

Did the farmer <u>harvest</u> corn and soybeans?

The farmer **planted** corn and soybeans.

Did the <u>plumber</u> plant corn and soybeans?

The **farmer** planted corn and soybeans.

Did the farmer plant corn and <u>wheat</u>?

The farmer planted corn and **soybeans**.

He baked a cake for Keith's birthday.

Did he <u>buy</u> a cake for Keith's birthday?

He **baked** a cake for Keith's birthday.

Did he bake a cake for <u>Jeff's</u> birthday?

He baked a cake for **Keith's** birthday.

Did he bake a <u>pie</u> for Keith's birthday?

He baked a **cake** for Keith's birthday.

Did he bake a cake for <u>Thanksgiving</u>?

He baked a cake for **Keith's birthday**.

Clinician/Caregiver	**Client**
	Dan and Dave helped us move.
Did Dan and <u>Jim</u> help you move?	Dan and **Dave** helped us move.
Did Dan and Dave <u>make</u> you move?	Dan and Dave **helped** us move.
Did Dan and Dave help you <u>pack</u>?	Dan and Dave helped us **move**.
	The nurse brought his pills and water.
Did the <u>doctor</u> bring his pills and water?	The **nurse** brought his pills and water.
Did the nurse <u>drop</u> his pills and water?	The nurse **brought** his pills and water.
Did the nurse bring his <u>breakfast</u> and water?	The nurse brought his **pills** and water.
Did the nurse bring his pills and <u>coffee</u>?	The nurse brought his pills and **water**.
	It is quiet at the lake in the morning.
Is it quiet at the <u>river</u> in the morning?	It is quiet at the **lake** in the morning.
Is it quiet at the lake in the <u>evening</u>?	It is quiet at the lake in the **morning**.
Is it <u>noisy</u> at the lake in the morning?	It is **quiet** at the lake in the morning.
	They planted an herb garden last year.
Did they plant an herb <u>forest</u> last year?	They planted an herb **garden** last year.
Did they plant a <u>vegetable</u> garden last year?	They planted an **herb** garden last year.
Did they plant an herb garden <u>this</u> year?	They planted an herb garden **last** year.
Did they <u>photograph</u> an herb garden last year?	They **planted** an herb garden last year.

Clinician/Caregiver	**Client**
	Michelle and Verity worked on Saturday.
Did <u>Barb</u> and Verity work on Saturday?	**Michelle** and Verity worked on Saturday.
Did Michelle and Verity <u>play</u> on Saturday?	Michelle and Verity **worked** on Saturday.
Did Michelle and Verity work on <u>Sunday</u>?	Michelle and Verity worked on **Saturday**.
	June visits her grandchildren each weekend.
Does June visit her <u>nieces</u> each weekend?	June visits her **grandchildren** each weekend.
Does June <u>call</u> her grandchildren each weekend?	June **visits** her grandchildren each weekend.
Does June visit her grandchildren each <u>Wednesday</u>?	June visits her grandchildren each **weekend**.
Does <u>Kim</u> visit her grandchildren each weekend?	**June** visits her grandchildren each weekend.
	Janice showed Karl how to write the report.
Did Janice <u>tell</u> Karl how to write the report?	Janice **showed** Karl how to write the report.
Did Janice show <u>Gary</u> how to write the report?	Janice showed **Karl** how to write the report.
Did Janice show Karl how to write the <u>letter</u>?	Janice showed Karl how to write the **report**.
Did Janice show Karl how to <u>type</u> the report?	Janice showed Karl how to **write** the report.

Clinician/Caregiver	**Client**
	The vet said Ginny could pick up her dog.
Did the <u>mail carrier</u> say Ginny could pick up her dog?	The **vet** said Ginny could pick up her dog.
Did the vet say <u>Trish</u> could pick up her dog?	The vet said **Ginny** could pick up her dog.
Did the vet say Ginny could <u>drop off</u> her dog?	The vet said Ginny could **pick up** her dog.
	Keri answered the phone with a cheery voice.
Did <u>Hannah</u> answer the phone with a cheery voice?	**Keri** answered the phone with a cheery voice.
Did Keri answer the <u>door</u> with a cheery voice?	Keri answered the **phone** with a cheery voice.
Did Keri answer the phone with a <u>grumpy</u> voice?	Keri answered the phone with a **cheery** voice.
	Brenna's car broke down on Main Street.
Did Brenna's <u>truck</u> break down on Main Street?	Brenna's **car** broke down on Main Street.
Did <u>Lissa's</u> car break down on Main Street?	**Brenna's** car broke down on Main Street.
Did Brenna's car <u>get hit</u> on Main Street?	Brenna's car **broke down** on Main Street.
Did Brenna's car break down on <u>Walnut</u> Street?	Brenna's car broke down on **Main** Street.

(Note to SLP: The remaining sentences are not marked for stress. The patient has to decide where to put the stress to answer your questions. Copy only the right side of each page for the patient. That way, the patient can't get visual cues from seeing the underlined words in your questions.)

Clinician/Caregiver	Client
	Laurie told Tammy she would send the package.
Did Laurie tell <u>Jane</u> she would send the package?	Laurie told Tammy she would send the package.
Did Laurie tell Tammy she would <u>pick up</u> the package?	Laurie told Tammy she would send the package.
Did Laurie tell Tammy she would send the <u>letter</u>?	Laurie told Tammy she would send the package.
	Gina has two jobs after school.
Does Gina have <u>three</u> jobs after school?	Gina has two jobs after school.
Does Gina have two jobs <u>before</u> school?	Gina has two jobs after school.
Does <u>Adam</u> have two jobs after school?	Gina has two jobs after school.
	Sarah moved to Indiana in the spring.
Did Sarah move to <u>Kentucky</u> in the spring?	Sarah moved to Indiana in the spring.
Did Sarah <u>vacation in</u> Indiana in the spring?	Sarah moved to Indiana in the spring.
Did Sarah move to Indiana in the <u>fall</u>?	Sarah moved to Indiana in the spring.

Clinician/Caregiver	**Client**
	Their new home in Tampa has a pool.
Does their new <u>apartment</u> in Tampa have a pool?	Their new home in Tampa has a pool.
Does their new home in <u>Orlando</u> have a pool?	Their new home in Tampa has a pool.
Does their new home in Tampa have a <u>patio</u>?	Their new home in Tampa has a pool.
	She found Grover standing in the road.
Did <u>he</u> find Grover standing in the road?	She found Grover standing in the road.
Did she <u>lose</u> Grover standing in the road?	She found Grover standing in the road.
Did she find <u>Serena</u> standing in the road?	She found Grover standing in the road.
Did she find Grover standing in the <u>field</u>?	She found Grover standing in the road.
	Clarissa took her father to the store this morning.
Did Clarissa take her <u>mother</u> to the store this morning?	Clarissa took her father to the store this morning.
Did Clarissa <u>drive</u> her father to the store this morning?	Clarissa took her father to the store this morning.
Did Clarissa take her father to the <u>bank</u> this morning?	Clarissa took her father to the store this morning.
Did Clarissa take her father to the store <u>last night</u>?	Clarissa took her father to the store this morning.
	Alexander's gray cat was very sly.
Was Alexander's <u>white</u> cat very sly?	Alexander's gray cat was very sly.
Was Alexander's gray <u>dog</u> very sly?	Alexander's gray cat was very sly.
Was Alexander's gray cat very <u>smart</u>?	Alexander's gray cat was very sly.

218

Clinician/Caregiver	**Client**
	She turned the wallet in to Lost and Found.
Did she turn the <u>purse</u> in to Lost and Found?	She turned the wallet in to Lost and Found.
Did <u>he</u> turn the wallet in to Lost and Found?	She turned the wallet in to Lost and Found.
Did she turn the wallet in to the <u>police</u>?	She turned the wallet in to Lost and Found.
	Doris reads the paper every morning.
Does Doris <u>deliver</u> the paper every morning?	Doris reads the paper every morning.
Does Doris read a <u>magazine</u> every morning?	Doris reads the paper every morning.
Does Doris read the paper every <u>evening</u>?	Doris reads the paper every morning.
	Mandy was walking down the driveway.
Was Mandy walking <u>up</u> the driveway?	Mandy was walking down the driveway.
Was Mandy walking down the <u>sidewalk</u>?	Mandy was walking down the <u>driveway</u>.
Was <u>Cassidy</u> walking down the driveway?	Mandy was walking down the driveway.
	They studied Macbeth in college.
Did they <u>read</u> Macbeth in college?	They studied Macbeth in college.
Did the study <u>Hamlet</u> in college?	They studied Macbeth in college.
Did they study Macbeth in <u>high</u> school?	They studied Macbeth in college.

Most declarative sentences fall in pitch at the end. Sometimes we use a sentence in a questioning way. If so, the voice goes up slightly at the end.

Read a sentence and let your voice fall at the end. Then read it again and make it sound like you're asking a question by making your voice go up at the end.

Lucy wants to go.
The play was wonderful.
Alice climbed to the top.
Drew picked up the book.
Arly answered the phone.
Give Aaron the shoe.
Bailey laughed at the joke.
Our appointment is tomorrow.
It was a beautiful day.
We sat near the front.

He went to work.
We don't have any.
The doctor released him.
Please pass the potatoes.
They took a walk.
They went on vacation.
They drove by the school.
It's a beautiful day.
The cat sat in the sun.
Michael moved to the city.

Interrogatives (questions) can have the voice rise at the end of the question or fall at the end of the question. Read the following questions and make sure your voice falls at the end.

Where did you park the car?
What time did you get here?
What time is the game?
When will the doctor be here?
How do you know my name?
How much will it cost?
Where do you live?
How long have you been here?
Why was he so late?
Which dessert is the best?

Why didn't he call?
Which one fits the best?
Where does he work?
How long will it take?
How long is that boat?
Where did you buy your car?
What was the final score?
What is his daughter's name?
Where did he take you?
What time did she get here?

Read the following questions. Make your voice go up at the end.

Is the camera broken?
Is lunch ready?
Is it time to go now?
Have the cats been fed?
Did you walk the dog?
Is the restaurant open?
Do you have a quarter?
Do you like broccoli?
Are you going to the meeting?
Did they go to the movie?

Was the teacher mad?
Did anyone see him?
Is the door unlocked?
Do you go to work at eight?
Have you been waiting long?
Were the children on the porch?
Was anyone in front of you?
Is the movie over now?
Do you have any animals?
Did he have surgery?

Use one of the word lists to practice slowing your rate by carefully pronouncing each syllable as you say it. You can try tapping on the pacing board as you say each syllable or use a window card, moving the card along so that only one syllable shows in the window at a time. These lists are divided into three-, four-, and five-syllable words.

(Note to SLP: A word is not always divided at the actual syllable break, but where it should facilitate pronunciation pauses between syllables.)

Three-Syllable Words   Syllables

chewing gum	chew	ing	gum
fingernail	fing	er	nail
kangaroo	kan	ga	roo
illegal	il	le	gal
magazine	ma	ga	zine
marigold	mar	i	gold
regular	re	gu	lar
spaghetti	spa	ghet	ti
Thanksgiving	Thanks	giv	ing
carefully	care	ful	ly
waterfall	wa	ter	fall
autograph	au	to	graph
umbrella	um	bre	lla
difficult	dif	fi	cult
factory	fac	to	ry
family	fam	i	ly
fingerprint	fing	er	print
furniture	fur	ni	ture
physician	phy	si	cian
sandpaper	sand	pa	per
wonderful	won	der	ful
thunderstorm	thun	der	storm
chicken pox	chick	en	pox

Three-Syllable Words   Syllables

syllable	syl	la	ble
portable	por	ta	ble
October	Oc	to	ber
cucumber	cu	cum	ber
silverware	sil	ver	ware
radio	ra	di	o
rearrange	re	a	rrange
relative	rel	a	tive
rubber band	ru	bber	band
anyplace	an	y	place
recommend	re	com	mend
natural	na	tur	al
nursery	nur	se	ry
needlepoint	nee	dle	point
accomplish	a	ccom	plish
Kentucky	Ken	tuck	y

Four-Syllable Words   Syllables

companionship	com	pan	ion	ship
unimportant	un	im	por	tant
accidental	ac	ci	den	tal
fundamental	fun	da	men	tal
legislation	le	gis	la	tion
amplifier	am	pli	fi	er
exploration	ex	plor	a	tion
unemployment	un	em	ploy	ment
additional	a	ddi	tion	al
emotional	e	mo	tion	al
acceptable	ac	cep	ta	ble
convertible	con	ver	ti	ble
dependable	de	pen	da	ble
questionable	ques	tion	a	ble
life preserver	life	pre	ser	ver
librarian	li	bra	ri	an
locomotive	lo	co	mo	tive
arithmetic	a	rith	me	tic
magazine rack	ma	ga	zine	rack
Colorado	Co	lo	ra	do
kindergarten	kin	der	gar	ten
combination	com	bi	na	tion
coincidence	co	in	ci	dence
congratulate	con	gra	tu	late
emergency	e	mer	gen	cy
neurology	neu	ro	lo	gy
generation	gen	er	a	tion

Four-Syllable Words   Syllables

harmonica	har	mon	i	ca
helicopter	hel	i	cop	ter
agriculture	a	gri	cul	ture
geography	ge	o	gra	phy
coffee grinder	co	ffee	grin	der
disorganzed	dis	or	ga	nized
forgettable	for	gett	a	ble
graduation	gra	du	a	tion
grandfather clock	grand	fa	ther	clock
alligator	al	li	ga	tor
significant	sig	ni	fi	cant
infrequently	in	fre	quent	ly
refrigerate	re	frig	er	ate

The Source for Dysarthria   224

Five-Syllable Words

Syllables

disagreeable	dis	a	gree	a	ble
unapproachable	un	a	pproach	a	ble
vegetarian	ve	ge	tar	i	an
unavoidable	un	a	void	a	ble
refrigeration	re	fri	ger	a	tion
hospitality	hos	pi	ta	li	ty
Special Olympics	Spe	cial	O	lym	pics
appreciation	a	ppre	ci	a	tion
precipitation	pre	ci	pi	ta	tion
pronunciation	pro	nun	ci	a	tion
contemporary	con	tem	por	a	ry
appendectomy	a	ppen	dec	to	my
opportunity	o	ppor	tu	ni	ty
unpopulated	un	po	pu	la	ted
metropolitan	me	tro	pol	i	tan
opinionated	o	pin	ion	a	ted
hippopotamus	hi	ppo	pot	a	mus
developmental	de	vel	op	men	tal
manufacturing	man	u	fac	tur	ing
administration	ad	min	i	stra	tion
condominium	con	do	min	i	um
immediately	i	mmed	i	ate	ly
simultaneous	si	mul	tan	e	ous
unanimously	u	nan	i	mous	ly
Louisiana	Lou	i	si	an	a
coincidental	co	in	ci	den	tal
congratulations	con	gra	tu	la	tions

These phrases and sentences are marked by syllables. Tap each syllable as you say it. You can try tapping on the pacing board as you say each syllable or use a window card, moving the card along so that only one syllable shows in the window at a time.

A	bag	full	of	can	dy.	
When	did	it	be	gin?		
He	was	dig	ging	a	hole.	
Did	you	re	cog	nize	him?	
We	saw	the	kan	ga	roo.	
a	pack	of	chew	ing	gum	
Chil	dren	love	fin	ger	paints.	
We	went	there	on	Thanks	giv	ing.
He	read	Moth	er	Goose	to	her.
We	sub	scribe	to	ma	ga	zines.
An	ti	freeze	is	dan	ger	ous.
He	wears	flan	nel	shirts.		
I	have	had	e	nough	of	that.
That	is	ver	y	di	fi	cult.
An	swer	the	te	le	phone.	
a	so	lid	foun	da	tion	
ex	cel	lent	pho	to	graph	er
I	have	found	a	few	pen	nies.
a	bowl	of	hot	cer	e	al
They	are	the	un	der	dogs.	
com	for	ta	ble	shoes		
Op	por	tu	ni	ty	knocks.	
Grey	hounds	are	gen	tle		
Have	a	hap	py	New	Year.	
Don't	o	ver	sleep	to	mor	row.
Help	me	raise	the	win	dow.	

He	lives	in	Al	a	ba	ma.
She	has	a	fa	mil	iar	face.
That's	a	mis	lea	ding	state	ment.
The	grand	kids	brought	sleep	ing	bags.
Cleve	land	is	cold	in	win	ter.
She	teach	es	a	rith	me	tic.
a	sta	ble	e	con	o	my
Get	an	ed	u	ca	tion.	
The	he	li	cop	ter	land	ed.
Don't	con	fuse	the	i	ssue.	
The	ma	jor	i	ty	rules.	
I	im	a	gine	you	are	tired.
Do	you	have	an	ob	jec	tion?
Home	made	cook	ies	are	the	best.
Ex	tin	guish	the	fi	re	now!
Please	au	to	graph	your	pic	ture.
I	need	some	in	for	ma	tion.
That	is	not	my	sig	na	ture.
He	has	the	chick	en	pox.	
What	time	is	the	in	ter	view?
He's	a	veg	e	tar	i	an.
cin	na	mon	rolls	for	break	fast
pea	nut	bu	tter	and	jell	y

Ask the patient the following questions. After the patient answers, purposefully misstate the information back to the patient. Tell the patient to use stress to clarify her answer. For example, if you ask "Where were you born?" and the patient states "I was born in Frankfort," you then state "So you were born in Georgetown." Patient should repeat "No, I was born in **Frankfort**." Choose questions based on the patient's age, living status, interests, etc.

Personal/Biographical Questions

Where were you born?
What is your address?
How many children do you have?
Where did/do you work?
What did/do you like about your job?
How tall are you?
How far did you go in school?
What are the names of your children?
Tell me someplace you've been on vacation.
What do you like to watch on TV?
What do you eat for breakfast?
What kind of car do you drive?
Where do you get your car fixed?
What is your doctor's name?
Where is your doctor's office?
What do you do in your spare time?
How many grandchildren do you have?
What is your wife/husband/partner's name?
Where else have you ever lived?

Miscellaneous Questions

What's the weather usually like in Florida?
Why do children go to school?
Why do we pay taxes?
Where do people keep their money?
What do you do with scissors?
Why do we need refrigerators?
Why do cats purr?
When do you use an umbrella?
Where can you borrow books?
Who was Elvis Presley?
What is the weather like today?
Who is the President?
Who is the Governor of this state?

Alphabet Board for Alternative/Augmentative Communication

A	B	C	D	E	REPEAT
F	G	H	I	J	START AGAIN
K	L	M	N	O	END OF WORD
P	Q	R	S	T	END OF SENTENCE
U	V	W	X	Y	Z

1 2 3
4 5 6
7 8 9 0

From Yorkston, K. M., Beukelman, D., and Bell, K. *Clinical Management of Dysarthric Speakers*. San Diego: College Hill Press, 1988.

There are words in the English language which are spelled the same, but pronounced differently. The meaning changes when the pronunciation changes.

On the list below, the word is first listed as a noun or adjective. The stress should occur on the first syllable. The word is then listed as a verb and the stress should occur on the second syllable. A sentence is provided for each word. Read each word and its accompanying sentence.

address	What is his new address?
address	Please address the envelope for me.
baby-sit	She will baby-sit for extra money.
baby sit	Can that baby sit by himself?
blowout	A blowout caused the accident.
blow out	Blow out the candles on the cake.
conduct	The teacher says he has poor conduct.
conduct	He will conduct the orchestra.
content	What is the content of the book?
content	I am content to sit on the porch.
contrast	This picture has poor contrast.
contrast	Can you compare and contrast those ideas?
convert	She is a convert to this religion.
convert	Can you convert this fraction to a decimal?
convict	The convict wore an orange uniform.
convict	The jury did not convict him.
countdown	The countdown stopped at 18.
count down	Count down from 20 to 1.
defect	There is a major defect in this product.
defect	The ballerina wants to defect to America.
digest	She likes to read Reader's Digest.
digest	Give me time to digest my dinner.
discharge	She received an honorable discharge.
discharge	I had to discharge her.
extract	The cookies contain vanilla extract.
extract	Try to extract the splinter from my finger.

knockout	He won by a knockout.
knock out	Help me knock out the wall.
lookout	We climbed to the top of the lookout.
look out	Look out for falling rocks.
object	What is the object of this game?
object	The lawyer will object to that.
overlook	We stopped at the scenic overlook.
overlook	Don't overlook the details.
permit	You need a permit to build an addition.
permit	Will you permit me to help?
present	She received only one present on her birthday.
present	I have to present the idea to the boss.
produce	This grocery has fresh produce.
produce	He could not produce the evidence.
project	I am finishing the project.
project	Project the movie on the screen.
rebel	James Dean was a rebel without a cause.
rebel	The students will rebel at that new rule.
record	He still holds the record for the best time.
record	They will tape record the meeting.
setup	This seems like a setup to me.
set up	They set up the room for a banquet.
subject	Who is the subject of the investigation?
subject	I hate to subject you to more testing.
survey	They will conduct a survey.
survey	He is going to survey the property.
touchdown	He scored the winning touchdown.
touch down	The space station will touch down on the moon.

The English language contains some words which are compound nouns. They are similar to words that are spelled alike but mean something different when pronounced differently. These compound nouns can be split into two words where they turn into an adjective plus a noun (i.e., chalkboard versus chalk board).

Compound nouns should be stressed on the first syllable. An adjective plus a noun should have the stress on the second word. Use stress to make these sound different.

barefoot	I like to go barefoot.
bare foot	I put my bare foot in the water.
bluebook	What is the bluebook value?
blue book	I left my blue book at school.
bullfight	A bullfight is barbaric.
bull fight	Did that bull fight?
crossword	I like to work crossword puzzles.
cross word	He never says a cross word.
darkroom	The photographer is in the darkroom.
dark room	I like to sleep in a dark room.
greenhouse	He grows flowers in the greenhouse.
green house	He lives in the green house.
hardball	Are they playing softball or hardball?
hard ball	A bowling ball is a very hard ball.
hot plate	She kept it warm on a hot plate.
hot plate	Don't touch this. It's a hot plate.
ladybug	The ladybug landed on the flower.
lady bug	Don't let that lady bug you.
Lifesaver®	I would like a cherry Lifesaver®.
life saver	Your help is a real life saver.
shortstop	His position is shortstop.
short stop	I have to make a short stop at the post office.
supermarket	We shop at the local supermarket.
super market	That's a super market you took us to.
White House	The President lives in the White House.
white house	There is a white house on the corner.

There are eight basic ways to pronounce English words. There are other intonation patterns, particularly for four-syllable words. However, these are the main patterns and they will give you practice changing your intonation.

Pattern I: one-syllable words with your voice falling at the end of the word

shack	tape	grief	leash
shape	meet	grape	lunch
she	skate	march	job
shelf	state	meal	Jill
shine	vote	mean	jam
tag	wrote	milk	
take	grab	mall	
talk	group	lake	

Pattern II: two-syllable words with the stress on the second syllable (voice falls a little at the end)

garage	confirm	expand	afford
good-bye	amend	intend	award
affair	command	offend	
before	defend	aboard	

Pattern III: two-syllable words with the stress on the first syllable

gallon	flashlight	handful	furnace
going	flagpole	finish	fever
garden	breakfast	fireplace	

Pattern IV: three-syllable words with the stress in the middle

denial	detective	November	banana
department	duration	begonia	bandana
deposit	December	Kentucky	fanatic

Pattern V: major stress on the first syllable and secondary stress on the last syllable

Pattern VI: major stress on the first syllable and no stress on the other syllables

(These sound almost alike and have been combined.)

federal	daffodil	diagram	basketball
Canada	decorate	dinosaur	cucumber
medicine	dedicate	broccoli	president

Pattern VII: three-syllable words with no stress on the first two syllables and falling stress on the last syllable

absentee	overthrow	souvenir	interfere
afternoon	guarantee	submarine	volunteer
referee	introduce	intersect	
disappoint	understand	entertain	
disappear	overlook	intercept	

Pattern VIII: four-syllable words with the stress on the third syllable

Colorado	superficial	accidental
ballerina	disappearance	continental
revolution	independence	horizontal
operation	Cinderella	regulation

234

Each of the following sentences can carry a different meaning depending upon the intonation pattern you use. Read each sentence three times. First read it to make it sound as if you are happy, then as if you are sad, and then as if you are surprised.

Don and Emily got married.

Juanita is the winner.

Tiffany found a dollar.

Jamie caught it.

His team lost.

Sadie got the prize.

Terry won the award.

The book is scary.

Linda got the job.

Felicia bought the car.

Keith dropped it.

Terry cut down the tree.

Amanda brought home another cat.

Randy lost the keys.

Dianna won the contest.

Jimmy bought the house.

Leslye was accepted.

Lynn got promoted.

Casey ordered dessert.

Andy pushed him.

Examples of Documentation

Daily

Patient: P.J.

S: Patient states she has been practicing using a pause to indicate stress when answering questions from staff.

O: Patient seen for training and instruction in use of compensatory techniques to improve the ability to convey stress. Patient able to answer questions requiring a phrase response indicating stress by using a pause before the stressed word on 80% of attempts without cues. When asked to add increased pitch to indicate stress on these same responses, patient was able to do so on 50% of the attempts. Patient needs cues to combine the use of pitch and pause 50% of the time. Sample of conversational speech reveals patient is beginning to use pause time occasionally to indicate stress, but mostly on short responses.

A: Patient doing well with use of pause in structured situations, and is even beginning to use it a bit in conversational level speech. Patient responds to visual cues provided to add increased pitch to convey stress.

P: Continue with activities per plan to increase use of markers for stress.

Weekly

Patient: M.B.

Dates and units of treatment (15-minute sessions)

Monday	11/2	2 units
Tuesday	11/3	2 units
Wednesday	11/4	2 units
Thursday	11/5	patient not seen: ill
Friday	11/6	2 units

S: Patient seen for therapeutic intervention to address decreased intelligibility. He was ill on Thursday and could not be seen.

O: Patient seen for facilitation techniques to improve function of lips and tongue to increase strength of articulators.

        AR 20   At the beginning of the week, training and instruction provided on elevating tongue tip against tongue blade. Patient was able to do so for only three consecutive trials before fatigue greatly reduced the amount of strength patient could exert. By the end of the week, patient was completing 8 repetitions without a break.

AR 23   Patient had worked on this treatment objective last week, and was able to maintain lip closure against resistance on 3 of 10 trials at that time. Patient now able to maintain lip closure 7 of 10 trials.

AR 42, 43   Patient is able to complete these activities independently so they no longer need to be addressed in treatment. He can continue to practice on his own.

Patient is also seen for training and instruction in compensatory techniques to improve intelligibility of his speech.

AR 48   Patient is required to imitate phrase and sentence level stimuli with over-articulation. His performance is analyzed and he is given cues to increase oral movements during this activity. He is 75% accurate at phrase level and 60% at sentence level. These levels of accuracy increase to 85% and 70% respectively when patient looks in the mirror.

A: Analysis of patient's performance reveals he is showing greater strength in both the tongue and lips which will help increase precision of articulation of tongue and lip sounds. He is requiring fewer cues to over-articulate, but can only do this in imitation.

P: Continue with therapeutic intervention to increase strength of articulators and use of compensatory techniques. Introduce tape recorder during intelligibility exercises to help patient evaluate his performance.

Weekly with Percentages Only

Patient: I.J.

Dates seen and units
       04/08   (2, 2)
       04/09   (2, 2)
       04/10   (1, 0)
       04/11   (2, 2)
       04/12   (2, 2)

S: Patient indicates on letter board that she has been using the board to augment speech attempts with staff.

O: Patient seen for speech therapy b.i.d. for severely decreased intelligibility. She was seen only once on 04/10, and then for a short session as she was ill. Provided training and instruction in use of compensatory techniques needed to improve comprehension of her messages by staff and family. Also provided treatment with facilitation techniques to improve phonatory productions.

PH 1	80% for 8 seconds
PH 5	90%
PH 6	80%
PH 15	70% on short phrases
PR 4	70% on sentence level answers

A: Patient doing well with increasing phonatory effort during speech attempts. Beginning to see some carryover into spontaneous speech attempts with staff noting Ms. J is talking a little louder. The use of the alphabet board has been helpful in slowing her rate, and also provides staff and family with added cues about her message.

P: Continue per plan with facilitation of phonation and with compensatory techniques to improve intelligibility. Add treatment objective PR 5, using alphabet board in conversation.

Monthly

Patient: K.S.

During the past month of therapy, training and instruction were provided to increase strength, range of motion, and coordination of tongue and lip movements for more precise articulation of consonants. During these sessions, the patient's responses to treatment were analyzed and patient responded to suggestions to change his performance. Feedback was given regarding perceived strength of all movements. Patient is now completing all exercises independently except strength exercises, and his wife practices these with him.

We have focused our efforts on reducing hypernasality and improving articulation of specific phonemes. Patient has made significant progress on resonance treatment objectives (RSN 3, 4, 9, 11 and 12). He still needs cues to use exaggerated mouth opening, but is using increased loudness without cues.

At the beginning of the month, the patient was not intelligible beyond two-word phrases, and then only when the context was known. Now he can use the compensatory techniques and make himself known to staff with phrase-level responses.

Treatment has also focused on improved production of alveolar sounds at the phrase level (AR 46) and is producing /t, d, l/ with 70% accuracy in all positions when reading sentences. This is an increase from 50% accuracy on short phrases last month.

Patient will need continued treatment to transfer the use of compensatory strategies to reduce nasality into conversational level speech and to continue to improve production of specific phonemes.

Sample Progress Report/Re-certification

Patient R.J.

Physician

Facility Happy Hills SNF

Date of evaluation 07-02-97   Date of report 08-02-97

Date of last re-certification n/a

Medical Diagnosis S/P CVA — bilateral brain stem

Communicative Disorder Diagnosis moderate flaccid dysarthria

Functional Problems	Functional Communication Measure*	
	Initial Level	Current Level
speech production disorder	4	5
ability to swallow function		
comprehension of spoken language		
production of spoken language		
comprehension of written language		
production of written language		
cognitive communication		
other: voice	4	4

Treatment Objectives

RSP 2: Patient will use diaphragmatic breathing and prolong phonation of a vowel sound for 10 seconds. (f)

RSP 4: Patient will produce a vowel sound while pulling and maintain that phonation for 10 seconds. (f)

RSP 13: Patient will respond to verbal/visual cues to "let the air out slowly" when imitating a phrase-level utterance. (c)

Progress

Patient initially able to use diaphragmatic breathing and prolong /a/ 3 seconds. Can now prolong /a/ for 6 seconds.

Patient initially could prolong /a/ when pulling for only 2 seconds; has increased this to 7 seconds.

Patient initially able to "let air out slowly" when imitating phrase 20% of trials as compared to 70% currently.

PH 1:   Patient will complete breath hold and maintain pressure for 10 seconds. (f)

Patient can complete breath hold and maintain for 10 seconds, improved from initial attempts of 4 seconds caused by air wastage at vocal cords.

PH 5:   Patient will produce /a/ while pulling to increase resistance. (f)

Similar to treatment objective RSP 4, this treatment objective is also designed to increase valving. Patient can produce /a/ for 7 seconds with no breathiness heard.

PH 7:   Patient will produce continuous tone from bottom of pitch range to top of range. (f)

Patient can produce continuous tone on 60% of trials, though only 4 distinct pitches are heard. Initially patient could only produce 2 pitches on 50% of trials.

AR 17:   Patient will protrude tongue tip against tongue blade 9/10 trials. (f)

improved from 50% to 75%

AR 20:   Patient will elevate tongue tip against resistance 9/10 trials. (f)

improved from 40% to 65%

AR 21:   Patient will elevate tongue blade against resistance 9/10 trials. (f)

improved from 70% to 85%

AR 39:   Patient will maintain jaw opening and elevate tongue tip to alveolar ridge and to floor of mouth behind anterior/lower incisors 9/10 trials without a model. (f)

improved from 25% to 60%

AR 45:   Patient will produce the phonemes /t, d, s, l/ in words with indicated levels of accuracy; baseline scores in. (f)

/t/ now 70% all positions (50%)
/d/ now 70% initial and medial (60%)
/s/ now 75% all positions singletons (60%)
/l/ now 80% initial (60%)

EM 3:   Speaker and/or listener will eliminate or reduce background noise.

Patient now requesting visitors to turn off TV and close door to room approximately 80% of interactions. Initially, patient tried to talk over all background noise.

EM 6:   Speaker and/or listener will make sure that they are sitting/standing close to one another and looking at each other before communication begins.

Patient and wife always make sure they are seated near one another before patient begins speaking.

Narrative Interpretation: (relationship to long-term and short-term goals)   During the first month of
therapy, patient has made significant gains to improve strength of muscles for respiration and phonation. Paired with his
use of environmental modifications to decrease background noise, he is now able to be heard at about 3' when there is no
transient noise. He is also making significant progress in improving articulation of specific error sounds up to the word
level. He is not yet intelligible to strangers, but his wife is now understanding about 90% of what he says on the first try.
Initially she frequently had to ask for repetitions which frustrated the patient.

Positive Expectation to Continue: Patient is very motivated in therapy and his wife often plans her visits so
she can participate. He has already improved intelligibility and shows good prognosis for continued change.

Need for Continued Skilled Services: Without continued skilled intervention, patient will not be understood
by staff.

Change in Treatment Plan: (Goals/Frequency)   Reduced from b.i.d. to q.d. treatment since the wife can now take
over the muscle-strengthening exercises.

_____   _____   _____
         Speech-Language Pathologist   License #   Date

I certify the above patient requires therapy services, is under a plan of care established or reviewed
every 30 days by me, and requires the above treatment specified on a continuing basis with the following changes:

Physician Notice: (Circle one)   I do / do not find it necessary to see this patient within the next 30 days.

_____   _____
                Physician   Date

ASHA Functional Communication Measure for Speech Production	
Level 0	unable to test
Level 1	Production of speech is unintelligible.
Level 2	Spontaneous production of speech is limited in intelligibility; some automatic speech and imitative words or consonant/vowel (CV) combinations may be intelligible.
Level 3	Spontaneous production of speech consists primarily of automatic words or phrases with inconsistent intelligibility.
Level 4	Spontaneous production of speech is intelligible at the phrase level in familiar contexts; out of context speech is generally unintelligible unless self-cueing and self-monitoring strategies are applied.
Level 5	Spontaneous production of speech is intelligible for meeting daily living needs; out of context speech requires periodic repetition, rephrasing, or provision of a cue.
Level 6	Spontaneous production of speech is intelligible in and out of context, but the production is sometimes distorted.
Level 7	Production of speech is normal in all situations.

Sample Discharge Report

Patient __R.J.__		Physician __D.S. Arthria__
Date of Discharge __11-02-97__ Birthdate __01-09-28__		Date of Initial Evaluation __07-02-97__
Facility __Serenity Hills SNF__		Duration of Therapy __16 weeks__

Progress in Therapy/Goals Met: Patient has met all goals established. He can be understood by staff and family in conversation and is loud enough to be heard with background noise.

Goals Not Met: _____

Reason for Discharge/Patient's Current Status: Patient's speech is intelligible and fairly natural sounding. He remains mildly hypernasal (not addressed in therapy). Prosody improved as phonation improved.

Follow-Up Recommendations: If patient's condition should change, he will require a re-evaluation by a speech-language pathologist, but it is not suspected at this point.

_____   _____   _____
Speech-Language Pathologist   License #   Date

_____   _____
Physician   Date

Glossary

anarthric	inability to produce speech
aneurysm (cerebral)	a ballooning or dilation of a thin-walled section or sections of a cerebral artery. Aneurysms are usually situated on major arteries, particularly at branching points.
anticholinergic	these drugs reduce Parkinson's symptoms by blocking acetylcholine receptors
antipsychotic drugs	neuroleptic drugs for the treatment of psychosis. Common drugs include Thorazine® (chlorpromazine), Mellaril® (thioridazine), Haldol® (haloperidol), and Clozaril® (clozapine). These can lead to a variety of extrapyramidal symptoms.
arteriovenous malformation (AVM)	congenital malformations that allow communication between an artery and vein. These AVMs have a tendency to bleed.
ataxia	defect of posture and gait characterized by incoordination (must occur in the absence of apraxia, paresis, rigidity, spasticity or involuntary movement)
athetosis	a form of hyperkinesia involving repetitive, involuntary, slow gross movements. It usually involves the extremities as well as the face and trunk.
auto-immune disorder	disorder in which the body reacts to its own tissue
autosomal dominant condition	an inherited condition in which transmission of a dominant gene causes a characteristic to be expressed
Babinski	a reflex elicited by scraping the sole of the foot. A positive Babinski results in upturning of the big toe and the other toes fan. The presence of a positive Babinski confirms an upper motor neuron lesion of the spastic type.
basal ganglia	a group of subcortical structures associated with motor control of tone and posture. The three main structures are the caudate nucleus, putamen, and globus pallidus. They are part of the extrapyramidal system.
bradykinesia	The terms *hypokinesia* (reduced movement) and *akinesia* (absence of movement) are sometimes used interchangeably with the term *bradykinesia*.

bulbar palsy	damage to the cranial nerves resulting in flaccid dysarthria
carotid endarterectomy	procedure that removes material which has been deposited on the inner walls of the artery, in this case the carotid arteries
central nervous system	the nerves contained within the brain and spinal cord; also called the neuraxis
cerebellopontine	leading from the cerebellum to the pons
cerebellum	the part of the brain concerned with maintaining proper posture and balance in walking, sequential movements like those in eating, and rapid alternating movements like those in speech
chorea	a form of dystonia characterized by irregular spasmodic, involuntary movements of limbs or facial muscles
collagen	a substance found in connective tissue in the body and used for injection into a paralyzed vocal fold
contralateral	pertaining to the opposite side (e.g., nerves on one side of the brain that cross (decussate) and control sensory and motor functions on the opposite side of the body)
corticobulbar tract	in the pyramidal system, comprised of upper and lower motor neurons and is the voluntary pathway for the movements of speech muscles
corticopontine tract	in the pyramidal system
corticospinal tract	in the pyramidal system; comprised of upper motor neurons and controls distal muscles
cryptococcal meningitis	infectious disease caused by a fungus that spreads from the lungs to the brain and central nervous system
decussates/decussation	to cross over in the form of an X. Some cranial nerves, described as *contralateral*, cross over as they leave the brain and travel to the opposite side of the body.
demyelinating	process that destroys the myelin sheath which protects the axons
distal muscles	muscles in the distal extremities (e.g., hands, feet, etc.) as opposed to proximal muscles which are muscles near or on the trunk of the body (e.g., deltoid, quadriceps)

dopaminergic drugs	drugs which restore the balance between dopamine and acetylcholine; used to treat Parkinson's disease
dopaminergic neurons	nerve cells which produce dopamine
dyskinesia	involuntary movement disorders usually associated with a lesion of the extrapyramidal system
dystonia musculorum deformans	a disorder in which muscular contractions cause distortions of the spine and hip; a childhood disorder that may be accompanied by dysarthria in its later stages
dystonia	a form of dyskinesia in which the limbs are in a distorted static posture because of excess tone. These postures are slow and bizarre, often involving twisting and turning.
essential voice tremor	an organic vocal tremor which is distinguished from pathologic tremors such as those associated with Parkinsonism.
extrapyramidal	one of two major systems in the central nervous system; comprised of a set of pathways that connect subcortical motor nuclei including the basal ganglia
fasciculations	small movements of a muscle (i.e., contractions of a number of muscle fibers which are supplied by a single nerve filament). These occur in atrophied muscles and indicate lower motor neuron damage.
focal dystonia	localized impairment of muscle tone
Guillain-Barré Syndrome	a disease whose cause is not known. Typically characterized by acute onset of peripheral nervous system dysfunction. Muscles of the face, pharynx, or eyes are occasionally affected first and more than half of individuals with this disorder have facial weakness, dysphagia, and flaccid dysarthria.
herpes zoster	an acute viral disease which is characterized by inflammation of dorsal root ganglia and eruption of vesicles along distribution of cutaneous nerve
hyperkinetic	increased muscle activity
hypertonia	abnormally increased tone displayed in spastic muscles
hypokinetic	abnormally diminished motor functions or activity
hypotonia	reduced muscle tone

245

idiopathic	without a known cause
inhalatory stridor	audible sound when person inhales; caused by obstruction of the airway. This can be one or both vocal cords being paralyzed at or near midline, by an obstruction on one of the cords, or an obstruction supra- or sub-glottally
internal carotid	large arteries (one on either side of the neck) which supply blood to the brain
intramedullary	within the bone marrow, spinal cord or medulla oblongata
ipsilateral	pertaining to the same side (e.g., nerves in the brain that eventually control sensory and motor functions on the same side of the body)
jaw jerk reflex	a primitive deep muscle stretch reflex; also called *maxillary reflex*; may be a confirmatory sign of bilateral UMN disease
lacunar	small infarcts in the small penetrating arteries of the brain
lacunar state	applied to patients who have had frequent lacunar infarcts. These patients may have dysarthria (often spastic), dementia, loss of control of affect, and/or dysphagia.
leukoencephalitis	inflammation of the white matter of the brain or spinal cord. This disease rarely occurs and exhibits signs only in corticospinal and corticobulbar tracts. There is no lower motor neuron involvement as there is in ALS.
lower motor neurons	send motor axons into the peripheral nerves, both cranial and spinal; damage to the lower motor neurons results in hypotonic or flaccid movement
Lyme disease	acute, recurrent inflammatory infection transmitted by ticks
manometer	an instrument to measure the pressure of liquids
Meige's Syndrome	a rare disorder which includes dyskinesia of the eyelids, face, and tongue
meningioma	a benign tumor in the meninges (e.g., the three membranes covering the brain and spinal cord which include the dura mater, arachnoid, and pia mater)
mononucleosis	an infectious disease characterized by formation of excess mononuclear leukocytes in the blood

The Source for Dysarthria　　　　　246

muscular dystrophy	a neurological disorder marked by progression of muscle weakness. In later stages, a flaccid dysarthria may appear. This occurs mainly in children, but can occur in adults.
myoclonus	contractions of part of a muscle, the whole muscle, or a group of muscles
myopathy	muscle disease in which muscles lose strength and bulk
nasolabial fold	the two folds of skin between the outer edge of the nose and corner of the mouth
neoplasm	a tumor
neuraxis	another term for the central nervous system; composed of the brain and spinal cord
neuroleptic	antipsychotic agent which can cause tardive dyskinesia or Parkinson's syndrome
neuropathy	lower motor neuron disease of peripheral nerves often caused by diabetes, vitamin deficiencies, etc.
neurotoxic	an agent that has a destructive or poisonous effect on the nervous system
ophthalmoparesis	paralysis of the eye muscles; also called *ophthalmoplegia*; vertical ophthalmoparesis means the patient cannot look up and down
orthostatic hypotension	blood pressure which drops suddenly upon standing
paryoxysmal ataxic dysarthria	a condition associated with multiple sclerosis in which the individual has brief episodes of ataxic dysarthria
peripheral nervous system	the nerves outside the central nervous system
pharyngeal plexus	the point in the pharynx at the upper border of the middle pharyngeal constrictor where the pharyngeal branch of the vagus merges with branches of the glossopharyngeal and external laryngeal nerves
poliomyelitis	inflammation of the gray matter of the spinal cord
pontine nuclei	nerve cells in basilar part of the pons where impulses are transmitted between cerebrum and cerebellum

primary lateral sclerosis	a disease difficult to distinguish from ALS; characterized by corticospinal and corticobulbar tract signs
progressive bulbar palsy	a syndrome of LMN weakness in cranial nerve muscles in which dysarthria and dysphagia are present
prosthodontist	a specialist concerned with making dental appliances
pseudobulbar affect	causes patients to laugh or cry easily and seemingly without provocation
psuedobulbar palsy	resulting from bilateral damage to the corticobulbar tract usually with involvement of speech, chewing, and swallowing
ptosis	paralytic drooping, often refers to the upper eyelid
pyramidal system	one of two major systems in the central nervous system; controls voluntary movement
rigidity	inflexibility or stiffness
snout reflex	primitive reflex similar to sucking reflex
spasmodic torticollis	dystonia of the cervical muscles which cause torsion of the neck
spasticity	muscular hypertonicity with increased resistance to stretch
substantia nigra	a mass of gray matter from the upper border of the pons into the subthalamus region; part of the basal ganglia
Syndenham's Chorea	a simple chorea (i.e., a nervous disorder with involuntary and irregular movements)
Tardive dyskinesia	a form of dyskinesia with bizarre movements of mouth, face, jaw, and tongue. It often develops after prolonged use of neuroleptic drugs.
thalamus	a structure in the brainstem responsible for certain subcortical speech and language functions
tremor	a form of dyskinesia; rhythmic involuntary actions
trigeminal neuralgia	sudden brief episodes of pain in the face which can indirectly affect speech

upper motor neurons	nerves that are contained within the brain, brain stem, and spinal cord; damage to upper motor neurons results in spastic or hypertonic movement
vascular	pertaining to the blood vessels
vertibrobasilar system	one of two systems (carotid being the other) that supplies blood to the brain
Wallenberg's Lateral Medullary Syndrome	a specific type of brainstem stroke which leads to palatal, pharyngeal, and laryngeal weakness with dysarthria and dysphagia

The Source for Dysarthria　　　　249

References

Chapter 1

Canter, G.J. "Speech Characteristics of Patients with Parkinson's disease, II, Physiological Support for Speech." *Journal of Speech and Hearing Disorders*, Vol. 30, No. 44, 1965, (217-224)

Darley, S.L., Aronson, A.E., and Brown, J.R. *Motor Speech Disorders*. Philadelphia: Saunders, 1975.

Darley, F. L. "Forward." *Clinical Dysarthria*, San Diego: College Hill Press, 1983.

Duffy, J.R. *Motor Speech Disorders: Substrate Differential Diagnosis Management*. St. Louis: Mosby Year Book, Inc., 1995.

Love, R., and Webb, W. *Neurology for the Speech-Language Pathologist*. Stoneham, MA: Butterworth Publishers, 1986.

Netsell, R. "Speech Motor Control: Theoretical Issues with Clinical Impact." *Clinical Dysarthria*, San Diego: College Hill Press, 1983.

Rosenbek, J.C. and LaPointe, L.L. "The Dysarthrias: Description, Diagnosis, and Treatment. In Johns, D. (ed.) *Clinical Management of Neurogenic Communication Disorders*, Austin, TX: PRO-ED, 1985.

Rosenbek, J.C., Till, J.A., Gerratt, B.R. and Wertz, R.T. "Dysarthria: Standardized Measurement Workshop." Veterans Administration Regional Medical Education Center Workshop, Long Beach, CA, 1991.

Wertz, R.T. and Rosenbek, J.C. "Where the Ear Fits: A Perceptual Evaluation of Motor Speech Disorders." In Webb, W. (ed.) *Seminars in Speech and Language: Oral Motor Dysfunction in Children and Adults*. Vol. 13, No. 1, February 1992, pp. 25-37.

Yorkston, K.M., Beukelman, D.R., and Bell, K.R. *Clinical Management of Dysarthric Speakers*. Boston: Little Brown & Co., 1988.

Yorkston, K.M. "Supplement on Treatment Efficacy Part I." *Journal of Speech and Hearing Research*, October 1996, pp. 46-57.

Chapter 2

ASHA National Outcomes Measurement System (NOMS) for Speech-Language Pathology and Audiology. American Speech-Language-Hearing Association, Rockville, MD, 1995.

Coster, W.J., and Haley, S.M. (1992). "Conceptualization and measurement of disablement in infants and young children." *Infants and Young Children*, Vol. 4, No. 4, 1992, pp. 11-22.

Darley, S.L., Aronson, A.E., and Brown, J.R. *Motor Speech Disorders*. Philadelphia: Saunders, 1975.

Duffy, J.R. *Motor Speech Disorders: Substrate Differential Diagnosis Management.* St. Louis: Mosby Year Book, Inc., 1995.

Enderby, P.M. *Frenchay Dysarthria Assessment.* Austin, TX: PRO-ED, 1983.

Lubinski, R. "Dysarthria: A Breakdown in Interpersonal Communication" in Vogel, D. and Cannito, M. (eds.) *Treating Disordered Speech Motor Control*, Austin, TX: Pro Ed, 1991.

McNeil, M.R. "A Critical Appraisal of Instrumentation Methods in the Evaluation and Management of Dysarthria." Presented at the 3rd Bi-Annual Clinical Dysarthria Conference, Tucson, AZ, February 1986.

Netsell, R. (1983). "Speech Motor Control: Theoretical Issues with Clinical Impact." *Clinical Dysarthria*, San Diego, College Hill Press, 1983.

Orlikoff, R.F. "The Use of Instrumental Measures in the Assessment and Treatment of Motor Speech Disorders." In Webb, W. (ed.) *Seminars in Speech and Language: Oral Motor Dysfunction in Children and Adults.* Vol. 13, No. 1, February 1992, pp. 25-37.

Rosenbek, J.C. and LaPointe, L.L. "The Dysarthrias: Description, Diagnosis, and Treatment. In Johns, D. (ed.) *Clinical Management of Neurogenic Communication Disorders*, Austin, TX: PRO-ED, 1985.

Theodoros, D.G., Murdoch, B.E., and Stokes, P.D. "Variability in the perceptual and physiological features of dysarthria following severe closed head injury: an examination of five cases." *Brain Injury*, Vol. 9, No. 7, 1995, pp. 671-696.

Wertz, R.T. and Rosenbek, J.C. "Where the Ear Fits: A Perceptual Evaluation of Motor Speech Disorders." In Webb, W. (ed.) *Seminars in Speech and Language: Oral Motor Dysfunction in Children and Adults.* Vol. 13, No. 1, February 1992, pp. 25-37.

World Health Organization. International classification of impairments, disabilities, and handicaps. Geneva: World Health Organization, 1980.

Yorkston, K.M., Beukelman, D.R., and Traynor, C.D. *Computerized Assessment of Intelligibility of Dysarthric Speech.* Tigard, OR: C.C. Publications, 1984.

Yorkston, K.M., Beukelman, D.R., and Bell, K.R. *Clinical Management of Dysarthric Speakers.* Boston: Little Brown & Co., 1988.

Yorkston, K.M. and Beukelman, D.R. *Assessment of Intelligibility of Dysarthric Speech.* Tigard, OR: C.C. Publications, 1981.

Chapter 3

American Speech-Language-Hearing Association. Code of Ethics. *Asha*, Vol. 36, Suppl. 13, March 1994, pp. 1-2

American Speech-Language-Hearing Association: Report: Augmentative and Alternative Communication, *Asha*, Vol. 33, Suppl. 5, 1991, pp. 9-12.

Ansel, B., McNeil, M., Hunker, C., and Bless, D. "The Frequency of Verbal and Acoustic Adjustments Used by Cerebral Palsied Dysarthric Adults When Faced With Communicative Failure." *Clinical Dysarthria*, San Diego: College Hill Press, 1983.

Berry, W. and Sanders, F. "Environmental Education: The Universal Management Approach for Adults with Dysarthria." *Clinical Dysarthria*, San Diego: College Hill Press, 1983.

Canter, G.J. "Speech Characteristics of Patients with Parkinson's disease, II, Physiological Support for Speech." *Journal of Speech and Hearing Disorders*, Vol. 30, No. 44, 1965, pp. 217-224.

Duffy, J.R. *Motor Speech Disorders: Substrate Differential Diagnosis Management.* St. Louis: Mosby Year Book, Inc., 1995.

Keatley, A. and Wirz, S. "Is Twenty Years Too Long? Improving Intelligibility in Long-Standing Dysarthria: A Single Case Treatment Study." *European Journal of Disorders of Communication*, Vol. 29, 1994, pp. 183-202.

Linebaugh C.W. "Treatment of Flaccid Dysarthria." In Perkins, W.H. (ed.) *Current Therapy of Communication Disorders: Dysarthria and Apraxia*, New York, Thieme Stratton, 1983.

McHenry, M.A., Wilson, R.L., and Minton, J.T. "Management of Multiple Physiologic System Deficits Following Traumatic Brain Injury." *Journal of Medical Speech-Language Pathology*, Vol. 2, No. 59, 1994.

McHenry, M., and Wilson, R. "Case Study: The Challenge of Unintelligible Speech Following Traumatic Brain Injury." *Brain Injury*, Vol. 8, No. 4, 1994, pp. 363-375.

Netsell, R. "Speech Motor Control: Theoretical Issues with Clinical Impact." *Clinical Dysarthria*, San Diego: College Hill Press, 1983.

Netsell, R. "Speech Physiology.: *Normal Aspects of Speech, Hearing, and Language*, Englewood Cliffs, NJ: Prentice Hall, 1973.

Rosenbek, J.C. and LaPointe, L.L. "The Dysarthrias: Description, Diagnosis, and Treatment. In Johns, D. (ed.) *Clinical Management of Neurogenic Communication Disorders*, Austin, TX: PRO-ED, 1985.

Ross, E.D., et al. "How the Brain Integrates Affective and Propositional Language into a Unified Behavioral Function: Hypothesis Based on Clinicoanatomic Evidence." *Archives of Neurology*, Vol. 38, No. 745, 1981.

Sarvela, P.D., Sarvela, J.L. and Odulana, J. "Knowledge of Communication Disorders Among Nursing Employees." *Nursing Homes*, Vol. 38, Nos. 1-2, October 1989, pp. 21-24.

Simpson, M.B., Till, J.A. and Goff, A.M. "Long Term Treatment of Severe Dysarthria: A Case Study." *Journal of Speech and Hearing Disorders*, Vol. 53, 1988, pp. 433-440.

Smith, C.R. and Scheinberg, L.C. "Clinical Features of Multiple Sclerosis." *Seminars in Neurology*, Vol. 5, No. 85, 1985.

Van Riper, C. *Speech Correction: Principles and Methods.* 5th ed. Englewood Cliffs, NJ: Prentice Hall, 1972.

Yorkston, K.M. "Supplement on Treatment Efficacy Part I." *Journal of Speech and Hearing Research*, October 1996, pp. 46-57.

Yorkston, K.M., Beukelman, D.R., and Bell, K.R. *Clinical Management of Dysarthric Speakers.* Boston: Little Brown & Co., 1988.

Yorkston, K.M., Miller, R.M. and Strand, E.A. *Management of Speech and Swallowing in Degenerative Disorders.* Tuscon: Communication Skill Builders (a divison of The Psychological Corporation), 1995.

Chapter 4

Aten, J.L. "Spastic Dysarthria: Revising Understanding." *Journal of Head Trauma Rehabilitation*, Vol. 3, 1988, pp. 63-73.

Duffy, J.R. *Motor Speech Disorders: Substrate Differential Diagnosis Management.* St. Louis: Mosby Year Book, Inc., 1995.

Dworkin, J.P. *Motor Speech Disorders: A Treatment Guide.* St. Louis: Mosby Year Book, Inc., 1991.

Hammen, V.L. and Yorkston, K.M. "Effective Instruction on Selected Aerodynamic Parameters in Subjects with Dysarthria and Control Subjects." In Till, J.A., Yorkston, K.M., and Beukelman, D.R. (eds.) *Motor Speech Disorders: Advances in Assessment and Treatment*, Baltimore: Paul H. Brookes Publishing, 1994.

Hixon, T.J., Hawley, J.L., and Wilson, K.J. "An Around-The-House Device for the Clinical Determination of Respiratory Driving Pressure: A Note on Making the Simple Even Simpler." *Journal of Speech and Hearing Disorders*, Vol. 47, No. 413, 1982.

Linebaugh, C.W. "Treatment of Flaccid Dysarthria." In Perkins, W.H. (ed.) *Current Therapy of Communication Disorders: Dysarthria and Apraxia*, New York: Thieme Stratton, 1983.

McHenry, M.A., Wilson, R.L., and Minton, J.T. "Management of Multiple Physiologic Systems Deficits Following Traumatic Brain Injury." *Journal of Medical Speech-Language Pathology*, Vol. 2, No. 59, 1994.

Netsell, R. and Hixon, T. "A Non-invasive Method for Clinically Estimating Subglottal Air Pressure." *Journal of Speech and Hearing Disorders*, Vol. 43, 1978, pp. 326-330.

Netsell, R. "Expiratory Checking and Therapy for Individuals with Speech Breathing Dysfunction." Presentation at American Speech-Language-Hearing Association Annual Convention, 1992, San Antonio, TX.

Putnam, A.H.B. and Hixon, T.J. "Respiratory Kinematics in Speakers with Motor Neuron Disease." In McNeil, N., Rosenbek, J., and Aronson, A.E. (eds.) *The Dysarthrias*, San Diego: College Hill Press, 1984.

Rosenbek, J.C. and LaPointe, L.L. "The Dysarthrias: Description, Diagnosis, and Treatment." In Johns, D. (ed.) *Clinical Management of Neurogenic Communication Disorders*, Austin, TX: PRO-ED, 1985.

Simpson, M.B. "Long-term treatment of severe dysarthria." *Journal of Speech and Hearing Disorders*, 53, 1988, pp. 433-440.

Yorkston, K.M., Beukelman, D.R., and Bell, K.R. *Clinical Management of Dysarthric Speakers*. Boston: Little Brown & Co., 1988.

Chapter 5

Aronson, A.E. *Clinical Voice Disorders*, New York: Thieme Stratton, 1990.

Aten, J.L. "Spastic Dysarthria: Revising Understanding." *Journal of Head Trauma Rehabilitation*, Vol. 3, 1988, pp. 63-73.

Boone, D.R. and McFarlane, F.C. *The Voice and Voice Therapy*. 4th ed. Englewood Cliffs: Prentice Hall Inc., 1998.

Darley, S.L., Aronson, A.E., and Brown, J.R. *Motor Speech Disorders*. Philadelphia: Saunders, 1975.

Dworkin, J.P. *Motor Speech Disorders: A Treatment Guide*. St. Louis: Mosby Year Book, Inc., 1991.

Greene, M.C.L. and Watson, B.W. "The Value of Speech Amplification in Parkinson's disease Patients." *Folia Phoniatrica*, Vol. 20, No. 4, 1968, pp. 250-257.

Ramig, L.O. "The Role of Phonation in Speech Intelligibility: A Review and Preliminary Data from Patients with Parkinson's disease." In R.D. Kent (ed.) *Intelligibility in Speech Disorders: Theory, Measurement and Management*, 1992.

Ramig, L.O. "Speech Therapy for Patients with Parkinson's disease." In Koller, W. and Paulson S. (eds.) *Therapy of Parkinson's disease*, 2nd ed. New York: Marcel Dekker Inc., 1996

Ramig, L.O., Bonitati, C.M., Lemke, J.H., and Horii, Y. "Voice Treatment for Patients with Parkinson's disease: Development of an Approach and Preliminary Efficacy Data." *Journal of Medical Speech-Language Pathology*, Vol. 2, 1994, pp. 191-210.

Ramig, L.O., Countryman, S., Thomspon, L.L., and Horii, Y. "A Comparison of Two Forms of Intensive Speech Treatment in Parkinson's disease." *Journal of Speech and Hearing Research*, Vol. 38, 1995, pp. 1232-1251.

Ramig, L.O., Pawlas, P., and Countryman, S. *Lee Silverman Voice Treatment: A Practical Guide for Treating Voice and Speech Disorders in Parkinson's disease.* Iowa City, IA: National Center for Voice and Speech, University of Iowa, 1995.

Robertson, S. and Thompson, F. "Speech Therapy in Parkinson's disease: A Study of the Efficacy and Long-Term Effect of Intensive Treatment." *British Journal of Disorders of Communication*, Vol. 19, 1984, pp. 213-224.

Scott, S. and Caird, F.L. "Speech Therapy for Parkinson's disease." *Journal of Neurology and Neurosurgery and Psychiatry*, Vol. 46, 1968, pp. 140-144.

Simpson, M.B. "Long-Term Treatment of Severe Dysarthria." *Journal of Speech and Hearing Disorders*, Vol. 53, 1988, pp. 433-440.

Smith, M.E., Ramig, L.O., Dromey, C., Perez, K., and Samandari, R. "Intensive Voice Treatment in Parkinson disease: Laryngostroboscopic Findings." *Journal of Voice*, Vol. 9, No. 4, 1995, pp. 453-459.

Yorkston, K. "Treatment Efficacy: Dysarthria." *Journal of Speech and Hearing Research*, Vol. 39, 1996, pp. 46-57.

Chapter 6

Aten, J.L. "Spastic Dysarthria: Revising Understanding." *Journal of Head Trauma Rehabilitation*, Vol. 3, 1988, pp. 63-73.

Aten, J., McDonald, A., Simpson, M., and Gutierrez, R. "Efficacy of Modified Palatal Lifts for Improved Resonance." In McNeil, M., Rosenbek, J., and Aronson, A. (eds.) *The Dysarthrias: Physiology, Acoustics, Perceptions, Management.* Boston: College Hill Press, 1984.

Bedwinek, A.P. and O'Brian, R.L. "A Patient Selection Program for the Use of Speech Prosthesis in Adult Disorders." *Journal of Communication Disorders*, Vol. 18, 1985, pp. 169-182.

Bookshire, R.H. *An Introduction to Neurogenic Communication Disorders.* St. Louis: Mosby Year Book, Inc., 1992.

Duffy, J.R. *Motor Speech Disorders: Substrate Differential Diagnosis Management.* St. Louis: Mosby Year Book, Inc., 1995.

Dworkin, J.P. *Motor Speech Disorders: A Treatment Guide.* Chicago: Mosby Year Book, Inc., 1991.

The Source for Dysarthria 256

Dworkin, J.P. and Johns, D.F. "Management of Velopharyngeal Incompetence in Dysarthria: A Historical Review." *Clinical Otolaryngology*, Vol. 5, No. 61, 1980, pp. 61-74.

Gonzalez, J.B. and Aronson, A.E. "Palatal Lift Prosthesis for Treatment of Anatomic and Neurologic Palatopharyngeal Insufficiency." *Cleft Palate Journal*, Vol. 7, No. 91, 1970, pp. 91-104.

Hammen, V.L. and Yorkston, K.M. "Effective Instruction on Selected Aerodynamic Parameters in Subjects with Dysarthria and Control Subjects." In Till, J.A., Yorkston, K.M., and Beukelman, D.R. (eds.) *Motor Speech Disorders: Advances in Assessment and Treatment*, Baltimore: Paul H. Brookes Publishing, 1994.

Hardy, J., et al. "Management of Velopharyngeal Dysfunction in Cerebral Palsy." *Journal of Speech and Hearing Disorders*, Vol. 34, No. 123, 1969, pp. 123-137.

Johns, D.F. "Surgical and Prosthetic Management of Neurogenic Velopharyngeal Incompetency in Dysarthria." In Johns, D.F. (ed.) *Clinical Management of Neurogenic Disorders*, New York: Little Brown, 1985.

Kuehn, D.P. and Wachtel, J.M. "CPAP Therapy for Treating Hypernasality Following Closed Head Injury." In Till, J.A., Yorkston, K.M., and Beukelman, D.R. (eds.) *Motor Speech Disorders: Advances in Assessment and Treatment*, Baltimore: Paul H. Brookes Publishing, 1994.

Linebaugh, C.W. "Treatment of Flaccid Dysarthria." In Perkins, W.H. (ed.) *Current Therapy of Communication Disorders: Dysarthria and Apraxia*. New York: Thieme-Stratton, 1983.

McHenry, M.A., Wilson, R.L., and Menton, J.T. "Management of Multiple Physiologic System Deficits Following Traumatic Brain Injury." *Journal of Medical Speech-Language Pathology*, Vol. 2, No. 59, 1994.

Netsell, R. and Rosenbek, J. *Treating the Dysarthrias. Speech and Language Evaluation in Neurology: Adult Disorders.* New York: Grune and Stratton, 1985.

Rosenbek, J.C. and LaPointe, L.L. "The Dysarthrias: Description, Diagnosis, and Treatment. In Johns, D. (ed.) *Clinical Management of Neurogenic Communication Disorders*, Austin, TX: PRO-ED, 1985.

Simpson, M.B., Till, J.A., and Goff, A.M. "Long-term Treatment of Severe Dysarthria: Case Study." *Journal of Speech and Hearing Disorders*, Vol. 53, 1988, pp. 433-440.

Thompson, E.C. and Murdoch, B.E. "Disorders of nasality in subjects with upper motor neuron tpe dysarthria following cerebrovascular accident." *Journal of Communication Disorders*, Vol. 28, No. 3, 1995, pp. 261-276.

Yorkston, C.M. "The Summary of Treatment Efficacy for Dysarthria." *Journal of Speech and Hearing Research*, Vol. 39, 1996, pp. 46-57.

Yorkston, K.M., Beukelman, D.R., and Bell, K.R. *Clinical Management of Dysarthric Speakers.* Boston: Little Brown & Co., 1988.

Yorkston, K.M., et al. "The Effects of Palatal Lift Fitting on the Perceived Articulatory Adequacy of Dysarthric Speakers." In Yorkston, K.M. and Beukelman, D.R. (eds.) *Recent Advances in Clinical Dysarthria*, Austin, TX: PRO-ED, 1989.

Chapter 7

Aten, J.L. "Spastic Dysarthria: Revising Understanding." *Journal of Head Trauma Rehabilitation*, Vol. 3, 1988, pp. 63-73.

Barlow, S.M. and Abbs, J.H. "Force Transducers for Evaluation of Labial, Lingual, and Mandibular Function in Dysarthria." *Journal of Speech and Hearing Research*, Vol. 26, No. 616, 1983.

Darley, S.L., Aronson, A.E., and Brown, J.R. *Motor Speech Disorders*. Philadelphia: Saunders, 1975.

DePaul, R. and Brookes, B. "Multiple Orofacial Indices in Amyotrophic Lateral Sclerosis." *Journal of Speech and Hearing Research*, Vol. 36, No. 1158, 1993.

Duffy, J.R. *Motor Speech Disorders: Substrate Differential Diagnosis Management*. St. Louis: Mosby Year Book, Inc., 1995.

Dworkin, J.P. *Motor Speech Disorders: A Treatment Guide*. St. Louis: Mosby Year Book, Inc., 1991.

Enderby, P. and Crow, E. "Long-term Recovery Patterns of Severe Dysarthira Following Head Injury." *British Journal of Disorders of Communication*, Vol. 25, 1990, pp. 341-354.

Fairbanks, G. *Voice and Articulation Drill Book*. New York: Harper and Row, 1960.

Froeschels, E. "A Contribution to the Pathology and Therapy of Dysarthria Due to Certain Cerebral Lesions." *Journal of Speech Disorders*, Vol. 8, No. 301, 1943.

Linebaugh, C.W. "Treatment of Flaccid Dysarthria." In Perkins, W.H. (ed.) *Current Therapy of Communication Disorders: Dysarthria and Apraxia*, New York: Thieme Stratton, 1983.

Rosenbek, J.C. and LaPointe, L.L. "The Dysarthrias: Description, Diagnosis, and Treatment. In Johns, D. (ed.) *Clinical Management of Neurogenic Communication Disorders*. Austin, TX: PRO-ED, 1985.

Yorkston, K.M., Beukelman, D.R., and Bell, K.R. *Clinical Management of Dysarthric Speakers*. Boston: Little Brown & Co., 1988.

Chapter 8

Adams, S.G. "Accelerating Speech in a Case of Hypokenetic Dysarthria: Descriptions and Treatment." In Till, J.A., Yorkston, K.M., and Beukelman, D.R. (eds.) *Motor Speech Disorders: Advances in Assessment and Treatment*, Baltimore: Paul H. Brookes Publishing, 1995.

Aten, J.L. "Spastic Dysarthria: Revising Understanding." *Journal of Head Trauma Rehabilitation*, Vol. 3, 1988, pp. 63-73.

Barnes, G. J. "Suprasegmental and Prosodic Considerations in Motor Speech Disorders." *Clinical Dysarthria*, San Diego: College Hill Press, 1983.

Berry W. and Goshorn, E. "Immediate Visual Feedback in the Treatment of Ataxic Dysarthria: A Case Study." In Berry, W. (ed.) *Clinical Dysarthria*, Boston: College Hill Press, 1983.

Bellaire, K., Yorkston, K.M., and Beukelman, D.R. "Modification of Breath Patterning to Increase Naturalness of a Mildly Dysarthic Speaker." *Journal of Communication Disorders*, 1986, pp. 271-280.

Beukelman, D.R. and Yorkston, K.M. "A Communication System for the Severely Dysarthric Speaker with an Intact Language System." *Journal of Speech and Hearing Disorders*, Vol. 27, 1977, pp. 265-266.

Caligiuri, M.P. and Murry, T. "The Use of Visual Feedback to Enhance Prosodic Control in Dysarthria." In Berry, W. (ed.) *Clinical Dysarthria*, Boston: College Hill Press, 1983.

Craig, S. and Sikorski, L. *Succeed with Effective English Communicaiton: Intonation Patterns.* Anaheim, CA: Craig and Ford, Inc., 1985.

Crow, E. and Enderby, P. "The Effects of an Alphabet Chart on the Speaking Rate and Intelligibility of Speakers with Dysarthria." In Yorkston, K.M. and Beukelman, D.R. (eds.) *Recent Advances in Clinical Dysarthria*, Austin, TX: PRO-ED, 1989.

Fairbanks, G. *Voice and Articulation Drill Book*. New York: Harper and Row, 1960.

Hammen, V.L., Yorkston, K.M., and Minifie, F.D. "Effects of Temporal Alternations on Speech Intelligibility in Parkinsonian Dysarthia." *Journal of Speech and Hearing Research*, Vol. 37, No. 2, 1994, pp. 244-253.

Hanson, W.R. and Metter, E.J. "DAF Instrumental Treatment for Dysarthria in Progressive Supernuclear Palsy: A Case Report." *Journal of Speech and Hearing Disorders*, Vol. 45, No. 268, 1980.

Hanson, W.R. and Metter, E.J. "DAF Speech Rate and Modification in Parkinson's Disease: A Report of Two Cases." In Berry, W.R. (ed.) *Clinical Dysarthria*, Austin, TX: PRO-ED, 1983.

Helm, N. "Management of Palilalia With a Pacing Board." *Journal of Speech and Hearing Disorders*, Vol. 44, 1979, pp. 350-353.

Henderson, A., Goldman-Eisler, F., and Skarbek, A. "Sequential Temporal Patterns in Spontaneous Speech." *Language and Speech*, Vol. 9, No. 207, 1966.

Johnson J.A. and Pring T.R. "Speech Therapy and Parkinson's disease: A Review and Further Data." *British Journal of Disorders of Communication*, Vol. 25, No. 183, 1990.

LeDorze, G., Ouellet, L., and Ryalls, J. "Intonation and Speech Rate in Dysarthric Speech." *Journal of Communication Disorders*, Vol. 27, No. 1, 1994, pp. 1-18.

Lehiste, I. *Suprasegmentals*. Cambridge, MA: M.I.T. Press, 1970.

Liberman, P. *Intonation, Perception, and Language*. Cambridge, MA: M.I.T. Press, 1967.

Linebaugh, C.W. "Treatment of Flaccid Dsyarthria." In Perkins, W.H. (ed.) *Current Therapy of Communication Disorders: Dysarthria and Apraxia*. New York: Thieme Stratton, 1983.

McHenry, M. and Wilson, R. "Case Study: The Challenge of Unintelligible Speech Following Traumatic Brain Injury." *Brain Injury*, Vol. 8, No.4, 1994, pp. 363-375.

Murry, T. "Treatment of Ataxia Dysarthria." In Perkins, W.H. (ed.) *Current Therapy of Communication Disorders: Dysarthria and Apraxia*, New York: Thieme Stratton, 1983.

Nalling, K. and Horner, J. "Reorganizing Neurogenic Articulation Disorders by Modifying Prosody." Presentation at the American-Speech-Language-Hearing Association Annual Convention, Atlanta, 1979.

Netsell, R. *Speech Physiology. Normal Aspects of Speech, Hearing, and Language*. Englewood Cliffs, NJ: Prentice Hall, 1973.

Ramig, L.O. "Acoustic Analysis of Phonation in Patients with Huntington's Disease: Preliminary Report." *Annals of Otology, Rhinology, and Laryngology*, Vol. 95, No. 3, 1986, pp. 288-293.

Robin, D.A., Klouda, G.V., and Hug, L.N. "Neurogenic Disorders of Prosody." In Vogel, D. and Cannito, M.P.(eds.) *Treating Disordered Speech Motor Control*, Austin, TX: PRO-ED, 1991.

Rosenbek, J.C. and LaPointe, L.L. "The Dysarthrias: Description, Diagnosis, and Treatment. In Johns, D. (ed.) *Clinical Management of Neurogenic Communication Disorders*, Boston: Little Brown, 1985.

Shapiro, B. and Danly, M. "The Role of the Right Hemisphere in the Control of Speech Prosody in Prepositional and Affective Context." *Brain and Language*, Vol. 25, 1985, pp. 19-36.

Simmons, N. "Acoustic Analysis of Ataxic Dysarthia: An Approach to Monitoring Treatment." In Berry, W. (ed.) *Clinical Dysarthria*, San Diego: College Hill Press, 1983.

Turner, G.S. and Weismer, G. "Characteristics of Speaking Rate in the Dysarthria Associated with Amyotrophic Lateral Sclerosis." *Journal of Speech and Hearing Research*, Vol. 36, No. 6, 1993, pp. 1134-1144.

Vance, J.E. "Prosodic Deviation in Dysarthria: A Case Study." *European Journal of Disorders of Communication*, Vol. 29, No. 1, 1994, pp. 61-76.

Yorkston, K.M. "Supplement on Treatment Efficacy Part I." *Journal of Speech and Hearing Research*, Vol. 39, 1996, pp. 46-57.

Yorkston, K.M., Beukelman, D.R., and Bell, K.R. *Clinical Management of Dysarthric Speakers*. Boston: Little, Brown, and Company, 1988.

Yorkston, K.M., Beukelman, D.R., Minifie, F.D. and Sapir, F. "Assessment of Stress Patterning." In McNeil, M.R., Rosenbek, J.C. and Aronson, A.E. (eds.) *The Dysarthrias: Physiology, Acoustics, Perception and Management*, San Diego: College Hill Press, 1984.

Yorkston, K.M., Hammen, B.L., Beukelman, D.R., and Traynor, C.D. "The Effect of Rate Control on the Intelligibility and Naturalness of Dysarthric Speech." *Journal of Speech and Hearing Disorders*, Vol. 55, 1990, pp. 550-561.

Yorkston, K.M. and Beukelman, D.R. "Ataxic Dysarthria: Treatment Sequences Based on Intelligibility and Prosodic Considerations." *Journal of Speech and Hearing Disorders*, Vol. 46, No. 398, 1981.

Yorkston, K.M., et al. "The Effect of Rate Control on the Intelligibility and Naturalness of Dysarthric Speech." *Journal of Speech and Hearing Disorders*, Vol. 55, No. 550, 1990.

Equipment and Suppliers

Electronic Speech Enhancement, Inc.
143 McDonnell Blvd, Building B
St. Louis, MO 63042
1-888-463-7353
FAX: 314-298-9608

✔ Speech Enhancer™

Kay Elemetrics Corp.
2 Bridgewater Lane
Lincoln Park, NJ 07035-1488
1-800-289-5297
FAX: 201-628-6363

✔ Visi-Pitch™

Bruce Medical Supply
411 Waverly Oaks Road
Waltham, MA 02154-9166
1-800-225-8446
FAX: 617-894-9519

✔ personal voice amplifiers

Luminaud, Inc.
8688 Tyler Blvd.
Mentor, OH 44060
1-800-255-3408
FAX: 440-255-2250

✔ personal voice amplifiers

Communication Skill Builders
a division of The Psychological Corporation
555 Academic Ct.
San Antonio, TX 78204-2498
1-800-211-8378
FAX: 1-800-232-1223

✔ pacer/tally for pacing speech and
   tallying responses

PRO-ED, Inc.
8700 Shoal Creek Blvd.
Austin, TX 78758
1-800-897-3202
FAX: 1-800-397-7633

✔ See-Scape™
✔ Frenchay Dysarthria Assessment Test
✔ The Assessment of Intelligibility of
   Dysarthric Speech
✔ The Computerized Assessment of
   Intelligibility of Dysarthric Speech

Applied Symbolix
800 North Wells St.
Chicago, IL 60610
1-800-676-7551
FAX: 312-787-3828

✔ Boston Stimulus Board
✔ Pocket Pacing Board

1-09-11